29¢

Writing Research Papers

Second Edition

Writing Research Papers

A Complete Guide   Second Edition

James D. Lester
Austin Peay State University

Scott, Foresman and Company   Glenview, Illinois

Dallas, Tex. Oakland, N.J. Palo Alto, Cal. Tucker, Ga. Brighton, England

Library of Congress Cataloging in Publication Data

Lester, James D.
Writing Research Papers.

Includes bibliography and index.
1. Report writing. I. Title.
LB2369.L4   1976   808'.023   75-25949
ISBN: 0-673-07990-2

TABLE OF CONTENTS

PREFACE

The aims of the Second Edition of *Writing Research Papers* are primarily those of the first: (1) to tell beginning researchers everything they need to know when sitting down to write a paper—from how to choose a topic, organize the paper functionally, and write clear expository prose to what kind of paper to use, what size margins to employ, and similar mechanical details; and (2) to direct the material to *all* undergraduate students—those in biology, for example, as well as those in freshman English. To help fulfill these aims, I have incorporated numerous helpful suggestions offered by the many instructors who have used the First Edition. As a result of their comments, I hope this edition is an even more useful guide and reference tool than its predecessor.

This new edition also adheres to the stylistic principles of the second edition of the *MLA Style Sheet*, a feature introduced in the 1971 Diamond Printing of *Writing Research Papers*. In certain instances, however, this text offers instructors and students a choice of following strictly the *MLA Style Sheet* or of employing a more traditional format. For term papers, for example, the *MLA Style Sheet* recommends double-spacing quotations, even long indented ones, and double-spacing footnotes and placing them on separate sheets at the end of the work. In contrast, this book offers the traditional practices of single-spacing long indented quotations and single-spacing footnotes at the bottom of each page, while informing students that they may be asked to follow strictly the *MLA Style Sheet* guidelines, which are explained wherever necessary within the text.

For the sake of greater clarity and usefulness, several improvements over the First Edition have been made. In Chapter 1 the sections on restricting a topic and forming a preliminary thesis sentence have been expanded because these elements are the foundation upon which purposeful research and a well-organized paper rest. Former Chapters 2 and 3 ("The Working Bibliography" and "The Library") have been combined into the new Chapter 2 ("Gathering Data") to reflect more accurately the preliminary research process as an ongoing and unified operation.

Chapter 3 includes new examples of note-taking methods, an expansion of the sections on summary note cards and quotation note cards, plus an attempt to delineate more sharply the subtle and often confusing differences between plagiarism and the acceptable use of source material.

Chapter 4 has undergone several important changes. At the request of several instructors, the outlining section now includes an example of the decimal outline. In order for the text to conform more closely to its aims, the material on writing with unity, coherence, and clarity has been condensed, and the section "Writing in the Proper Tense," which deals directly with a problem students continually face in the research paper, has been expanded. "Handling Reference Material" has been completely reworked, while "Handling Problems of Format" now explains in more detail the specifics of setting up the title page, outline, opening, body, conclusion, and bibliography. A new section in this chapter, "Handling Technicalities of Preparing the Manuscript," treats in alphabetical order many mechanical items students often need to be reminded of—margins, footnote numbering, paper, underlining, spacing, and so on. Finally, the chapter features a new sample research paper, examples from which are scattered throughout the chapter to serve as models for solving such knotty problems as the integration of quotations within the body of the paper.

Chapter 5, "Footnoting," has two new features. I have added examples of the footnote form to be employed for subsequent references—those after the first full one—and have taken special care to illustrate especially difficult or unusual examples of these subsequent notes. The section "Specimen Footnotes—Periodicals" is now expanded and arranged by type, with descriptive headings added to distinguish journals with continuous pagination from those with separate pagination and to illustrate the distinctions between the form of notes for "magazines" and "journals." I have also clarified the troublesome section on footnotes for books published as part of a series.

The bibliography materials of Chapter 6 have also been expanded and revised, particularly the sample bibliography entries for periodicals. Chapter 7, "Documentation of Science Papers," has been updated but still basically follows the prevailing style manuals for each discipline, be it, for example, the *CBE Style Manual* for biology or the *Style Manual* of the American Institute of Physics.

To the glossary, Appendix I, which explains additional research terms not included in the text, I have added two new entries, "Names of Persons" and "Punctuation." Supplementing the entire book and especially the section on locating important reference works is Appendix II, which has been completely revised and updated to include the latest and most important reference materials in a variety of academic disciplines. An additional feature is the inclusion of important reference works on black literature and women's studies.

At the request of many teachers, an *Instructor's Manual* to accompany the Second Edition is available. The manual features research questions and exercises for the student, all geared to the organization of the text. It can be used by those instructors who wish to test the progress of their students in nearly every phase of the research paper project.

It is impossible to list here all those instructors and students who have responded so favorably to the First Edition, but to them I owe a debt of thanks. In addition I am deeply grateful to various people for their help and encouragement along the way: Ted Owens and William Elkins, who inspired the original manuscript; my editor, Stan Stoga; student Glenda Durdin for her research paper; many colleagues at Austin Peay State University for their help with Appendix II; critics and reviewers Patricia Ann Carlson of the United States Naval Academy, Walter Cummins of Fairleigh Dickinson University, Carol Cunningham of Bakersfield College, Elmer Ericson of Weber State College, William A. C. Francis of the University of Akron, James Ledford of Broward Community College, Bonnie Robinson of Golden West College, and especially Dorothy Schlegel of Norfolk State College. Most of all I thank Martha, Jim, and Mark, the family.

J. D. Lester

THE PRELIMINARIES 1

Introduction

■ Why write a research paper? The answer is twofold. First, you add new information to your personal storehouse of knowledge by collecting and investigating facts and opinions about a limited topic from various sources. Second, you add to the knowledge of others by effectively communicating the results of your research in the form of a well-reasoned answer to a scholarly problem or question.

Perhaps more importantly, learning to master research techniques will be of great help in your other courses and in your life after college. Since you will probably face several instances in your career that will require careful research, you should acquire the techniques for retrieving information, knowing where and how to find it, and using it to your best advantage as soon as possible. Sound research means going beyond encyclopedia articles and getting into special indexes and reference books, scholarly journals, and specialized studies of all sorts. With today's sophisticated communications systems, there is an abundance (some would say an over-abundance) of information available to the researcher. Learning proper research techniques will help you identify and process the information you seek with a minimum of time and effort.

Another long-term advantage in doing a research paper will be learning to shape your material into coherent, logical patterns. Any adequate research assignment, whether in or out of the classroom, will ask you to inform, interest, and, in some cases, persuade the reader. You must be able to judge critically the merit of the evidence which you have compiled through careful research techniques and then be able to express precisely demonstrable conclusions about it. Such a task requires concentration and, more importantly, demands an imaginative molding of your material.

In this respect, it is all too easy to submit a poor manuscript. For example, you might attempt to compile a paper by paraphrasing a few authorities and by inserting quotations abundantly. But such a compilation would prove seriously inadequate since it would merely be presenting commonplace facts and opinions in a research paper format. In such a paper, the thesis—if there was one—would not be developed or explored. In other words, you would have offered a recital of investigations without the personal expression and explanation that is the ultimate purpose of all research writing.

Research techniques and the ability to shape the material derived from research—these are two of the more important things you will learn in writing your paper. Along with these, you should also acquire a working familiarity with research writing style and the handling of quoted materials. This book will help you: it explores the complete scope of research writing, including a sample paper and full information on style, format, and footnote and bibliography forms.

If you are concerned that your research is insignificant and your writing is inadequate, do not despair. The undergraduate research paper is primarily a learning and training experience. That is, you learn thoroughly a selected topic and train yourself in writing that generally conforms to an established style and format. At first the task may appear insurmountable: locating sources, reading books and articles, taking notes, footnoting source materials, outlining, writing, rewriting, typing, and proofreading. Perhaps at some point you will begin to question your ability to express yourself in English at all!

Obviously, you need to apply some kind of order to this procedure. This book will help you do that by providing basic research techniques, strategies for selecting and arranging evidence, and methods for presenting your ideas in a clear and logical fashion. College graduates are not expected to know everything; but they should possess the ability to find accurate information about any subject and to communicate their facts and conclusions to the reader. Self-reliant library research and competent writing will be valuable assets in meeting several kinds of demands: assignments in other courses, research articles for publication, seminar papers in graduate study, and reports and studies for business and industry.

Choosing a Topic

Perhaps the most important advice is to select a topic of interest to yourself. Your choice requires more than passing attention because you may discover, too late, that an impulsive choice has led you into a dull subject, insurmountable research problems, or disappointing results. Before deciding upon a final topic, ask yourself if you can live with that topic for several weeks of intensive study.

In addition, there are several other principles you should consider in the selection of a topic. The first thing to keep in mind is that the topic should offer opportunities for investigation, for discovery of something new, different, or original, and for the formulation of judgments. It should demand, therefore, much more than a brief investigation of one or two encyclopedias which, though they may get you started, will provide only a report at most and are not sufficient for investigative research. For example, subjects such as "Poetic Imagery" or "Auto Production" are seldom suitable because all reference sources would provide almost identical information, and you would have little opportunity for the discovery and formulation of judgments. Restricting yourself to a specific topic might help, such as "Poetic Imagery in the Poetry of Langston Hughes" or "Auto Production: A Key to America's Economy." You would then have a narrow topic demanding a careful scrutiny of the issues and the comments of experts in those respective fields.

The second principle requires that you be wary of topics that are too recent, too specialized, and too geographically removed for you to obtain adequate materials. First, a news item in this week's newspaper might appear interesting, but research materials would most likely be limited to recent articles and editorials in newspapers and popular magazines that would permit little depth for development. Most instructors prefer your topic to be one that critics, experts, and authorities have examined in books, scholarly reports, and learned journals found on library shelves, not at a corner newsstand. Second, some topics are so specialized and classified that research itself becomes the sole end. You may get as technical as you wish as long as you don't get so bogged down in technical jargon, procedures, etc., that the paper becomes a report rather than a research tool in which you draw some conclusions about the general significance of your topic. For example, a paper on the differences between Euclidian and non-Euclidian geometry would get rather technical; but as long as your instructor approves, you are capable, and the conclusions are valid, this topic seems to be a pretty good one. Third, a regional topic is permissible, even encouraged, if it centers around your own geographic region. For example, a student in Michigan might consider the ecological crisis in the Great Lakes area while a student in Louisiana might examine the same issue by focusing on Lake Pontchartrain. In short, select a topic for which you can readily obtain the material.

Research studies usually avoid certain topics. Avoid topics that can be handled only by restating the research material; avoid straight biography that summarizes a person's life, though acceptable topics may be developed on either the influence of a historical period on a person or the importance of one aspect of a person's work; avoid sensational topics that merely titilate, such as "Political Sex Scandals"; avoid topics that are too broad, such as "The U.S. Presidency"; and avoid topics that are not scholarly—there is seldom any place in research writing for such topics as "Fishing for Trout" or "The American Hot Dog." However, as you will see, all these topics can be the basis for valid papers if they are properly restricted by your thesis and then adequately developed.

Finally, you should select a topic that will permit you to express your reasoned judgments and your guarded opinions with support from your source materials. A thorough examination of all the available evidence should result in responsible, impartial findings. All topics are controversial to some degree, but guard against unsubstantiated personal opinion and prejudice. Bias has no place in the research paper which requires careful assimilation and presentation of the evidence to prevent any appearance of prejudice and unfounded rationalization. Therefore, you will need to be especially cautious in your assessment of findings about controversial topics such as abortion, gun control, and the death penalty.

In brief, research demands the search for and discovery of information, an evaluation of that information, a formulation of unbiased judgments, and a demonstrable conclusion. The topic you choose must offer an opportunity for full development of each of these four points.

Preliminary Reading

You will need a thorough acquaintance with your material before attempting to restrict the subject. To that end, your introductory reading will serve several purposes: it will provide an overview of the subject; it will furnish the beginning of a working bibliography (see pp. 11-15); it will enable you to determine the availability of relevant reference material; and it will make possible a judicious restriction of the subject.

This preliminary reading does not normally require taking notes, since you cannot yet be certain of your needs. As a starting point, you might begin with a book or journal article recommended by your instructor or librarian (see pp. 15-35 for a full discussion of the use and resources of the library). You might also start with a general survey, such as *Literary History of the United States* (see Appendix II, pp. 155-87, for a list of general reference works and journals in your field). Or you may begin with an encyclopedia, a biographical dictionary, or some other general reference work, as listed below:

ENCYCLOPEDIAS

Chambers's Encyclopaedia. 4th ed. 15 vols. Fairview Park, N.Y.: Maxwell Scientific International, 1968.

Collier's Encyclopedia. 24 vols. New York: Collier, 1965.

Columbia Encyclopedia. 3rd ed. New York: Columbia Univ. Press, 1963.

Encyclopaedia Britannica. 15th ed. 30 vols. Chicago: Encyclopaedia Britannica, 1974.

Encyclopedia Americana. 30 vols. New York: Encyclopedia Americana, 1974. Rev. annually.

BIOGRAPHICAL DICTIONARIES
Universal

Deceased

Chambers's Biographical Dictionary. Rev. ed. New York: St. Martin's Press, 1969.
Webster's Biographical Dictionary. Rev. ed. Springfield, Mass.: Merriam, 1972.

Living

Current Biography. New York: H. W. Wilson, 1940-date. Cumulated Index 1940-70.
Current Biography, Yearbooks. New York: H. W. Wilson, 1946-date.
Dictionary of International Biography. Cambridge, England: Melrose, 1974.
A Dictionary of Universal Biography of All Ages and People. Ed. Albert M. Hyamson. 2nd ed. New York: Dutton, 1951.
Index to Women of the World from Ancient to Modern Times: Biographies and Portraits. Ed. Norma O. Ireland. Westwood, Mass.: Faxon, 1970.
International Who's Who. London: Europa Publs. and Allen & Unwin, 1935-date.
International Who's Who 1974-75: Covers the Five Continents. 38th ed. New York: International Publications Service, 1974.
Twentieth Century Authors: A Biographical Dictionary of Modern Literature. Ed. Stanley J. Kunitz and Howard Haycraft. New York: H. W. Wilson, 1942. Supplement 1955.
Webster's Biographical Dictionary. Rev. ed. Springfield, Mass.: Merriam, 1972.
Who's Who in the World. New ed. Chicago: A. N. Marquis, 1973.

American

Deceased

Dictionary of American Biography, 1927-1972. 16 vols. New York: Scribner's, 1973.
National Cyclopaedia of American Biography. 50 vols. Ann Arbor: Univ. Microfilms, 1967.
Who Was Who in America. 6 vols. Chicago: A. N. Marquis, 1951-68.

Living

Biography News: A Compilation of News Stories and Feature Articles from American News Media Covering Personalities of National Interest in All Fields. Detroit: Gale, 1974-date. With Cumulative Index.
Contemporary Authors. Detroit: Gale, 1962-date.
Encyclopedia of American Biography. Ed. John A. Garraty. New York: Harper & Row, 1974.
National Cyclopaedia of American Biography. 50 vols. Ann Arbor: Univ. Microfilms, 1967.
Webster's American Biographies. Ed. Charles Van Doren. Springfield, Mass.: Merriam, 1974.
Who's Who in America. Chicago: A. N. Marquis, 1899-date.
Who's Who of American Women. Chicago: A. N. Marquis, 1958-date.
Who's Who in Colored America: A Biographical Dictionary of Notable Living Persons of Negro Descent in America. Rpt. of 1927 ed. Ann Arbor: Finch Press.

British

Deceased

Burke's Landed Gentry. 18th ed. 3 vols. New York: International Publications Service, 1965-69.
Dictionary of National Biography. Ed. Leslie Stephen and Sidney Lee. 63 vols. 1882-1953; rpt. New York: Oxford Univ. Press, 1971.
Who Was Who: Companion to Who's Who. 6 vols. New York: St. Martin's Press, 1952-62.

Living

Who's Who. London: Black, 1849-date.

ALMANACS AND YEARBOOKS

The American Yearbook: A Record of Events and Progress. New York: Appleton, 1911-51.
The Americana Annual: An Encyclopedia of Current Events. New York: Americana Corporation, 1923-date.
The Annual Register: A Review of Public Events at Home and Abroad. London: Longmans, Green, 1761-date.
Britannica Book of the Year. Chicago: Encyclopaedia Britannica, 1938-date.
Collier's Year Book. New York: Crowell-Collier, 1939-date.
Facts on File: A Weekly Synopsis of World Events. New York: Facts on File, 1940-date.
Information Please Almanac. New York: Simon & Schuster, 1947-date.
Kane, Joseph Nathan. *Facts About the Presidents.* 3rd ed. New York: H. W. Wilson, 1974.
Kane, Joseph N. *Famous First Facts: A Record of First Happenings, Discoveries and Inventions in the United States.* 3rd ed. New York: H. W. Wilson, 1964.
The Negro Almanac. Ed. Harry A. Ploski and Ernest Kaiser. Rev. ed. New York: Bellewether, 1971.
The New International Year Book: A Compendium of the World's Progress, 1907-date. New York: Dodd, Mead, 1908-date.
Notable Names in American History. 3rd ed. Clifton, N.J.: James T. White, 1973.
Official Associated Press Almanac. Ed. Dan Perkes. Maplewood, N.J.: Hammond, 1973-date.
The Statesman's Year-Book: Statistical and Historical Annual of the States of the World. London: Macmillan, 1864-date.
The World Almanac and Book of Facts. New York: Newspaper Enterprise Association, 1868-date.
Yearbook of the United Nations. Lake Success, N.Y.: United Nations, 1947-date.

ATLASES AND GAZETTEERS

Adams, James T. *Atlas of American History.* New York: Scribner's, 1943.
The Atlas of the Universe. Chicago: Rand McNally, 1970.
Atlas of World History. Ed. R. R. Palmer. Chicago: Rand McNally, 1970.
Bartholomew, John W. *Advanced Atlas of Modern Geography.* 8th ed. New York: McGraw-Hill, 1956.
Cleveland, William A. *Britannica Atlas: Geography Edition.* Chicago: Encyclopaedia Britannica, 1972.
Commercial Atlas and Marketing Guide. Chicago: Rand McNally, 1972.

Goode's World Atlas. Ed. Edward B. Espenshade. 12th ed. Chicago: Rand McNally, 1964.

Hammond World Atlas. Maplewood, N.J.: Hammond, 1971.

The National Atlas of the United States of America. Washington, D.C.: Dept. of Interior, 1970.

National Geographic Atlas of the World. 3rd, rev. ed. Washington, D.C.: National Geographic Society, 1970.

The New York Times Atlas of the World. In collaboration with *The Times of London.* New York: Harper & Row, 1972.

Oxford Economic Atlas of the World. 4th ed. London: Oxford Univ. Press, 1972.

Oxford World Atlas. Ed. Saul B. Cohen. New York: Oxford Univ. Press, 1970.

Shepherd, W. R. *Historical Atlas.* 9th ed. New York: Barnes & Noble, 1964.

The Times Atlas of the World. Comprehensive ed., produced by *The Times of London* and John Bartholomew & Son. Boston: Houghton Mifflin, 1967.

DICTIONARIES

The American College Dictionary. Rev. ed. New York: Random House, 1967.

Fowler, Henry W., and F. G. Fowler, eds. *The Concise Oxford Dictionary of Current English.* Rev. E. McIntosh. 5th ed. Oxford: Clarendon Press, 1964.

Funk and Wagnalls Standard College Dictionary. New York: Funk and Wagnalls, 1973.

Murray, James A. H., et al., eds. *Oxford English Dictionary.* 12 vols. Oxford: Clarendon Press, 1933. Supplement.

Random House Dictionary of the English Language: The Unabridged Edition. Ed. Jess Stein. New York: Random House, 1967.

The Shorter Oxford English Dictionary. Ed. William Little et al. 3rd ed. 2 vols. New York: Oxford Univ. Press, 1973.

Webster's New World Dictionary of the American Language. Cleveland: Collins-World, 1974.

Webster's New Collegiate Dictionary. Rev. ed. Springfield, Mass.: Merriam, 1973.

Webster's Third New International Dictionary: The Great Library of the English Language. Springfield, Mass.: Merriam, 1972.

Weekley, Ernest. *A Concise Etymological Dictionary of Modern English.* Rev. ed. New York: Dutton, 1952.

BOOKS OF USAGE, SYNONYMS, AND DIALECT

Americanisms: A Dictionary of Selected Americanisms on Historical Principles. Ed. Mitford M. Mathews. Chicago: Univ. of Chicago Press, 1966.

Berrey, Lester V., and Melvin Van den Bark. *The American Thesaurus of Slang.* 2nd ed. New York: Crowell, 1953.

A Dictionary of American English on Historical Principles. Ed. Sir William Craigie and J. R. Hulbert. 4 vols. Chicago: Univ. of Chicago Press, 1936-44.

Fowler, H. W. *A Dictionary of Modern English Usage.* Rev. Sir Ernest Gowers. 2nd ed. Oxford: Clarendon Press, 1965.

Nicholson, Margaret. *Dictionary of American-English Usage: Based on Fowler's Modern English Usage.* New York: Oxford Univ. Press, 1957.

Partridge, Eric. *A Dictionary of Slang and Unconventional English.* 7th ed. New York: Macmillan, 1970.

Perrin, Porter G. *Writer's Guide and Index to English.* Rev. Wilma R. Ebbitt. 5th ed. Glenview, Ill.: Scott, Foresman, 1972.

Roget's Thesaurus of English Words and Phrases. Rev. Robert A. Dutch. New ed. New York: St. Martin's Press, 1964.

Webster's Dictionary of Synonyms. Springfield, Mass.: Merriam, 1942.

Wentworth, Harold, and Stuart B. Flexner, eds. *Dictionary of American Slang.* New York: Crowell, 1960. Supplement.

This initial reading need not be extensive since it is intended to provide only a general survey. You will have accomplished your purpose in preliminary reading when you have enough understanding of your material to decide on the restricted phase of it which you wish to pursue.

Restricting the Subject

You should not be too ambitious in what you attempt to cover. For one reason, research writing requires you to probe deeply and to present accurately facts and ideas that demonstrate the validity of your contentions. Your support for various judgments and opinions will be effective only if detailed. Furthermore, you will realize no sense of accomplishment if you present only vague, indefinite statements about a too extensive, too generalized subject.

Another reason why you should limit your subject to a specific problem or question is that the research paper is a comparatively short work, often no more than about ten typewritten pages in length, excluding title page, outline, and bibliography. The subject, accordingly, should be one that can be handled within these limitations of space, not one that would require twenty or thirty pages for adequate presentation.

For example, you could not deal adequately with "Edgar Allan Poe: His Poetic Genius," but you should get along well with "The Role of the Narrator in 'The Raven.' " Rather than attempting "The Ecology Problem," you might write effectively about "The Ecological Effects of Fish Kills on the Cottonwood River." And though "American Inflation" is probably unmanageable, "The Effects of Inflation Upon College Tuition" might well be within your range.

This restriction of subject requires meticulous study of all available sources. For example, let us say you are assigned the general subject area of the U.S. Presidency. A first step in restriction could be to limit the topic to one President—Gerald R. Ford. You would discover, however, that there is an overwhelming amount of written data about Ford. Therefore, you would want to limit yourself to one aspect of Ford's administration—for example, his fight against inflation. At this point you should read the related documents, articles, and books, noting particularly all material about inflation. You might then decide that Ford's economic controls were effective or ineffective. Either way, you have a manageable topic in "President Ford and His Economic Controls." You may, of course, go one step further and limit your study to a specific economic factor, such as Ford's Cost of Living Council.

If you need specific tools for narrowing a subject, consider the following techniques:

1. Examine the table of contents and index of your textbook, which are divided into major headings.

2. Read an encyclopedia entry which provides a summary of major issues about a subject as well as a brief bibliography listing of new sources.

3. Check the library's card catalog (see pp. 29-34) which, under subject headings, will indicate study areas. This search will also reveal the number and kinds of books available on a topic.

4. Relate your subject to your own special interests. If your general subject is poetry and your special interest is ecology, you might join the two by studying poems about ecology and nature in general. In like manner, you might join the subject "Crime" with your interest in detective fiction, or you might join the subject "The State Legislature" with legislation affecting your special interest—for example, marijuana, abortion, or tuition and fees.

Remember that it is usually the uninformed, uncertain writer who feels he or she must take refuge in the "safety" of a large, generalized, unrestricted subject.

Developing a Preliminary Thesis Sentence

The next great influence upon the success of your work is your development of a *preliminary* thesis sentence to limit even further the scope of your study. As you progress more and more deeply into your subject, you will need more than ever the unity of a central purpose. Early in your work it will be all right to have a sentence which begins with "The purpose of this paper is ..."; but you are warned against phrasing it so in the formal paper. Also, remember that your preliminary thesis will both control and, to a certain extent, be controlled by your research. It will always be subject to change as you progress in your research.

After note-taking and just before you start writing your first draft, you will arrive at a *final* thesis sentence that will be your controlling force. The final thesis sentence should unite your various findings, serve as the nerve center for all your paragraphs, and lead toward your demonstrable conclusions at the end of the paper.

Let us look at two possibilities. If your general topic is "Demand for Energy Production in the U.S." and you have restricted it to the effects of the energy crisis upon the environment, then your purpose is to examine the critical issues in this push-pull debate. Does the energy crisis require that we sacrifice the environment? Should we allow pollution in order to heat our homes? Can we have a safe, clean environment and also drive our automobiles at will? Asking such questions during research and note-taking will ultimately lead to your final thesis—for example, "The demands for energy production in the United States will expand environmental pollution and delay, perhaps forever, our chances for clean air and water."

If your general topic is Robert Frost's poetry and you have narrowed it to a study of his imagery, then you can ask such questions as: Is there an image or image cluster that appears often? Is it a significant image in several important poems? Asking many questions like these will eventually lead to your final thesis—for example, "As an image, 'snow' is suggestive of mystery in Robert Frost's poetry."

The earlier the preliminary thesis is formulated, the earlier a satisfactory working limitation will be set on note-taking. Remember that you may change your working thesis sentence as you progress. You should not bind yourself, early in your work, to a thesis you cannot support or do not believe. In fact, you cannot properly state your final thesis until after you complete note-taking and are ready to begin writing the paper. Nevertheless, a preliminary central idea, expressed in one or two sentences, will aid you in the organization of facts, limit your note-taking, and eliminate needless research.

The Working Bibliography

■ Early in your research you ought to begin developing a working bibliography, which is a list of reference sources that you will eventually investigate for information about your subject. Therefore, during your preliminary reading you should begin writing bibliography cards for all references that show promise of giving clues about your topic. Specifically, you need to watch for bibliographies and footnotes that list new source materials. Most books of critical evaluation will contain extensive bibliographies at the end of chapters or at the end of the book. Journal articles usually have footnotes at the bottom of the page and a bibliography at the end. General reference works, such as encyclopedias and biographical dictionaries, normally offer brief bibliographies at the end of each entry.

Suppose your topic concerns some aspect of Benjamin Franklin's political activities. Your preliminary reading of *Encyclopaedia Britannica* will uncover not only a brief biography but also the following bibliography:

Fig. 1: From *Encyclopaedia Britannica*

MAJOR WORKS

POLITICAL AND ECONOMIC: *A Modest Enquiry into the Nature and Necessity of a Paper Currency* (1729); *Plain Truth; or Serious Considerations on the Present State of the City of Philadelphia* (1747); *Proposals Relating to the Education of Youth in Pensilvania* (1749); *Observations Concerning the Increase of Mankind* (1755); *The Way to Wealth* (1757); *The Interest of Great Britain Considered with Regard to Her Colonies and the Acquisition of Canada and Guadaloupe* (1760); *Positions to be Examined Concerning National Wealth* (1769); *Journal of the Negotiations for Peace* (1782).

RELIGIOUS, PHILOSOPHICAL, AND SCIENTIFIC: *A Dissertation on Liberty and Necessity, Pleasure and Pain* (1725); *Articles of Belief and Acts of Religion* (1728); *Experiments and Observations on Electricity* (1751).

OTHER WORKS: *Poor Richard's* (1732–57), an almanac containing a number of famous maxims; Franklin's *Autobiography* (1771–88); "Information to those who would remove to America" (1784).

BIBLIOGRAPHY. *The Papers of Benjamin Franklin*, 15 vol., ed. by L.W. LABAREE *et al.* (1959–71), with 25 additional volumes expected, will be the definitive collection. *The Writings of Benjamin Franklin*, 10 vol., ed. by A.H. SMYTH (1905–07), has heretofore been the chief collection. The fullest biography is CARL VAN DOREN, *Benjamin Franklin* (1938); the best brief one is VERNER W. CRANE, *Benjamin Franklin and a Rising People* (1954). The most recent life is THOMAS FLEMING, *The Man Who Dared the Lightning: A New Look at Benjamin Franklin* (1971). An interesting specialized study is BRUCE INGHAM GRANGER, *Benjamin Franklin, An American Man of Letters* (1964).

(T.Hor.)

Since several of these sources will appear promising, you will want to begin making bibliography cards, such as:

**Fig. 2: Sample
Bibliography Card**

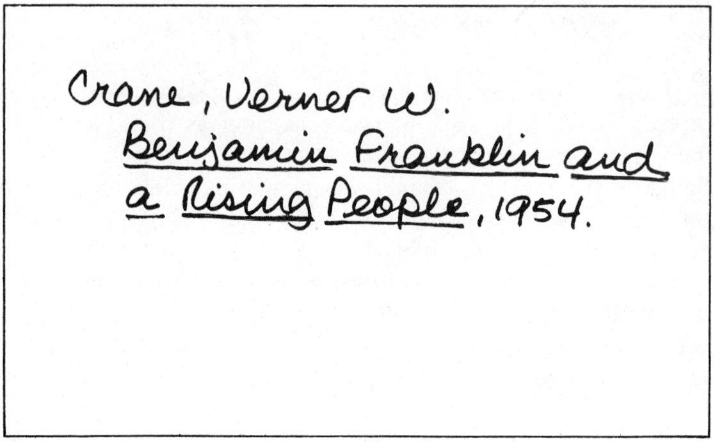

Crane, Verner W.
Benjamin Franklin and
a Rising People, 1954.

Later, at the card catalog, you can insert the proper library call number (see pp. 29-32) and the missing publication information (see Figure 3, p. 13). Then, when you are ready to study this particular book, your card provides the information for finding it. In addition, your card will have the necessary data for the final bibliography.

As you discover each new reference, you should record the bibliographical data onto *individual*, three-by-five-inch index cards. (But if you have a system that works well for you, by all means use it, provided, of course, that your system is accurate and efficient.) Individual cards have one great advantage over other systems: you can shuffle and arrange them to keep them in alphabetical order.

As you record information, check carefully to make certain that each card includes the following:

1. *Author's name*, followed by a period. Arrange the name in inverted order, surname first, for alphabetizing purposes. Provide the name in the fullest form available, e.g., "Hart, Thomas P.," not "Hart, T. P."

2. *Title of the work*, followed by a period. Enclose within quotation marks titles of articles, essays, chapters, sections, short poems, stories, and songs. Underline titles of books, journals, pamphlets, newspapers, plays, movies, long poems, and operas.

3. *Publication information.* For a book: the place, followed by a colon; the publisher, followed by a comma; the date, followed by a period. For a journal article, the name of the journal, followed by a comma; the volume number in Arabic numerals; the date in parentheses, followed by a comma; the page(s), followed by a period. Spell in full titles of periodicals, e.g., *Journal of Higher Education,* not *J. of Higher Ed.*

4. *Other items of documentation* as necessary (see Chapter 6, pp. 119-35, for exact information about positioning these items on the card):

- name of the editor or translator
- edition used, whenever it is not the first
- series number
- number of volumes with this particular title
- volume number if one of two or more

5. *Library call number* of a book or magazine, placed in the upper right-hand corner of the card. This item is valuable when you are ready to search out and read your sources.

6. *A personal note,* at the bottom of the card, as to the type of material to be found in this source or any special aspect it presents.

Specimen Bibliography Cards

In addition to the examples provided below, you may also study the bibliographical entries in Chapter 6.

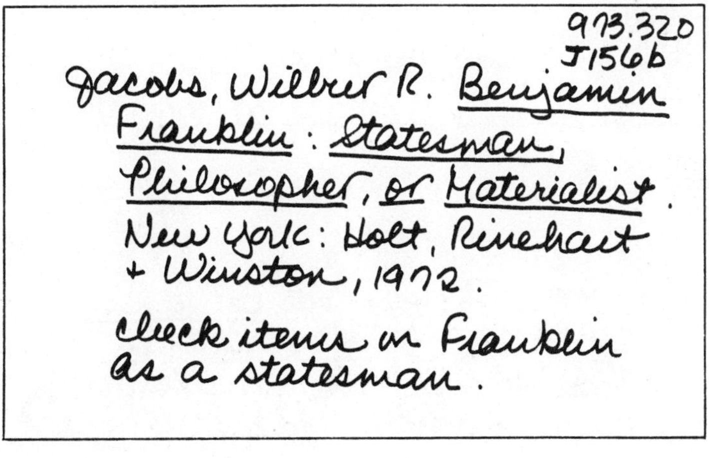

Fig. 3: Card for an Entire Book

> 973.320
> J156b
> Jacobs, Wilbur R. Benjamin
> Franklin: Statesman,
> Philosopher, or Materialist.
> New York: Holt, Rinehart
> + Winston, 1972.
> check items on Franklin
> as a statesman.

Fig. 4: Card for a Journal Article

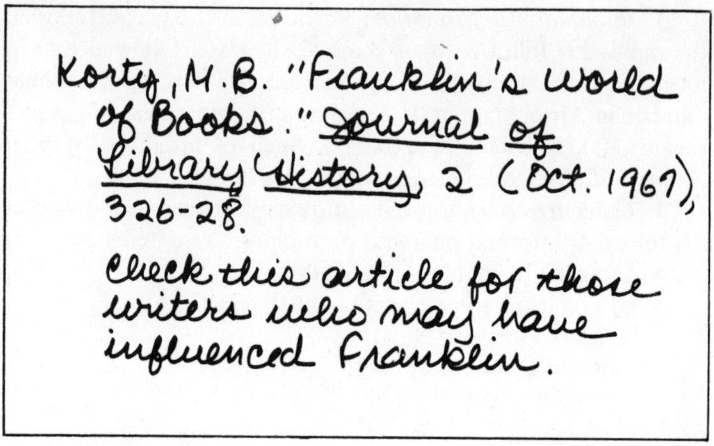

Korty, M.B. "Franklin's World of Books." _Journal of Library History_, 2 (Oct. 1967), 326-28.

Check this article for those writers who may have influenced Franklin.

Fig. 5: Card for Entry Found in _Essay and General Literature Index_

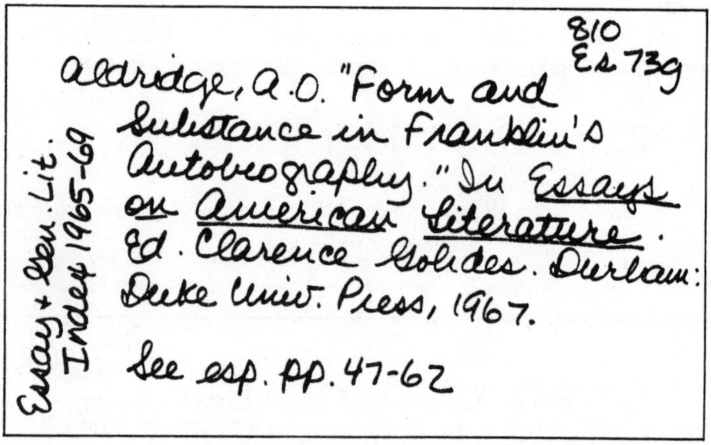

810
Es739

Aldridge, A.O. "Form and Substance in Franklin's Autobiography." In _Essays on American Literature_. Ed. Clarence Gohdes. Durham: Duke Univ. Press, 1967.

See esp. pp. 47-62

Essay + Gen. Lit. Index 1965-69

Fig. 6: Card for an Editor

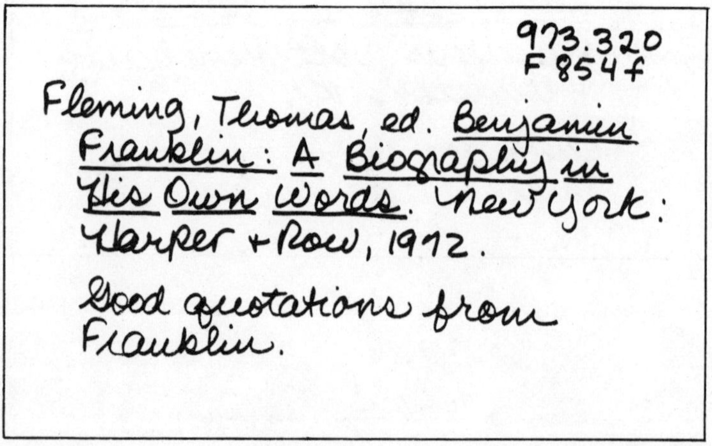

973.320
F854f

Fleming, Thomas, ed. _Benjamin Franklin: A Biography in His Own Words_. New York: Harper + Row, 1972.

Good quotations from Franklin.

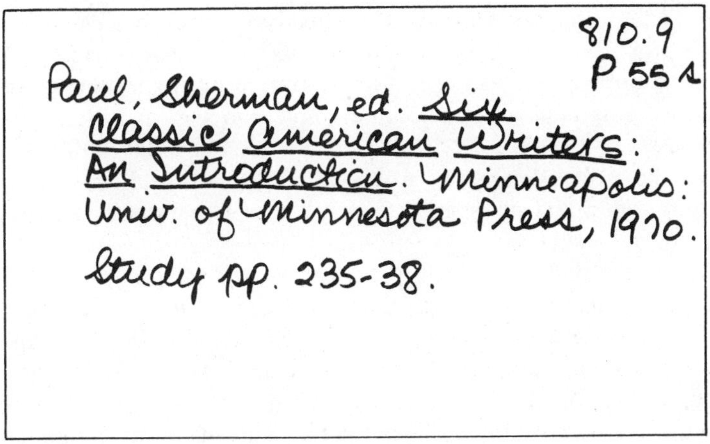

Fig. 7: Card That Refers to a Portion of a Book

Paul, Sherman, ed. *Six Classic American Writers: An Introduction*. Minneapolis: Univ. of Minnesota Press, 1970. Study pp. 235-38.

810.9
P 55 s

The Library Reference Room

You will need a system of library study that will save time and produce results. Adding a few sources to your bibliography during preliminary reading is only incidental to your main bibliographical development. After preliminary reading and your selection of a restricted topic, you will need to investigate thoroughly all avenues of approach to the subject. To that end, you should follow established procedures which direct you to the important bibliographies and indexes in your library's reference room. In these books you will discover a vast array of source material. Your stack of bibliography cards will grow rapidly, providing a valuable index to the range and scope of past and present scholarship related to your subject.

The step-by-step method of investigation that follows in this chapter should provide a basis for thorough coverage of your topic: it takes you first to bibliographies and indexes, then to the card catalog, and finally to the books and articles themselves. Following this system will ensure efficiency and skill in the preparation of your paper.

Before beginning formal research, you may wish to tour the library to learn its organization. Your tour should include the information desk, the reference room, the card catalog, the periodicals rooms, the stacks (if they are open to undergraduates), and other speciality areas such as microfilm room, photocopying area, listening area for records and tapes, and the viewing room for films and film loops.

Experienced researchers usually begin their investigation in the reference room. There they gather a list of sources from bibliographies, indexes, and other works of reference. Later, at the card catalog, they supplement their list and record call numbers. Only then do they begin serious reading for note-taking.

You may employ this same procedure. Already you should have a few bibliography cards that you recorded during your preliminary reading in encyclopedias and other general works. Now you need to expand this small list into a full working bibliography. Keep in mind, however, that bibliographies and indexes in the reference room do not provide information for note-taking; rather, they direct you to books, pamphlets, and articles in collections, magazines, and newspapers where you will find detailed treatment of your topic.

Bibliographies and indexes classify their listings according to individual systems that vary from work to work. Before using any index, you should study its preliminary pages to determine its system of abbreviations, symbols, and classification. And, since indexes appear weekly, bimonthly, monthly, and yearly, you should look closely at the date of publication of each one you select. For example, if your topic concerns a contemporary problem, you would want to concentrate on recent listings, but if your subject is a historical figure like Woodrow Wilson, you would want to examine earlier indexes, especially those for the years 1913-1921 when he was president.

Because reference works serve many students, you must not take them from the library. Rather, make notes from them and leave them on a table so that the librarians may return them to their proper position on the shelves.

BIBLIOGRAPHIES

In the reference room you will find separate bibliographies on a wide range of subjects. Some, like *A Shakespeare Bibliography,* are standard bibliographies that list sources in existence for some time. Others, like *Bibliographic Index,* are current bibliographies that list recent publications and that are kept up-to-date by supplements.

Bibliographies also appear within other works. As noted previously, encyclopedias usually contain brief bibliographies at the end of most articles. Critical and biographical studies often have bibliographies at the end of the book; for example, Thomas J. Fleming's *Man Who Dared the Lightning* has a four-page bibliography. Most scholarly journals maintain up-to-date bibliographies; history students depend upon *English Historical Review,* literature students look to the *MLA Bibliography,* biology students consult *Biological Abstracts.*

As a beginning researcher, you need a comprehensive listing of major reference materials in your subject field. To that end, Appendix II of this manual contains lists of standard reference works and journals in the following subject areas: applied sciences (pp. 155-60), art (pp. 160-61), biological sciences (pp. 161-63), business (pp. 163-64), education (pp. 164-

65), English language and literature (pp. 165-69), foreign languages (pp. 169-73), health and physical education (pp. 173-75), home economics (p. 175), music (pp. 176-77), philosophy (pp. 177-78), psychology (pp. 178-79), religion (pp. 179-80), social sciences (pp. 180-86), and speech and drama (pp. 186-87). A brief glance at these lists will show you that they contain titles of major bibliographies in all these disciplines.

Then, for thorough coverage of your field, examine the following reference sources; each of these books functions as a bibliography that offers a list of other bibliographies:

Barton, Mary N., and Marion V. Bell, eds. *Reference Books: A Brief Guide for Students and Other Users of the Library.* 7th ed. Baltimore: Enoch Pratt Free Library, 1970.

Besterman, Theodore. *A World Bibliography of Bibliographies.* 4th ed. 5 vols. Lausanne: Societas Bibliographica, 1965.

Murphey, Robert W. *How and Where to Look It Up: A Guide to Standard Sources of Information.* New York: McGraw-Hill, 1958.

Shores, Louis. *Basic Reference Sources.* Ed. Lee Ash. Library Reference Series. Rpt. of 1954 ed. Boston: Gregg, 1972.

Walford, Arthur J., ed. *Guide to Reference Material.* 3rd ed. London: Library Association, 1973.

Winchell, Constance M. *Guide to Reference Books.* 8th ed. Chicago: American Library Association, 1967. Supplements, 1965-66, 1967-68, and 1969-70.

Let us assume you wish to proceed with the investigation of Ben Franklin begun earlier in this chapter. You would first examine the listings under "History" (pp. 183-84), "Political Science" (pp. 184-85), and "American Literature" (pp. 165-66) in Appendix II and perhaps one or two of the books listed immediately above. As a result, you would find such works as:

American Historical Association. *Guide to Historical Literature.* Ed. George F. Howe and others. New York: Macmillan, 1961.

Beers, Henry P. *Bibliographies in American History.* New York: H. W. Wilson, 1942.

Northup, Clark S. *A Register of Bibliographies of the English Language and Literature.* New York: Hafner, 1962.

Examining these and other books like them, you would then search for special bibliographies of Franklin. In this case, fortunately, there are two bibliographies exclusively concerned with our subject:

Ford, Paul Leicester. *Franklin Bibliography: A List of Books Written by, or Relating to, Benjamin Franklin.* Brooklin: n.p., 1889. Rev. by R. R. Bowker in *Library Journal,* XIV, 425.

"List of Works Relating to Benjamin Franklin Published Since the Franklin Bicentenary." Washington D.C.: Library of Congress, 1924.

However, if your thorough investigation uncovers the fact that no bibliography devoted solely to your subject exists, you will still have plenty of other reference material to work with. Even with the Franklin bibliographies above, you would need up-to-date reference sources because new discoveries are made regularly, even about such historical figures as Benjamin Franklin. Scholars are constantly reinterpreting such things as his writings, the circumstances surrounding him during his age, and the effect he had upon others.

Therefore, in addition to such special bibliographies you should also examine:

> *Bibliographic Index: A Cumulative Bibliography of Bibliographies.* New York: H. W. Wilson, 1938-date.

Although *Bibliographic Index* originally covered only the years 1937-42, it is kept current by supplements. It is therefore valuable for bringing your investigation of a topic up-to-date. A sample entry from *Bibliographic Index* of 1971 uncovers these sources:

Fig. 8: From *Bibliographic Index, 1971.* 1. Subject heading **2.** Entry of book that contains a bibliography on Franklin **3.** Specific pages on which bibliography is located

FRANKLIN, Benjamin, 1706-1790
1— Fleming, Thomas J. Man who dared the
      lightning; a new look at Benjamin Frank-
      lin. Morrow '71 p515-20
    Wright, Esmond. Benjamin Franklin and
      American independence. English univs. press
2—   '66 p 175-6 annot

                    about
    Korty, M. B. Franklin's world of books.
      J Lib Hist 2:326-8 O '67

                by and about
    Hillesheim, James W. and Merrill, George D.
      eds. Theory and practice in the history of
      American education; a bk. of readings.
3—   Goodyear pub. co. '71 p 120-2
    Paul, Sherman, ed. Six classic American
      writers; an introduction. Univ. of Minn.
      press '70 p235-8

Each entry in *Bibliographic Index* directs you to the specific bibliographic section within a critical study. In other words, by consulting this text, you would have discovered not only five books about Franklin but also five additional bibliographic lists. For example, a bibliography on Franklin will be found on pp. 515-20 of Thomas J. Fleming's *Man Who Dared the Lightning* and on pp. 175-76 of Esmond Wright's *Benjamin Franklin and American Independence.* This information should be noted on a bibliography card, as follows:

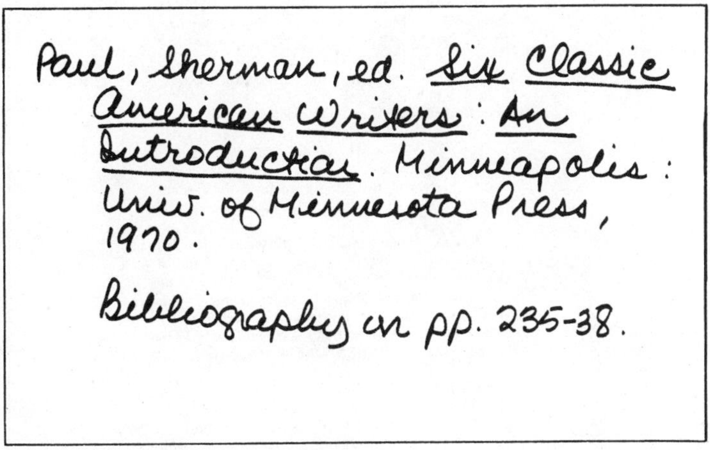

Fig. 9: Card Listing a Bibliographic Source

Paul, Sherman, ed. *Six Classic American Writers: An Introduction.* Minneapolis: Univ. of Minnesota Press, 1970.

Bibliography on pp. 235-38.

Another reference aid of this general nature is *Bulletin of Bibliography and Magazine Notes* (Boston: F. W. Faxon, 1897-date). The first page of each volume contains an index.

TRADE BIBLIOGRAPHIES

You may also want to use the trade bibliographies, which are works intended primarily for use by booksellers and librarians. As a researcher, you will find them helpful in three ways: to discover sources which may not be listed in other bibliographies or in the card catalog of your library; to locate facts of publication, such as place and date; and, especially, to learn if a book is in print.

Subject Guide to Books in Print (New York: Bowker, 1957-date) supplies a subject index that enables you to discover new sources. For example, the 1974 edition contains an extensive listing about Benjamin Franklin; a small portion follows:

Fig. 10: From _Subject Guide to Books in Print_
1. Subject **2.** Dates of subject's life span **3.** Author **4.** Title **5.** Date of publication **6.** Price **7.** Publisher **8.** Library of Congress Number **9.** International Standard Book Number (used when ordering) **10.** Paperback book

```
1
2      FRANKLIN, BENJAMIN, (1706-1790)
         Aldridge, Alfred O. Benjamin Franklin & Nature's God.
           1967. 7.50 (ISBN 0-8223-0002-8). Duke.
         — —Franklin & His French Contemporaries. 1956. 10.00x
           (ISBN 0-8147-0003-9). NYU Pr.
3        Amacher, Richard E. Benjamin Franklin. 1962. pap. 2.45
           (T12, Twayne). Coll & U Pr.
4        — Benjamin Franklin. (U. S. Authors Ser, No. 12). (gr.
           10 up). 6.50. Twayne.
         Barbour, Frances M., ed. Concordance to the Sayings in
5          Franklin's Poor Richard. LC 73-20460 1974. 15.00
           (ISBN 0-8103-1009-0). Gale.
         Bigelow, ed. Works of Ben Franklin, 12 vols. 180.00.
           Somerset Pub.
         Bowen, Catherine D. The Most Dangerous Man in
           America: Scenes from the Life of Benjamin Franklin.
6          1974 8.95 (ISBN 0-316-10396-9, Pub. by Atlantic
           Monthly Pr). Little.
         Buxbaum, Melvin H. Benjamin Franklin & the Zealous
           Presbyterians. 1974. price not set (ISBN 0-271-01176-
7          9) Pa St U Pr.
         Clark, William B. Ben Franklin's Privateers: A Naval Epic
8          of the American Revolution. LC 74-90485. Repr. of
9          1956 ed. 11.00 (ISBN 0-8371-2262-7) Greenwood.
         Cohen, I. Bernard. Franklin & Newton: An Inquiry into
           Speculative Newtonian Experimental Science &
           Franklin's Work in Electricity As an Example Thereof.
           rev ed. 1973. 15.00x (ISBN 0-674-31801-3). Harvard U
           Pr.
         Country Beautiful Editors & Marks, D'Arlyn, eds. The
           Most Amazing American: Benjamin Franklin. LC 73-
           75989. (America's Founding Fathers Ser.). (Illus.).
           1973. 12.95 (ISBN 0-87294-035-7). Country Beautiful.
         Crane, Verner W. Benjamin Franklin & A Rising People.
           (The Library of American Biography). 1954. 5.00
10         (ISBN 0-316-16011-3); pap. 2.95 (ISBN 0-316-16012-
           1, 1962). Little.
         Crowther, James G. Famous American Men of Science.
           facs. ed. LC 69-18925. (Essay Index Reprint Ser).
           1937. 14.25 (ISBN 0-8369-0040-5). Bks for Libs.
         Currey, Cecil B. Code Number 72: Ben Franklin, Patriot
           or Spy? LC 72-7497. (Illus.). 1972. 7.95 (ISBN 0-13-
           139493-2). P-H.
```

Many items from this _Subject Guide to Books in Print_ will lend themselves to your study. Therefore, bibliography cards should be made for the most promising, as in this sample card:

Fig. 11: Sample Bibliography Card for Source Found in _Subject Guide to Books in Print_
The publisher's full name and city are listed in a separate section of _Books in Print_

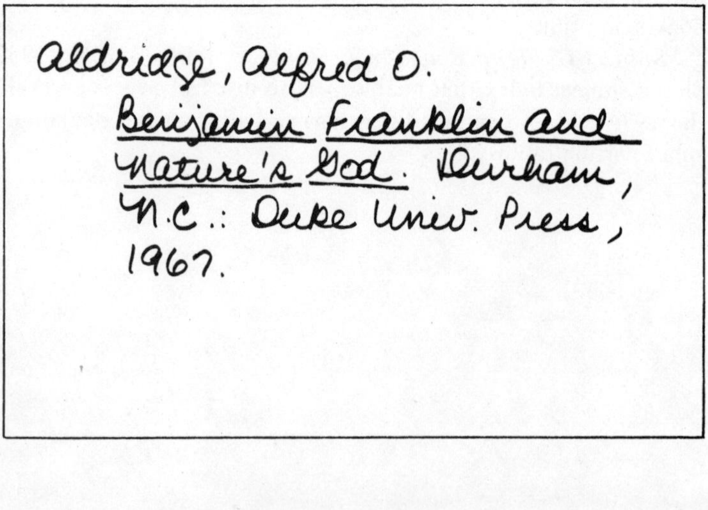

Aldridge, Alfred O.
Benjamin Franklin and
Nature's God. Durham,
N.C.: Duke Univ. Press,
1967.

In like manner, you should become familiar with *Books in Print* (New York: Bowker, 1948-date). This work provides an author-title index to the *Publishers' Trade List Annual* (New York: Bowker, 1874-date), a list of books currently in print. Also, *Publishers' Weekly* (New York: Bowker, 1872-date) offers current publication data. In short, you cannot overlook the trade bibliographies as a possible source of information. Others are:

Paperbound Books in Print. New York: Bowker, 1955-date.

> Since the publication of paperback books is increasing annually and since important books are occasionally found *only* in paperback form, you may find this text a necessary tool.

Cumulative Book Index. Minneapolis [later New York]: H. W. Wilson, 1900-date.

> This work lists books by author, subject, editor, and translator. Use it to find complete publication data or to locate *all* material in English on a particular subject.

The National Union Catalog: A Cumulative Author List. Ann Arbor: Edwards, 1953-date.

> Basically, this work is the card catalog in book form; that is, it provides a list representing the Library of Congress printed cards and also titles reported by other libraries. It supplements the *Library of Congress Catalog.*

Library of Congress Catalog: Books: Subjects. Washington, D.C.: Library of Congress, 1950-date.

> This catalog complements *The National Union Catalog* by supplying a subject classification. Separate volumes are available for the years 1950-54, 1955-59, 1960-64, and annually thereafter.

General Catalogue of Printed Books. London: Trustees of the British Museum, 1881-date.

> This British publication serves a corresponding function to *The National Union Catalog.* Such listings are available for most nations.

Union List of Serials in Libraries of the United States and Canada. 3rd ed. New York: H. W. Wilson, 1965. Supplements, *New Serial Titles,* Washington, D.C.: Library of Congress, 1953-date.

> You may consult this work to determine if a nearby library has a magazine that is unavailable in your library.

Ulrich's International Periodicals Directory. Ed. Merle Rohinsky. 15th ed. New York: Bowker, 1973.

> This work is a guide to current periodicals, both domestic and foreign.

INDEXES

A general index furnishes the page number(s) of another book or magazine where you will find specific information. Fundamentally, there are three types: indexes to materials in books and collections, indexes to literature in periodicals, and indexes to materials in newspapers.

Indexes to Books and Collections

First, you should recall *Bibliographic Index* (see pp. 18-19), which refers you to books or collections as well as bibliographies. In addition, you should familiarize yourself with:

> *Essay and General Literature Index, 1900-1933.* New York: H. W. Wilson, 1934. Supplements, 1934-date.
>
> *Biography Index: A Quarterly Index to Biographical Material in Books and Magazines.* New York: H. W. Wilson, 1946/47-date.

The first index directs you to material within books and collections of a biographical and/or critical nature. Note the following entry from a supplement of *Essay and General Literature Index:*

Fig. 12: From *Essay and General Literature Index*
1. Subject 2. Article by Franklin 3. Book in which Franklin's essay appears 4. Designates that following essays are *about* Franklin, rather than essays written *by* him 5. Author of essay about Franklin 6. Title of the essay 7. Book in which the essay appears

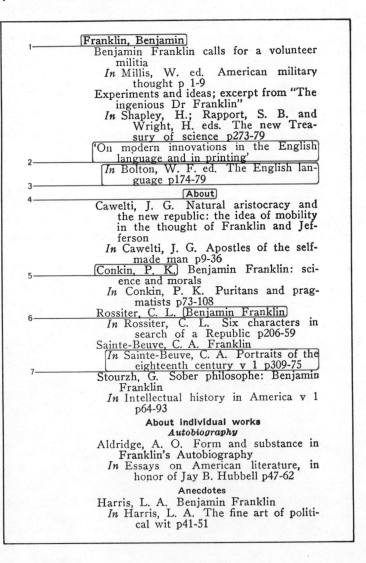

Franklin, Benjamin
    Benjamin Franklin calls for a volunteer militia
        In Millis, W. ed. American military thought p 1-9
    Experiments and ideas; excerpt from "The ingenious Dr Franklin"
        In Shapley, H.; Rapport, S. B. and Wright, H. eds. The new Treasury of science p273-79
    'On modern innovations in the English language and in printing'
        In Bolton, W. F. ed. The English language p174-79
    About
        Cawelti, J. G. Natural aristocracy and the new republic: the idea of mobility in the thought of Franklin and Jefferson
            In Cawelti, J. G. Apostles of the self-made man p9-36
        Conkin, P. K. Benjamin Franklin: science and morals
            In Conkin, P. K. Puritans and pragmatists p73-108
        Rossiter, C. L. Benjamin Franklin
            In Rossiter, C. L. Six characters in search of a Republic p206-59
        Sainte-Beuve, C. A. Franklin
            In Sainte-Beuve, C. A. Portraits of the eighteenth century v 1 p309-75
        Stourzh, G. Sober philosophe: Benjamin Franklin
            In Intellectual history in America v 1 p64-93
            About individual works
                Autobiography
        Aldridge, A. O. Form and substance in Franklin's Autobiography
            In Essays on American literature, in honor of Jay B. Hubbell p47-62
            Anecdotes
        Harris, L. A. Benjamin Franklin
            In Harris, L. A. The fine art of political wit p41-51

Note that this index sends you to essays *within* books that you might otherwise overlook; for example, J. G. Cawelti's essay appears in *Apostles of the Self-Made Man* and P. K. Conkin's essay appears in a book with the deceptive title *Puritans and Pragmatists*. The publishers and dates for these entries are found in a "List of Books Indexed" at the end of each volume of *Essay and General Literature Index.*

Biography Index is a good starting point if your study involves a famous person. It gives clues to biographical information for people of all lands. (However, for the years 1900-47 you should see *Essay and General Literature Index.)* Note the following short excerpt from *Biography Index:*

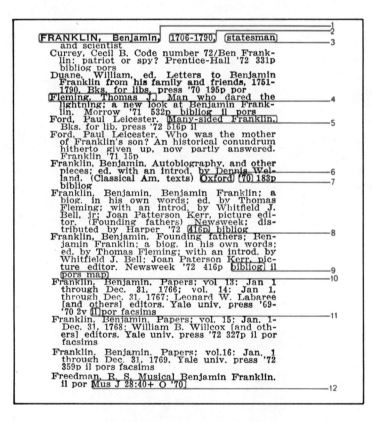

Fig. 13: From
Biography Index
1. Subject 2. Dates of subject's birth and death 3. Subject's profession 4. Author of the biography 5. Title of the biography 6. Publisher 7. Date of publication 8. Number of pages 9. Contains a bibliography 10. Contains portraits and a map 11. Illustrated 12. Publication data for a periodical

Most indexes published by the H. W. Wilson Company use this same code system. Specifically, note the code for journal volumes and page numbers—"23:81-91 D'71." To conform to the suggestions in this manual, you will want to record this data differently on your bibliography card, as follows:

Morris, R. B. "Meet Dr. Franklin." American Heritage, 23 (Dec. 1971), 81-91.

When looking for biographical information, you should also consult a good biographical dictionary (see p. 4).

Another important index is the cumulated subject and author indexes to *Dissertation Abstracts International* (Ann Arbor: Univ. Microfilms, 1970-date; formerly *Microfilm Abstracts,* 1938-51, and *Dissertation Abstracts,* 1952-69). Issue No. 12, Part II, of each volume contains the cumulated subject and author indexes for Issues 1-12 of the volume's two sections—A, Humanities and Social Sciences, and B, Sciences and Engineering. The *Comprehensive Dissertation Index* lists dissertations from 1861 to 1972 according to subject matter. For example, Volume 29 includes the following entries for Benjamin Franklin:

FRANKLIN
AN ANNOTATED CHECKLIST OF THE LETTERS OF
FRANKLIN BENJAMIN SANBORN (1831-1917)—
CLARKSON, JOHN W., JR. (PH.D. 1971 COLUMBIA
UNIVERSITY) X1971, p.222
FRANKLIN AND CREVECOEUR: INDIVIDUALISM AND
THE AMERICAN DREAM IN THE EIGHTEENTH
CENTURY— AGEE, WILLIAM HERBERT (PH.D. 1969
UNIVERSITY OF MINNESOTA) 600p. 31/01-A, p.380
70–01830
BENJAMIN FRANKLIN AND HIS BIOGRAPHERS: A
CRITICAL STUDY— KUSHEN, BETTY SANDRA (PH.D.
1969 NEW YORK UNIVERSITY) 317p. 30/09-A,
p.3946   70–03081
BENJAMIN FRANKLIN AND THE ZEALOUS
PRESBYTERIANS— BUXBAUM, MELVIN (PH.D. 1968
UNIVERSITY OF CHICAGO) X1968, p.172
SPIRITUAL AUTOBIOGRAPHY IN SELECTED WRITINGS
OF SEWALL, EDWARDS, BYRD, WOOLMAN, AND
FRANKLIN: A COMPARISON OF TECHNIQUE AND
CONTENT— MILLAR, ALBERT EDWARD, JR. (PH.D.
1968 UNIVERSITY OF DELAWARE) 362p. 29/06-A,
p.1873   68–15542
BENJAMIN FRANKLIN: A STUDY IN SELF-
MYTHOLOGY— WHITE, CHARLES WILLIAM (PH.D.
1967 HARVARD UNIVERSITY) X1967, p.175
THE GROWTH OF THE BENJAMIN FRANKLIN IMAGE:
THE PHILADELPHIA YEARS — SAPPENFIELD, JAMES
ALLEN (PH.D. 1966 STANFORD UNIVERSITY) 233p.
27/10-A, p.3469   67–04426
FRANKLIN'S STYLE: IRONY AND THE COMIC— CLASBY,
NANCY TENFELDE (PH.D. 1966 THE UNIVERSITY OF
WISCONSIN) 273p. 28/02-A, p.622   66–09892

An abstract of the eighth entry, "Franklin's Style: Irony and the Comic" by Nancy Tenfelde Clasby, is to be found in Vol. 28, No. 2A, p. 622, of *Dissertation Abstracts International*. A portion of that abstract follows:

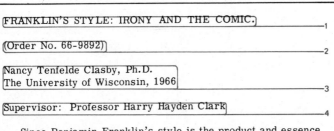

Fig. 16: From *Dissertation Abstracts International* **1.** Title of dissertation **2.** Order number if you desire to buy a copy of the work **3.** Author, school, and date **4.** Faculty chairman of the dissertation committee **5.** Price of microfilm copy of the dissertation **6.** Price of Xerox copy of the dissertation **7.** Total number of pages of the dissertation

FRANKLIN'S STYLE: IRONY AND THE COMIC. —1

(Order No. 66-9892) —2

Nancy Tenfelde Clasby, Ph.D.
The University of Wisconsin, 1966 —3

Supervisor: Professor Harry Hayden Clark —4

Since Benjamin Franklin's style is the product and essence of a lifetime of expressive action, an analysis of it should bring us closer to an understanding of his extremely complex man. My dissertation is aimed at collating and interpreting those elements of his style which will help to fill in the outlines of the figure which modern Franklin scholars have only begun to discover. There are three parts to this dissertation: the first deals with the expressive character of certain elements of style, the second with Franklin's mind, the source of expression, and the third, and longest, section presents and interprets statistics on such features of his style as parallelism, metaphor and tone. The comic and ironic tones which inform so much of Franklin's best work are treated at length in the third section.

••• ••• ••• ••• ••• ••• ••• ••• ••• ••• ••• ••• ••• •••

Reservations about the eighteenth-century world and its values did not, however, dull Franklin's passion for communication. In life, Franklin was an eiron, a maskmaker whose activities were shaped to present various appearances when seen from various angles. He made sure that people saw only those aspects of himself that they were capable of recognizing as parts of some coherent personality. In its myriad delicate adjustments to varied audiences his prose bears the marks of the same consuming effort to clarify, to make sense. The style is concrete and direct, never abstract, seldom merely decorative. It aims at the attractive statement of certain limited truths, and its aspect changes as Franklin adopts various masks. Beneath the multiple surface characteristics of the style, however, is a radical unity, a gestalt which reflects in miniature the quality and direction of a lifetime of communicative gestures. The whole effort of this paper, in its various parts, is directed toward a clarification of the full outlines of a carefully structured life and style. —5

Microfilm $3.55; Xerography $12.40; 273 pages. —7
—6

An abstract, of course, is only a brief summary of the entire work. If the dissertation is pertinent to your topic or if you plan an exhaustive investigation, you may wish to order a copy of the complete work from University Microfilms, Inc. To that end, information at the end of the abstract stipulates the cost of microfilm and Xerox copies of the complete dissertation.

Indexes to Literature in Periodicals

Because they provide four types of information better than any other source, you must use articles in periodicals. Understandably, they contain: the most recent materials on any subject; obscure, temporary, or extremely new materials; the climate of opinion of a particular period; and supplements to professional literature. Remember, too, that materials often appear as journal articles before their publication in book form.

There are two main types of periodicals: general periodicals (for example, *Time, Ladies' Home Journal, Reader's Digest*) and professional journals (for example, *American Historical Review, Journal of Psychology,* or *National Tax Journal*). You will use both types, of course, but you should depend mainly upon the learned journals whose treatment of topics is more critically detailed.

As an index to articles in periodicals, you should first investigate:

Readers' Guide to Periodical Literature. New York: H. W. Wilson, 1900-date.

A sample entry follows:

Fig. 17: From *Readers' Guide to Periodical Literature*
1. Subject **2.** A piece by Franklin himself **3.** Designates that the following articles are *about* Franklin **4.** Title of article **5.** Author **6.** Illustrated with portraits **7.** Indicates a review: Van Doren's book *Benjamin Franklin* was reviewed in *Commonweal* by J. Cournos **8.** Name of periodical and publication data

FRANKLIN, Benjamin — 1
Benjamin Franklin meets the press; excerpts from his writings. por facsim Scholastic 67:14-15 Ja 12 '56
Benjamin Franklin on his religious faith; letter to Ezra Stiles. Am Heritage 7:105 D '55 — 2
Excerpts from his voluminous writings. por N Y Times Mag p76 Ja 15 '56
Farther experiments and observations in electricity; excerpt from Experiments and observations on electricity. bibliog Science 123:47-50 Ja 13 '56
From Ben's letters. Time 67:90 Ja 30 '56
Mr Franklin, self-revealed. facsim Life 40: 74-7+ Ja 9 '56

about — 3
Americana page. Hobbies 61:100 Jl '56
Ben Franklin: an affectionate portrait, by N. B. Keyes. Review
Sat R 39:16 Ja 21 '56. W. M. Wallace
Ben Franklin, trail blazer for inventors. P. Lee. il pors map Pop Mech 105:99-102+ Ja '56 — 4
Benjamin and the bell. M. Alkus. Ladies Home J 72:180 Ap '55 — 5
Benjamin Franklin and the French alliance; adapted from Secret war of independence. H. Augur. il por Am Heritage 7:65-88 Ap '56 — 6
Benjamin Franklin, by C. Van Doren. Review
Commonweal 63:497 F 10 '56. J. Cournos — 7
Benjamin Franklin in modern life and education. T. Woody. Sch & Soc 84:102-7 S 29 '56
Benjamin Franklin the diplomat. por U S Dept State Bul 34:50-1 Ja 9 '56
Benjamin Franklin's grand design; Albany plan of union. R. B. Morris. il por map Am Heritage 7:4-7+ F '56 — 8

Again, you would want to write out bibliography cards for those entries that look promising, as in the following example:

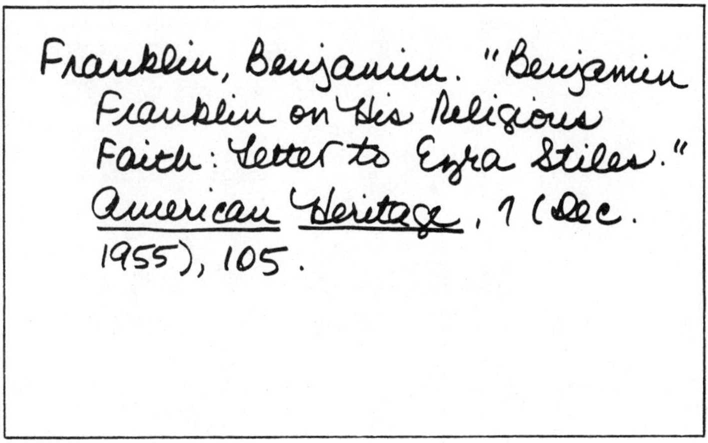

Franklin, Benjamin. "Benjamin Franklin on His Religious Faith: Letter to Ezra Stiles." American Heritage, 7 (Dec. 1955), 105.

Fig. 18:
Bibliography Card
for Entry Taken
from *Readers'
Guide to Periodical
Literature*

In most instances, this index directs you to general periodicals, though since 1953 certain scientific periodicals have been included. If you wish a more in-depth examination of the scholarly journals, such as *New England Quarterly* and *Political Science Quarterly,* you should investigate the following (listed in chronological order):

> *International Index.* Vols. 1-18. New York: H. W. Wilson, 1907-65.
> *Social Sciences and Humanities Index.* Vols. 19-61. New York: H. W. Wilson, 1965-74.
> *Humanities Index.* Vols. 1-   . New York: H. W. Wilson, 1974-date.
> *Social Sciences Index.* Vols. 1-   . New York: H. W. Wilson, 1974-date.

Both the new *Humanities Index* and the *Social Sciences Index* supersede the *Social Sciences and Humanities Index.* The *Humanities Index* now serves as an index to articles in 260 magazines in the following fields: archaeology, classical studies, area studies, folklore, history, language and literature, literary and political criticism, performing arts, philosophy, religion, and theology. *Social Sciences Index* catalogs articles in 263 magazines in these fields: anthropology, economics, environmental science, geography, law and criminology, medical sciences, political science, psychology, public administration, and sociology.

Because it is so new, an examination of the *Humanities Index,* of course, would produce few sources on Benjamin Franklin; an examination of one of its predecessors, say the 1960-62 issue of the *International Index,* would produce better results:

Fig. 19: From
International Index
1. Subject **2.** Title of
article **3.** Author
4. Name of journal
and publication data

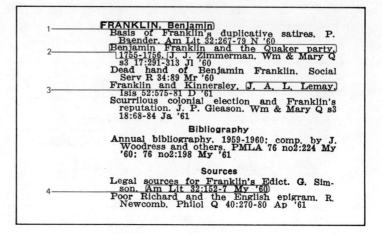

You may also need to investigate:

Nineteenth Century Readers' Guide to Periodical Literature, 1890-1899 [with
supplementary indexing, 1900-22]. 2 vols. New York: H. W. Wilson, 1944.
Poole's Index to Periodical Literature, 1802-1881. Rev. ed. Boston: Houghton
Mifflin, 1891. Supplements cover the years 1882-1906.
> With this work you may locate information on materials from 1802-1906.
> Note that *Poole's Index* has only a subject classification. See, however,
> Marion V. Bell and Jean C. Bacon, *Poole's Index Date and Volume Key*
> (Chicago: Association of College and Reference Libraries, 1957) for an
> alphabetical title listing.

Newspaper Indexes

Newspapers are an excellent source of information. Therefore, you
should familiarize yourself with the *New York Times Index* (New York:
New York Times, 1913-date). It not only indexes the *New York Times* but
also indirectly indexes most other newspapers by revealing the date on
which the same news was probably reported in other newspapers. Many libraries have the *New York Times* on microfilm. A sample entry from the
New York Times Index follows:

**Fig. 20: From *New
York Times Index***
1. Subject **2.** Cross
reference **3.** Title of
newspaper article
4. Date, section
number, and page
number (November
25, Section 8, p. 22)

For British newspapers a similar index is the *Official Index* [to *The London Times*] (London: Times, 1907-date). It is available in most American libraries.

Pamphlet Indexes

The principal index to most pamphlet material is:

Vertical File Index: A Subject and Title Index to Selected Pamphlet Material. New York: H. W. Wilson, 1932/35-date.

Your library may not own many of the items listed, but the catalog gives a description of each entry, the price, and the means by which you may order it.

Finding the Call Number

Sometime before completing your work in the reference room, you probably will want to begin preliminary investigations of some of the more promising sources you have listed on your bibliography cards. For that purpose you should turn to the card catalog, which specifies the location of all books in the library. (For periodicals most libraries have a separate, smaller catalog, sometimes called a *cardex.*) With your bibliography cards arranged alphabetically, you can easily find and record the call number for each book. If, after exerting sufficient effort, you cannot locate a catalog card, you may seek help from a librarian.

For each book you will usually find in the catalog at least three separate entries, filed under: (1) the author's name, printed on the first line (see p. 30); (2) the title of the work, typed in black ink at the top of the card (see p. 30); and (3) the subject, typed in red ink at the top of the card (see p. 33). Additional catalog cards are filed for coauthors, translators, editors, and illustrators, and for other subject headings.

MAIN ENTRY CARD

As you go through the card catalog you will quickly discover that there is a main entry card for each book you are seeking, usually filed under the author's name. For example:

Fig. 21: Main Entry Card (Author Card)
1. Classification number 2. Author number 3. Author 4. Life span of author 5. Title 6. Editor 7. Place of publication 8. Publisher 9. Date of publication 10. Technical description: size, number of pages, illustrations, etc. 11. Note on contents of book 12. Separate card also filed under editor's name 13. Publisher of this card 14. Order number-Library of Congress 15. Library of Congress Call Number and date

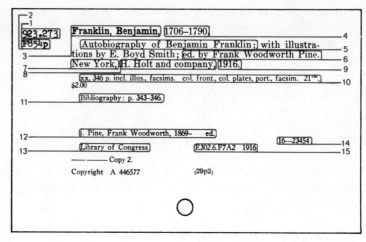

You may gather several kinds of information from this main entry card. Specifically, you should record the *complete* call number—in this case, $\frac{923.273}{F854p}$. Do not copy the first line only! You must have the full number, usually consisting of two (and sometimes three) lines of symbols. In addition, you should record any bibliographical notations, such as "Bibliography: p. 343-46." Data of this sort can direct you to additional sources.

TITLE CARD

Another card is always filed alphabetically by the book title:

Fig. 22: Title Card
1. Title, usually typed in black ink 2. Main entry card filed under "Newcomb, Benjamin H." 3. Subject headings under which you will find this same card

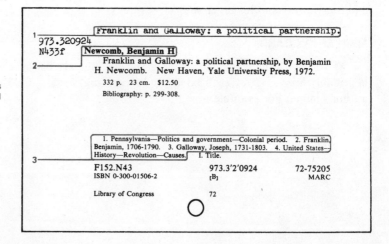

A third type of card found in the catalog is the subject card—but we will come to that in a moment.

THE CALL NUMBER

The library classifies and arranges its books by the call number, which is usually a combination of the Dewey Decimal System and the Cutter Author Number. In a call number such as $\frac{973.320924}{N433f}$, the first line is the Dewey Decimal Number, and the second line is the Cutter Author Number. The Dewey system divides all books into ten general classifications:

```
000-099  General Works
100-199  Philosophy
200-299  Religion
300-399  Social Sciences
400-499  Language
500-599  Pure Science
600-699  Technology (Applied Sciences)
700-799  The Arts
800-899  Literature
900-999  History
```

The Dewey system then divides each of these ten general classes into ten smaller divisions. For example, the general literature classification (800-899) is broken down into:

```
800-809  General Works [on Literature]
810-819  American Literature
820-829  English Literature
830-839  German Literature
840-849  French Literature
850-859  Italian Literature
860-869  Spanish Literature
870-879  Latin Literature
880-889  Greek and Classical Literature
890-899  Literature of Other Languages
```

Next, American Literature (810-819) is divided into the following classifications:

```
810  American Literature (General)
811  Poetry
812  Drama
813  Fiction
814  Essays
815  Speeches
816  Letters
817  Satire and Humor
818  Miscellany
819  Minor Related Literature
```

Immediately below the Dewey classification number, most libraries also insert an author number, a set of letters and numerals based on the Cutter Three-Figure Author Table. For example, "N433f" is the author number for Newcomb's *Franklin and Galloway*. The letter "N" is the initial of the author's last name; next the Cutter table stipulates the Arabic numeral "433"; and the lowercase "f" designates the first important letter(s) in the title to distinguish this entry from similar books by Newcomb. Thus, the complete call number for Newcomb's book is $\frac{973.320924}{N433f}$. You must use both items to locate the book.

Some libraries employ the Library of Congress classification system, which features capital letters followed by Arabic numerals to designate the subdivisions. The major divisions of the Library of Congress system follow:

A   General Works and Polygraphy
B   Philosophy and Religion
C   History and Auxiliary Sciences
D   History and Topography
     (excluding America)
E-F   History: America
G   Geography and Anthropology
H   Social Sciences
J   Political Science
K   Law
L   Education
M   Music
N   Fine Arts
P   Language and Literature
Q   Science
R   Medicine
S   Agriculture and Plant and Animal Husbandry
T   Technology
U   Military Science
V   Naval Science
Z   Bibliography and Library Science

An example of this system might be as follows:

TD   Environmental Technology
833   Air Pollution
.H48   Author Number

This call number for the Library of Congress system directs the researcher to the following book: Howard E. Hesketh, *Understanding and Controlling Air Pollution,* 2nd ed. (Ann Arbor, Michigan: Ann Arbor Science Publishers, 1974). In contrast, the Dewey classification number would be $\frac{628.53}{H461u}$.

Using the Catalog as an Index

The card catalog indexes all important subject areas by means of subject cards and tabular headings. This is the third kind of card to be found in the catalog. For example, if your subject is Benjamin Franklin, you would discover under "United States History" an index to all books in the library on this subject. Note the following subject card:

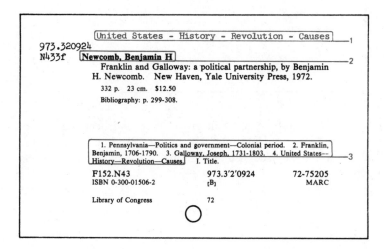

Franklin and Galloway: a political partnership, by Benjamin H. Newcomb. New Haven, Yale University Press, 1972.

Fig. 23: Subject Card

1. Subject heading, usually typed in red ink
2. Main entry card filed under "Newcomb, Benjamin H."
3. Other subject headings under which you will find this same card

The library makes a subject card of this nature for every topic developed within each book. As shown above, the library will index this same book by Newcomb under these additional subject headings:

> Pennsylvania—Politics and government—Colonial period
> Franklin, Benjamin, 1706-1790
> Galloway, Joseph, 1731-1803

In other words, the card catalog of your library is, among other things, a subject index to the books it lists.

Other Catalog Cards

Always be alert for special kinds of catalog cards. Temporary cards are of a different color and usually indicate that a book is not in circulation. However, ask the librarian about the book, for it may be available:

Fig. 24: Temporary Card

```
923.273
F8541ab      Franklin, Benjamin



             The autobiography of Benjamin
        Franklin, edited by Leonard W. Labaree
        and others.   New Haven, Yale University
        Press, 1964.

        Now on temporary display in the History
        Today book display in the Roberta White
        Reading Room, second floor.
```

Cross-reference cards refer you to alternate or related headings. There are two types. The "see" card indicates the correct heading under which material is listed, while the "see also" card directs you to related subjects that contain additional material:

Fig. 25: "See Also" Card

```
        United States--History--Revolution

           see also

        Pennsylvania--Politics and government--
           Colonial period
```

Your best procedure with the card catalog is a combination of practices: you can easily record call numbers while you search for new sources. For example, with your bibliography cards in hand, you should look first under the proper subject heading—"Franklin, Benjamin," in this instance. There you will find index cards for all books *by* Franklin that precede the books *about* him. At the same time, you will discover the call numbers for most of your sources. In addition, you may uncover new sources that supplement your working bibliography.

Getting Your Books and Periodical Articles

THE STACKS

Armed with the correct call numbers, you are now ready to locate your books in the stacks or, in the case of closed stacks, to request the books from a clerk. If a book is unavailable, you may request a "hold" on the book. When it returns, the librarian will reserve it for you.

THE RESERVE DESK

Recognizing the importance of certain books to their discipline, many instructors place them "on reserve" in the library so that a limited number of books will be available to many students. You will want to determine if any books necessary for your research are on reserve. To that end, you should ask the clerk at the desk to explain the filing system employed.

If you use a reserve book, you must usually read it in the library. Some libraries, however, permit overnight withdrawal of reserve books. But under no circumstances should you keep such a book for several days or hide it somewhere in the library for future use. These books must serve many students.

THE PERIODICALS ROOM

You will locate periodical articles in both bound and unbound volumes. The bound volumes, usually on open stacks, contain several issues within a hard cover. The unbound volumes are usually of recent publication. If periodicals are kept in closed stacks, you must provide the clerk with sufficient publication data.

Supplementing Library Materials

Without doubt the library is your best source of information when writing a research paper. But you may also find material in other places. For instance, you could write your U.S. Senator or Representative for one of the many booklets printed by the Government Printing Office. You will find a list of these materials, many of which are free, in a monthly catalog issued by the Superintendent of Documents, *United States Government Publications Monthly Catalog* (Washington, D.C.: GPO, 1895-date).

Also important are audiovisual materials: films, filmstrips, music, phonograph recordings, slides, and tape recordings. You may find these in the library or in some other location on or off campus.

Other good sources of information are: radio and television programs, lectures, letters, public addresses, personal interviews, and questionnaires.

■ All your work prior to actually writing the paper is organic and flexible. Therefore, after preliminary investigations, you need to take stock of your progress to that point. For example, as you gathered material for your working bibliography, you also should have uncovered and dipped into some of the more promising books and articles. Having gained from these an initial familiarity with your general subject, you should have framed a preliminary thesis sentence, thereby determining a little more accurately the direction of your future research. In addition, of course, you now should have in hand a good portion of your working bibliography, to which you will add new references as you come upon them while taking notes. Thus, your general subject will guide many aspects of your note-taking; but, at the same time, your note-taking will lead you to pin down the subject more specifically.

The Preliminary Outline

Before you progress very far in your note-taking, you should prepare a preliminary outline (write a final outline only *after* note-taking). It should be stressed that the preliminary outline is just that, a rough sketch of your major concerns, based upon ideas that you have absorbed while choosing and restricting your subject. It will serve the valuable purpose of giving order to your note-taking, thereby enabling you to choose quotes and material for paraphrase more wisely.

To develop the preliminary outline, you should follow two fairly simple steps: (1) jot down your ideas in a rough list, and (2) arrange the list into major and minor ideas. Suppose, for example, that your general topic is Lorraine Hansberry's drama *A Raisin in the Sun,* a play about a black family in a Chicago ghetto. Your rough list of ideas might look like this:

```
A problem play of escape from a ghetto
Relationship of Mama Younger and Walter, her son
Mama as dominant, a matriarch
Walter's frustrations in attempting to be the man of the
    house
Matriarchy as a theme of the drama
Is setting important?
Ruth and the theme of abortion
Beneatha as a black radical and revolutionary
```

Obviously, this list is not even a rough outline, but you now have your ideas on paper where you may examine them and find relationships among them. If you organize the items, grouping main topics and relating subordinate elements to them, you will, in turn, come up with a rough outline for your paper. Two possible arrangements are shown below:

Matriarchy in Lorraine
Hansberry's A Raisin in the
Sun

Matriarchy
    Matriarchy defined
    The history of matriarchy
    Matriarchy today
Women as matriarchs
    Mama Younger
    Beneatha Younger
    Ruth Younger
The effects of matriarchy
on the male
    Walter's emasculation
    Walter's rebellion
Search for harmony
    A collapsing family
    Mama's trust in Walter
    Walter's betrayal of
        that trust
Closing
    Walter's final emergence
        as a man
    Mama as a noble,
        inspirational figure

The Theme of Escape in
Lorraine Hansberry's A
Raisin in the Sun

The ghetto and its effects
    Ghetto conditions ex-
        plained
    The Youngers as a ghetto
        family
The dream of escape to a
better life
    Mama Younger's determi-
        nation to buy a house
    Beneatha's determination
        to be educated
    Ruth's desire for a home
        for her family
    Walter's liquor store
        scheme
The collapse of the dreams
    Walter's loss of the
        family fortune
    Walter's willingness to
        sell out to the white
        organization
Closing
    Walter's determination
        to stand as a man
    The family's determi-
        nation to escape the
        ghetto despite the loss
        of their money

Obviously, both "outlines" are sketchy, but they would serve the purpose of note-taking. Later, before actually writing the paper, you can develop a more formal outline. For now, however, you have a fairly good idea of what things to look for in books and articles—that is, a definition of matriarchy, the effects of ghetto life, and the sociological consequences of that life upon members of the Younger family.

Always be prepared to alter the outline as your focus on the subject sharpens. For example, if you decide that the theme of escape in *A Raisin in the Sun* would not prove fruitful, then adjust your outline and your thinking to a new direction, switching perhaps to the matriarchy theme.

When preparing a preliminary outline, remember that you may arrange it in one of two ways, either general to particular (deductive order) or particular to general (inductive order). If you arrange your materials deductively, you will present first a general statement (thesis) that you will afterwards support with specific details and instances. For example, the paper about *A Raisin in the Sun* might make some generalizations about matriarchy and then pinpoint particulars from the text. Similarly, you could use the deductive procedure in other kinds of research papers: stating the theme of a novel and then proving it with details from the work, presenting the conclusions of a laboratory experiment and then stating the particulars, or declaring the ruthlessness of a political dictator and then presenting evidence.

In other papers, however, you may wish to use the particular to general procedure. Using the inductive technique, you would reverse the process described in the paragraph above and present first the specifics of your argument and then work carefully toward a general conclusion. For example, the individual writing about *A Raisin in the Sun* might examine the characteristics of Mama Younger, Walter, and the others before arriving at any generalizations about matriarchy within the family. Such an arrangement, of course, would delay the expression of the thesis until late in the paper.

If your project demands it, you may want to use a more structured method of organization, such as cause and effect, comparison and contrast, chronological order, or process analysis. Because these methods call for fuller explanations than can be given here, you should consult any standard rhetoric book for a quick review.

Brief as they are, the rough outlines above would help you locate and record the important, necessary data and omit information that looks valuable but that, in fact, contributes little to your overall plan. Preliminary outlines are usually ragged and incomplete, but only you will see them. Such outlines represent roughly the best you can do before your note-taking is very far along.

You should not feel bound by this first outline. Instead, let it develop and grow; add new topics and discard others, rearrange your order, evaluate topics, and subordinate minor elements. In short, as your ideas materialize, you should allow your outline to expand accordingly. (Before writing your final outline, however, see pp. 52-55.)

Evaluating Your Source Material

You should skim all potentially relevant material to determine its relationship to your thesis and rough outline. When you discover something pertinent, you can then write accurate, detailed notes, recording only that material which will aid the development and clarification of your thesis.

Also, you should closely examine each book to see if it contains, in addition to its text, any of the following:

1. A *table of contents* that helps you discover the chapters that deal directly or indirectly with your topic. You may find, for example, that only one chapter is potentially useful.

2. A *preface* that may explain the presence or absence of certain material in the book.

3. An *introduction* that usually serves as a critical overview of the entire book, pinpointing the primary subject of the book and approaches taken toward it.

4. An *appendix* that offers additional materials of a supplementary nature not pertinent to the primary text but perhaps important to your study.

5. A *glossary* that lists and defines complex terminology within the subject area.

6. An *index* that, by listing specific concepts, events, and names mentioned in the text, helps you discover whether the book discusses your subject at all.

7. A *bibliography* and *footnotes* that suggest new sources for later investigation.

You should utilize the most recent, reliable sources of information. Since you are expected to form sound judgments based on the merit of your collected evidence, you should depend upon the most respected authorities in your subject area and should closely evaluate outdated or biased material. The most highly regarded or influential authorities on your topic are most likely not hard to find because they are usually mentioned again and again in the sources you uncover. For example, writers about women's liberation refer often to Kate Millet, a pivotal figure in the movement. If women's liberation is your subject, you certainly must look at Millet's *Sexual Politics*.

Whatever the field, the names of certain authors are going to come up again and again, and it would pay to look at their work. For example, in black studies there is Martin Luther King, Jr.; in early space rocketry there is Wernher von Braun; in James Joyce studies there is Richard Ellmann; in recent American history there is Arthur Schlesinger; and the list goes on. There are several methods of discovering the key people in your area: (1) ask your instructor; (2) watch for certain names that keep reappearing in scholarly materials; (3) if available, check the credentials of an author—Has the individual written several books? Is the individual a chairperson of a national committee on this subject? Has he or she had wide experience in this field? (4) consult reference sources that evaluate books or that index evaluations.

The *Book Review Digest* (New York: H. W. Wilson, 1905-date) is considered a reliable source for checking the critical reception of a book. Here is a portion of the 1970 edition which demonstrates several entries that summarize the reviews for Kate Millett's *Sexual Politics:*

Fig. 26: From *Book Review Digest*
1. Author, title, and facts of publication **2.** Call number, subject entry for card catalog, and Library of Congress number **3.** Description of the book **4.** Reviewer's evaluation of the book **5.** A review that the *Book Review Digest* has not summarized **6.** Facts of publication of the review—*Christian Science Monitor* (September 10, 1970), p. 15, 850 words

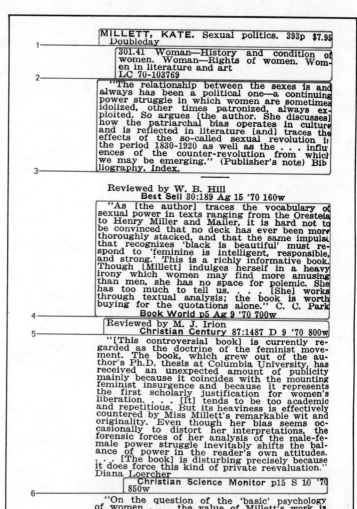

MILLETT, KATE. Sexual politics. 393p $7.95 Doubleday

301.41 Woman—History and condition of women. Woman—Rights of women. Women in literature and art
LC 70-103769

"The relationship between the sexes is and always has been a political one—a continuing power struggle in which women are sometimes idolized, other times patronized, always exploited. So argues [the author. She discusses] how the patriarchal bias operates in culture and is reflected in literature [and] traces the effects of the so-called sexual revolution in the period 1830-1920 as well as the . . . influences of the counter-revolution from which we may be emerging." (Publisher's note) Bibliography. Index.

Reviewed by W. B. Hill
Best Sell 30:189 Ag 15 '70 160w

"As [the author] traces the vocabulary of sexual power in texts ranging from the Oresteia to Henry Miller and Mailer, it is hard not to be convinced that no deck has ever been more thoroughly stacked, and that the same impulse that recognizes 'black is beautiful' must respond to 'feminine is intelligent, responsible, and strong.' This is a richly informative book. Though [Millett] indulges herself in a heavy irony which women may find more amusing than men, she has no space for polemic. She has too much to tell us. . . . [She] works through textual analysis; the book is worth buying for the quotations alone." C. C. Park
Book World p5 Ag 9 '70 700w

Reviewed by M. J. Irion
Christian Century 87:1487 D 9 '70 800w

"[This controversial book] is currently regarded as the doctrine of the feminist movement. The book, which grew out of the author's Ph.D. thesis at Columbia University, has received an unexpected amount of publicity mainly because it coincides with the mounting feminist insurgence and because it represents the first scholarly justification for women's liberation. . . . [It] tends to be too academic and repetitious. But its heaviness is effectively countered by Miss Millett's remarkable wit and originality. Even though her bias seems occasionally to distort her interpretations, the forensic forces of her analysis of the male-female power struggle inevitably shifts the balance of power in the reader's own attitudes. . . . [The book] is disturbing precisely because it does force this kind of private reevaluation." Diana Loercher
Christian Science Monitor p15 S 10 '70 850w

"On the question of the 'basic' psychology of women . . . the value of Millett's work is diminished by the effects of her missionarism. Results of animal behavior studies and research on the role of hormones, for instance, are either ignored, deemed irrelevant, or explained away on other terms when they indicate fundamental sex differences; yet where such research indicates equivalence of the sexes, it is heralded. Millett mentions John Money's conclusion that gender identity is a matter of social learning but neglects his finding that women given male hormones become more aggressive and sexually desirous. Such eclecticism is unfortunate. It is as if to consider the possibility of natural sex differences is equivalent to acknowledging female inferiority, a curious bias." N. R. McWilliams
Commonweal 93:25 O 2 '70 1500w

Arranged alphabetically by author, the *Book Review Digest* provides an evaluation of several thousand books each year.

You might also examine *Index to Book Reviews in the Humanities* or *Index to Book Reviews in the Social Sciences* (Williamston, Mich.: Phillip Thomson, 1960-date). Although these two works do not contain summaries of reviews or capsule evaluations, they provide additional reference information on current book reviews.

And you will find additional evaluation of source material in any of the following:

The Booklist. Chicago: American Library Association, 1905-date.

> This work offers a selective list of new books that will meet the needs of the average public library. Annotations make it valuable for student usage.

The Reader's Adviser. Rev. and enl. by Hester R. Hoffman. 11th ed. New York: Bowker, 1968.

> This work provides a systematic treatment of many books, as indicated by its subtitle: "a guide to the best in print in literature, biographies, dictionaries, encyclopedias, bibles, classics, drama, poetry, fiction, science, philosophy, travel, history."

United States Quarterly Book List. New Brunswick, N.J.: Rutgers Univ. Press, 1945-56.

> Critical annotations and biographies of the authors make this a valuable reference. However, you will not find recent material because it has ceased publication.

Finally, it will pay you to be curious and somewhat skeptical during research. Curiosity will keep you searching and tracking down facts from the library and other sources. Skepticism will prevent you from accepting the printed word as absolute. Analyze the printed page as you analyze the spoken word of instructors and friends. Verify and document your facts and findings. Your critical perception will enable you to interpret and report your findings in an interesting as well as a reliable manner.

Using Primary and Secondary Sources

Whenever possible, you should make use of primary sources—that is, the original works of an author. Primary sources include novels, short stories, poems, letters, diaries, notes, manuscripts, documents, and autobiographies. Remember, an author's own words are often the most valid source of information for both direct quotation and paraphrase.

On the other hand, you should also make extensive use of secondary sources—books and articles. Articles may be found in magazines, learned journals, and book-length critical studies. However, in reading these sources, you must judge carefully the difference between fact and opinion.

Just because a statement is in print does not validate it. You must learn to rely primarily on facts, and then base your own interpretations and opinions upon these. Still, if certain opinions or interpretations seem valuable to the discussion, you might wish to include them in the notes, though clearly labeled as opinion. In your later readings, perhaps, you will discover other authorities lending credence to an opinion. The weight of such evidence would then authenticate what, at first, seemed opinion.

Technique of Note Cards

As with the bibliography cards, you should be exact in recording note card information. The following system may prove helpful:

1. Write the notes legibly in ink—penciled notes become blurred because of repeated shuffling of the cards.

2. In general, use either four-by-six-inch or three-by-five-inch index cards for taking notes. (Some people prefer the four-by-six-inch cards to avoid getting them mixed up with the smaller bibliography cards.) Cards provide adequate space for most notes and, unlike large sheets of paper, are easily shuffled and rearranged.

3. Place only *one* item of information on each card. You may then shuffle and rearrange the cards during all stages of organization.

4. Since material on the back of a card may be overlooked, write on only one side of the card. However, if material should run a few lines beyond the one side on occasion, finish it on the back, but write "OVER" conspicuously on the face of the card. If you use two cards for one note, staple the two together to avoid their separation.

5. Before writing the note, indicate in an abbreviated form the source of the information. Use a brief form, inasmuch as full information on the reference is available on the bibliography card. The identification may be the title of the book, the name of the author, or both. (Some students prefer a key number system, which involves numbering each bibliography entry. When a particular reference is used, this key number is then placed on the card. The danger of this technique, however, is the possibility of losing the key.)

6. Always place the proper page number at the top of each note card, since the bibliography card will not contain this specific page reference needed for a footnote entry.

7. Also, label the note card to indicate the kind of information it contains. This label at the top of the card will speed arrangement of notes with the outline.

8. Finally, write the note, using one of four basic methods: summary, précis, paraphrase, or quotation. (See below for a discussion of each method.)

Methods of Note-Taking

SUMMARY

Many times you will want to write a brief sketch of your material without great concern for style or expression. You primarily need to put information on your card, quickly and concisely—there is no concern here for careful wording or exact paraphrase. The summary note serves this purpose. Later, if you need the material for your paper, you will write it in a clearer and more appropriate prose style.

Your chief purpose with the summary card, as well as with the other kinds of note cards, is to extract all significant facts. You must devote, at this time, sufficient energy to this task; otherwise, it will still remain to be done if you take the easy way and unthinkingly copy entire paragraphs verbatim. Also, you should remember that the summary requires a footnote when placed in the text. A sample note card follows:

```
Matriarchy defined          Baughman, pp. 80-81


A family situation with mother in control;
husband is absent or, if he is present, the
wife or mother still exercises control over
family affairs.
```

Fig. 27: Summary Note Card

This sort of summary note card is valuable for giving you a rough sketch of material you may need but can express more fluently when you write your first draft. For an example of how one student employed this note, see the sample research paper, p. 79.

Another type of summary card is one that briefly summarizes the plot of a drama or story that serves as your primary source. The following note demonstrates the plot summary card:

```
Hansberry                              A Raisin in the Sun

        The drama is a problem play that portrays
    a black family's determination to move out of a
    ghetto to a better life.  Mama Younger domi-
    nates the family, shaping and molding the fami-
    ly members, although each rebels in his own
    way, especially Walter who squanders the family
    inheritance and brings them to a crisis that
    threatens their survival.
```

Such a summary should be brief, offering only enough information to clarify the plot for your reader. Avoid writing a plot summary that extends beyond one paragraph. For an example of how one student employed this note, see the sample research paper, p. 79.

PRÉCIS

The précis is a very brief summary in your own words, differing from the rough summary in being more polished in style and differing from the paraphrase in being more concise. Try to write your précis in a polished form with complete sentences in formal English. (Only the rough summary allows abbreviations and sentence fragments.) Moreover, you must make certain that the précis is accurate not only in its content but also in its connotations. That is, you should preserve the essential truth of the reference material. Do not distort the material in any way or quote out of context, a suggestion which applies to all of your note-taking. You will have success with the précis if you:

1. Condense the original with precision and directness. Reduce a long paragraph into a few sentences, tighten an article into a paragraph, and summarize a longer work, such as a biography, into a few pages.

2. Preserve the tone of the original. If the original is humorous, for example, maintain that tone in the précis. In the same way, retain moods of satire, exaggeration, doubt, irony, and so on.

3. Limit the use of key words or phrases from the original, and write the précis in your own language. However, retain exceptional words and phrases from the original, enclosing them in quotation marks.

4. Provide a footnote locating the source of your material.

A sample précis note card follows:

```
Traditional view                    Frazier, 306-33
   of matriarchy


      Frazier's view of matriarchy is the tradi-
tional one, supported by most sociologists,
based on a theory that the black family was
matriarchal because of slavery, the migration
from rural to urban environments, and racial
prejudice.
```

Fig. 29: Précis Note Card

This note summarizes in a few words the substance of Frazier's position. The student has examined twenty-six pages of textual matter, determined its relevance, and quickly summarized it. For an example of how one student eventually used this précis, see the sample research paper, p. 80.

PARAPHRASE

You will probably write many notes in the form of paraphrase—restating, in your own style, the thought or meaning expressed by someone else. In other words, you borrow an idea, opinion, interpretation, or statement of an authority and rewrite it in your own language. Furthermore, you write the note in about the same number of words as the original, hence the distinction between paraphrase and précis, the latter being a very *brief* condensation.

Obviously, you should choose only important materials for such treatment. Material of doubtful importance should be summarized, while bulky references should be condensed with a précis. Also, it is generally wiser to paraphrase material rather than to indiscriminately fill card after card with directly quoted matter. One danger of relying primarily on quoted materials is that they may lead you into plagiarism (see pp. 48-51). Of course, you are saved from plagiarism in the use of paraphrase only if you credit the thoughts you have borrowed by means of a footnote. The point of view and the presentation may be yours, but the idea, you must always remember, belongs to the original author.

You will have success with paraphrasing if you:

1. Rewrite the original in your own style in about the same number of words.

2. Preserve the tone of the original by maintaining moods of satire, anger, humor, doubt, and so on.

3. Retain exceptional words and phrasing from the original.

4. In order to avoid any hint of plagiarism, provide a footnote in your paper indicating the source of your material.

Provided below is a short extract from *Black Rage* by William H. Grier and Price M. Cobbs, followed by a sample paraphrase note card that re-states their ideas.

> The black mother shares a burden with her soul sisters of three centuries ago. She must produce and shape and mold a unique type of man. She must intuitively cut off and blunt his masculine assertiveness and aggression lest these put the boy's life in jeopardy.[1]

Fig. 30: Paraphrase Note Card

```
     Matriarchal influence          Grier and Cobbs, 62
        on the black male


          Grier and Cobbs sense a commonly held and
     long-standing attitude among black matriarchs,
     who feel that they need to curb the natural
     tendencies of "masculine assertiveness and ag-
     gression" lest these qualities jeopardize their
     sons' lives and well-being.
```

The length of the note, thirty-seven words, is nearly the same length as the original material. For an example of how the student eventually used this paraphrase, see the sample research paper, p. 87.

QUOTATION

Students frequently overuse direct quotation in taking notes, and as a result they overuse quotations in the final paper. Probably only about 10 percent of your final manuscript should appear as directly quoted matter.

[1] William H. Grier and Price M. Cobbs, *Black Rage* (New York: Basic Books, 1968), p. 62.

Therefore, you should strive to limit the amount of exact transcribing of source materials while taking notes. The overuse of quotation indicates either that you do not have a clear focus on your subject matter and are jotting down verbatim just about everything related to your subject, or that you have inadequate source materials and are using the quotations only as padding. Originality in research writing requires a personal presentation of thoroughly assimilated material. Accordingly, it should be you speaking in the major portion of your paper, giving, of course, proper credit where credit is due.

Direct quotation is most necessary with primary sources, especially when you are discussing matters of style or content in your primary source. For example, the study of Lorraine Hansberry's *A Raisin in the Sun* would demand several direct quotations from the drama itself. With secondary sources, direct quotation is useful as corroboration for an assertion now and then, especially when you foresee its possible rejection by the reader. When quoting from secondary sources, therefore, look for material that is the best evidence on the subject, that is said with especially brilliant clarity, or that is subject to refutation.

You will have success with quotation note cards if you:

1. Place quotation marks around material that is directly quoted to distinguish it from paraphrases and the like.

2. Copy the exact words of the author, even to the retention of any errors in the original (see *sic*, pp. 63-64) or what might appear to be errors (see the use of *sic* in the sample research paper, p. 86). *Sic* is a term used within brackets to show that a quoted passage is reproduced precisely.

3. For special problems that you encounter, see "Handling Reference Material," pp. 59-68.

A sample note card that quotes a primary source follows:

Fig. 31: Quotation Note Card

```
Walter's frustration                    Raisin, 61


"Walter: Sometimes it's like I can see the
future stretched out in front of me——just plain
as day.  The future, Mama.  Hanging over there
at the edge of my days.  Just waiting for me——a
big, looming blank space——full of nothing."
```

See p. 86 of the sample research paper for an example of how one student used this quotation.

A sample note card, quoting a secondary source, follows:

**Fig. 32: Quotation
Note Card**

```
    Female agression as a key
       to black survival          Staples, BS, 1, 8



       "Black women have not been passive objects
    who were satisfied with watching their menfolk
    make history.  If they had been contented to
    accept the passive role ascribed to the female
    gender, then the travail of the past four cen-
    turies might have found the black race just as
    extinct as the dinosaur."
```

For an example of how one student employed this quotation, see the sample research paper, p. 80.

Avoiding Plagiarism

Fundamentally, plagiarism is the offering of the words or ideas of another person as one's own. While the most blatant violation is the use of another student's work, the most common is the intentional misuse of your reference sources. Since you will be working with the writings of others, it is important that you learn and adhere to certain ethical rules as to the use of reference material. One of the chief reasons for following these rules is that you want to avoid being falsely accused of plagiarism when your only error was unintentionally failing to acknowledge a source.

An obvious form of plagiarism is copying any direct quotation from your source material without providing quotation marks and without crediting the source. A more subtle form, but equally improper, is the paraphrasing of material or use of an original idea if that paraphrase or borrowed idea is not properly introduced and documented. Remember that another author's ideas, interpretations, and words are his or her property; they are protected by law and must be acknowledged whenever you borrow them. Consequently, your use of source materials requires that you conform to a few rules of conduct:

1. Acknowledge borrowed material within the text by introducing the quotation or paraphrase with the name of the authority from whom it was taken.

2. Enclose within quotation marks all quoted materials.

3. Make certain that paraphrased material is written in your own style and language. The simple rearrangement of sentence patterns is unacceptable.

4. Provide a footnote for each borrowed item.

5. Provide a bibliography entry for every book or magazine that appears in the footnotes.

The examples provided below should reveal the difference between genuine research writing and plagiarism. First, here is the original reference material; it is followed by three student versions, only one of which would *not* be called plagiarism:

Original Material

I don't think that black women can afford to be competitive with their men—especially now. Competing with them for jobs would just add to the problem that already exists. Black women have been able to find work when their husbands couldn't and have often been the head of the family not because they wanted to be but out of economic necessity. Some of those women's lib girls are asking for jobs that black men haven't been able to get.[2]

Student Version A (Unacceptable)

```
        Black women have usually been less discrim-
inated against than their male counterparts. For
example, black women have been able to find work
when their husbands couldn't and have often been
the head of the family not because they wanted to
be but out of economic necessity.
```

This piece of writing is plagiarism in a most deplorable form. The student has simply borrowed abundantly from the original source, even to the point of retaining the essential wording, and has provided no documentation whatever, which implies to the reader that these sentences are entirely his or her original creation.

[2] Marjorie Barnes as quoted by Renee Ferguson, *Washington Post*, 3 Oct. 1970; rpt. in *Black Women in White America*, ed. Gerda Lerner (New York: Pantheon, 1972), p. 589.

Student Version B (Unacceptable)

> Black women have usually been less dis-
> criminated against than their male counter-
> parts. For example, most black women have usu-
> ally been able to find jobs when their husbands
> couldn't. And they have sometimes been head of
> the household out of economic necessity, not
> because they wanted to be.[7]
>
> [7]Marjorie Barnes as quoted by Renee
> Ferguson, Washington Post, 3 Oct. 1970; rpt.
> in Black Women in White America, ed. Gerda
> Lerner (New York: Pantheon, 1972), p. 589.

This student's version is also plagiarism, even though the citation is carefully documented. He or she has obviously copied almost directly from the
source, changing only a few words and phrases. The student also fails to
introduce the borrowed materials; thus, the reader is uncertain about the
footnote. Does it refer to the entire paragraph or only the final sentence or
two? As a research writer, you may avoid these errors by introducing the
material as direct quotation or, if you prefer, as a scholarly paraphrase that
might include direct quotation of a few significant or well-worded phrases.

Student Version C (Acceptable)

> Black women have usually been less dis-
> criminated against than their male counterparts.
> For example, Marjorie Barnes points out that
> black women often find employment while their
> husbands cannot. She adds that "economic ne-
> cessity" has forced some of these women to be
> heads of households even though they did not
> seek the role.[7]
>
> [7]Marjorie Barnes as quoted by Renee
> Ferguson, Washington Post, 3 Oct. 1970; rpt. in
> Black Women in White America, ed. Gerda Lerner
> (New York: Pantheon, 1972), p. 589.

This version represents a satisfactory handling of the source material. (For an example of usage that employs more direct quotation, see the sample research paper, p. 81.) The authority is acknowledged at the outset, and the substance of the commentary is well expressed in the student's own language with one phrase directly quoted, so as to give full credit where the credit is due. The student has been wholly honest to the source material while effectively using that source for a particular purpose.

WRITING YOUR PAPER 4

■ During the course of research, you have been making judgments and comparisons and putting details into order and completing them. You are now ready to synthesize all research materials into a paper that will give the greatest possible clarity, orderliness, and meaning to your findings. But before beginning the actual writing, you should first formulate a detailed, exact outline.

The Final Outline

Your rough preliminary outline should now be expanded into a clear, logical plan that will guide the writing of your paper, especially your over-all arrangement and paragraph development. Remember that you are not bound by your original plan, which was only intended to guide research and note-taking. If you see possibilities in a new arrangement, you should, by all means, try it.

Since you will write your final outline for your instructor and other readers, you should follow recognized conventions. First, use the standard outline symbols:

```
I.
    A.
        1.
        2.
            a.
            b.
                (1)
                (2)
                    (a)
                    (b)
    B.
        1.
        2.
            a.
            b.
                (1)
                (2)
                    (a)
                    (b)
II.
```

And so on. Your indentation of each heading will indicate the importance of the material; that is, you will progress from major concepts to minor ones. The degree to which you continue the subheads will depend, in part, upon the complexity of your subject; but, as a general rule, you should seldom find it necessary to carry the subheads beyond the first series of small letters.

In addition, headings of like rank on the same margin should have an equal importance. And if you establish equal ideas, give them parallel form. Note the mistake in the following:

```
I. Spring sports
   A. To play baseball
   B. Tennis
   C. Track
```

Obviously, the infinitive phrase "To play baseball" is not parallel with the nouns "Tennis" and "Track." If A is a noun, then make B and C nouns also, or if you prefer, make them all infinitives; but do not mix the grammatical forms.

When you indent outline headings, you are subordinating your ideas. Thus, if you find yourself attempting to enter a single subhead, you obviously have one major idea and not several subordinate ones. Note the following:

```
I. Spring sports
   A. Baseball
      1. History
   B. Tennis
      1. History
   C. Track
      1. History
```

The writer intends to discuss the history of the sports and might rearrange the entries in the following manner:

```
Spring Sports
  I. The History of Baseball
     A. Origin
     B. Growth
     C. Maturity
 II. The History of Tennis
     A. Origin
     B. Growth
     C. Maturity
III. The History of Track
     A. Origin
     B. Growth
     C. Maturity
```

Since your introduction is first and your conclusion last, you need not insert such labels into your outline. Instead, you should name specifically the contents of that section (see sample outlines, pp. 54-55).

Because the thesis is the main idea of the entire paper and no other idea can rank equally with it, you should not label your thesis sentence as item I in the outline. Otherwise, you may find yourself searching fruitlessly for a parallel idea to put in II, III, and IV. Instead, you should write your thesis sentence separately, placing it above the outline proper.

You may write your outline in topic, sentence, or paragraph form, remembering, of course, that you cannot alternate forms within a given outline. With the topic outline, every heading is a noun phrase or its equivalent, a gerund phrase or an infinitive phrase. In the sentence outline, either every heading is a sentence or the major headings are nouns and the subheads are sentences. With the paragraph outline, every section is a paragraph; however, you will seldom use the paragraph outline, although it is valuable for papers that require multiple, complex details.

Reproduced below is a portion of the outline from the sample research paper "The Theme of Black Matriarchy in *A Raisin in the Sun*" (see pp. 76-77 for the complete topic outline) in topic, sentence, and paragraph forms.

```
Thesis sentence: Hansberry uses the sociological concept
                 of black matriarchy to create dramatic
                 conflict among the members of the
                 Younger family.
```

Topic Outline

```
    I. Black matriarchy as a sociological concept in A
       Raisin in the Sun

       A. Two views of the drama
          1. A problem play about escape from the ghetto
          2. A sociological drama about black matriarchy

       B. The history of black matriarchy
          1. Matriarchy defined
          2. The traditional views of matriarchy

       C. Reasons for today's matriarchy
          1. Women less discriminated against than men
          2. Women better educated than men
          3. Men crippled psychologically by self-reliant
             women

   II. The women in A Raisin in the Sun as matriarchs
```

Sentence Outline

```
    I. Black matriarchy is a viable sociological concept in
       A Raisin in the Sun.

       A. There is more than one view of the drama.
          1. It is a problem play about escape from the
             ghetto.
          2. It is also a sociological drama about black
             matriarchy.

       B. Historical views of black matriarchy have not
          always agreed.
          1. Matriarchy is defined as a family situation in
             which the woman has the predominant influence.
          2. The traditional view of Frazier suggests
             slavery as the primary cause for matriarchy.

       C. There are several reasons for the continuance of
          black matriarchy today.
          1. Black women are less discriminated against than
             black men.
          2. Women are better educated than men.
          3. The self-reliance of women has crippled black
             men psychologically.

   II. Two of the women in A Raisin in the Sun are
       matriarchs.
```

Paragraph Outline

I. Black matriarchy: the sociological concepts in A
Raisin in the Sun

A. This drama is first a problem drama about a
family's attempts to escape from the black ghetto.
It is also a sociological drama about matriarchal
effects on members of the Younger family.

B. The historical views of black matriarchy reveal
some disagreements. Basically it is defined as a
family situation in which the woman has the pre-
dominant influence. The traditional views of
Franklin Frazier have been most influential.
Frazier argued that the slave system gave rise to
the woman as the most forceful member of the black
family.

C. There are several reasons why black matriarchy is
still an essential feature of today's black family. First, black women have usually been less
discriminated against than their male counter-
parts. Second, black women have traditionally
been better educated than black men. Third, the
assertiveness and self-reliance developed through
necessity by the black female has had a crippling
effect on many black males.

II. Two women: the matriarchs of A Raisin in the Sun

Various outline forms that deviate from these classic models with
respect to indenting, spacing, numbering, and so on are possible. The most
popular deviation, especially in business and the sciences, is the decimal
outline (also known as the industrial numerical outline):

1. Black matriarchy as a sociological concept in A
Raisin in the Sun

1.1. Two views of the drama
1.1.1. A problem drama
1.1.2. A sociological drama

1.2. The history of black matriarchy
1.2.1. Matriarchy defined
1.2.2. The traditional views of matriarchy

1.3. Reasons for today's matriarchy
1.3.1. Women less discriminated against than men
1.3.2. Women better educated than men
1.3.3. Men crippled psychologically by self-
reliance of women
2. The women in A Raisin in the Sun as matriarchs

Although many scientific and business reports use the decimal system, you
should avoid it when doing conventional research papers. Because it is so
precise and thorough, it breaks the material down into multiple, fragmented
parts so that almost every sentence becomes a numerical subpart. A continuous numbering system tends to break down the organic relations found in
the classic outline form.

Preparing to Write

If you begin writing your paper at least one full week before it is due, you should have sufficient time for writing, revising, and rewriting. However, you should not rush into the writing; instead, you should (1) examine your thesis sentence and outline to see that they provide you with a well-rounded, logically organized plan of procedure; (2) examine your tone to see that it suits your topic, purpose, and audience; and (3) examine your note cards to see that support for your ideas is abundantly supplied.

Ask yourself, "Do I know my main idea and supporting ideas?" If in doubt, you must read your thesis sentence and your outline again. With an objective eye you should examine your ideas and their logical progression through the outline. At this point you cannot afford ambiguity because each of your paragraphs must develop and expand your thesis sentence.

Next ask yourself, "Do I know my purpose?" To answer this question, you must consider both the intellectual framework (what you want the reader to understand) and the emotional framework (what you feel and what you want the reader to feel). Thus, you will have to present your material from a selected perspective that will influence your handling of the subject and your audience's reaction to it.

For example, suppose your topic deals with world population and hunger. Obviously, you face an intellectual choice: you may defend or condemn the relief agencies of various governments. Complete objectivity is unlikely in a research paper which is, in fact, a form of argument. Moreover, you will determine your emotional framework by assuming either a detached or an involved position. For example, if you should select a detached approach, you would gain a degree of objectivity by giving an accurate, well-ordered presentation of both sides of the issue and by declaring your position with formal, controlled logic. If, on the other hand, you should assume an involved position, either pro or con, your presentation should be more persuasive, more demanding. You would need to avoid bias and prejudice, but you could be more subjective by condemning falsehoods, by destroying misconceptions, by rallying your audience to your cause, and by supporting your ideas with examples and comparisons that vividly portray the circumstances.

Moreover, with some topics you should consider the possibility of a humorous or a satiric approach, by which you relate, with tongue in cheek, the absurdity of a situation or you hold up to ridicule the foolishness of a condition, intending, thereby, to bring a new awareness of a problem to your reader.

Finally, ask yourself, "Do I have sufficient support from several sources for my contentions?" Since many undergraduates attempt to rely upon one major source, this question is a vital one. Remember, reliance upon the frequent use of one source is an all too apparent confession that your research has been too restricted in its scope. The presence of almost endless strings of "Ibid." entries in your footnotes reflects a lack of industry and initiative on your part. The footnotes of your text, as well as the text itself, will reflect the quality of your research. Your instructor expects that you will put labor into collecting and assimilating adequate material from many sources and that you will then blend these sources into a readable and effective whole.

WRITING WITH UNITY, COHERENCE, AND CLARITY

After many hours of considerable effort, you are ready to give expression to your ideas, to share them with others, and to convince your readers of the validity of your findings. In order for your paper to reflect the care and time you have devoted to it, you must write it in the best possible language. In most instances, readers will see only the finished product, upon which they will base their judgment of your findings and writing ability. Therefore, you should carefully construct your paper, always seeking unity, coherence, and clarity. Your paper will have *unity* if it explores one topic in depth, with each paragraph carefully expanding upon a single aspect of the topic. Your paper will have *coherence* if your controlling ideas and your research details and evidence all flow together and function as an interrelated whole. Coherence requires that quotations and paraphrases be logical extensions of your writing, not intrusions or mere padding. Coherence also demands the logical progression of your ideas by the repetition of key words, the exact usage of pronouns and synonyms, and the application of transitional words and phrases (for example, the use of such words as *also, furthermore, nevertheless, in addition,* and *thus*). Your paper will have *clarity* if you use precise prose that avoids excessive rhetorical splendor. Research writing is exact writing, featuring well-balanced sentences with proper subordination of minor elements and at the same time employing concrete, specific words.

WRITING IN THE PROPER TENSE

When you are dealing with an event or concept of the past, your overall approach to the material should be in the past tense, as in the following example:

> After slavery, the trials of emancipation
> had a disruptive effect on the black family as
> a unit because blacks were suddenly expected to
> change many of the social values taken on when
> they were slaves. One of these was the idea
> that the male should be the family head and
> chief provider. But, as with all new social
> values in any culture, this idea was slow in
> gaining acceptance by blacks; thus matriarchy
> is still an essential feature of today's black
> family.

Clearly, the use of the past tense is required with this material. But note the use of present tense in the following portion of that same paper:

> A Raisin in the Sun presents a realistic
> view of the differing aspects of black matri-
> archy and the conflicts it can produce. The
> character of Lena (Mama) exhibits most of the
> characteristics of the traditional black matri-
> arch. She directs family activities in her
> apartment. She controls the family wealth, a
> $10,000 insurance inheritance. She establishes
> guidelines on how the money will be spent.

The writer of these lines is concerned with a drama of the past, but since it continues in print, it continues into the present. Therefore, the writer uses the verbs *presents, exhibits, directs, controls,* and *establishes* rather than the past tense forms *presented, exhibited,* and so on. That is, the writer uses the historical present tense to indicate what is true at the present time and will remain true in the future.

In the same way, you should use the present tense for most comments or observations by authorities about a text under examination. Thus, use the present tense in referring to a view expressed by some quoted or paraphrased author, for the criticism is still in print and continues to be true in the present. Good usage demands "Richard Ellmann argues," "Professor Thompson writes," or "T. S. Eliot stipulates," rather than "Richard Ellman argued," "Professor Thompson wrote," or "T. S. Eliot stipulated."

Handling Reference Material

As you begin transferring your note material into your written text, you will have questions about the proper use of your references. For example, you will often ask yourself, "How should I use this note—as paraphrase or quotation?" Obviously, you cannot just copy all your notes directly into the text. The trick is to skillfully incorporate a paraphrase or short quotation into your own writing so that the outside source is not obtrusive and at the same time illuminates and supports your own conclusions. You will find that this task is vital to the success of your manuscript.

SHORT PROSE QUOTATIONS AND PARAPHRASES

There are two basic forms for incorporating quoted matter into the text. First, if the quotation is no more than four lines long, you may place it within the body of the text and enclose it within quotation marks.

Suppose, for example, that you have the following material on a note card:

```
Female aggression as key      Staples, BS, 1, 8
   to black survival


"Black women have not been passive objects who
were satisfied with watching their menfolk make
history.  If they had been contented to accept
the passive role ascribed to the female gender,
then the travail of the past four centuries
might have found the black race just as extinct
as the dinosaur."
```

There are several ways you could incorporate this material into your paper, but not all of them would be considered acceptable. Consider the following example:

Unacceptable

> If black women had accepted the "passive role ascribed to the female gender, then the travail of the past four centuries might have found the black race as extinct as the dinosaur."[5]
>
>   [5]Robert Staples, "The Myth of Black Matriarchy," The Black Scholar, 1 (Jan.–Feb. 1970), 8.

This style is not *wrong* but would be *unacceptable* to most instructors because the writer provides no introduction for the quotation. Use the names of your authorities in order to move smoothly from your own material to quoted matter.

Acceptable

> Even recent opponents of Frazier's views, like Robert Staples, admit that black women were not passive because "if they had been contented to accept the passive role ascribed to the female gender, then the travail of the past four centuries might have found the black race as extinct as the dinosaur."[5]
>
>   [5]Robert Staples, "The Myth of Black Matriarchy," The Black Scholar, 1 (Jan.–Feb. 1970), 8.

To see how one student eventually used this quoted material in context, see the sample research paper, p. 80. Other alternatives might be:

Robert Staples argues that if black women had
been "contented to accept the passive role ascribed to the female gender, then the travail
of the past four. . . ."

On the subject of black women as "passive ob-
jects," one critic states, "If they had been
contented to accept the passive role ascribed
to the female gender, then the travail of the
past four. . . ."

INTRODUCING SHORT QUOTATIONS AND PARAPHRASES

When introducing short reference material (four lines or less), you
should avoid repetition of a stereotyped phrase—for example, "Professor
Jones says." Rather, you should vary the method of formal introduction as
shown in the following:

One critic insists that Hansberry uses the drama
as. . . .

Hansberry portrays Walter Younger as. . . .

Ashley Montague suggests that women are superior
to. . . .

"Walter, that ain't none of our money," complains
Ruth as she. . . .

According to one critic, Hansberry centers her
drama around. . . .

The unemployment rate, according to figures by
Lee Rainwater and William L. Yancey, is two
times greater among blacks than among. . . .

One source declares that black females today
still. . . .

Two critics stipulate "that those Negro males who
perceive themselves as. . . ."

Ruth refuses her husband's plea, saying, "Walter,
that ain't none of our money."

Mama presses Ruth, "He finally come into his manhood today, didn't he?"

Other words that will give variety to your introductions are *accept, add,
admit, affirm, believe, confirm, mention, propose, rely, report, reveal,
state, submit, suggest, think,* and *verify.* However, you should avoid the
monotony of such introductions by alternating them with your own contentions and with a few long single-spaced quotations (see below, "Longer
Quotations," p. 65).

COMBINING PARAPHRASE AND QUOTATION

As shown above, it is a good practice to introduce your material by citing the name of the authority from which it is drawn. However, you must place a footnote index numeral at the end of paraphrased and quoted matter whether the name of the author appears in the text or not. In the following example the writer of the research paper about *A Raisin in the Sun* has obeyed these two rules. Additionally, this student has molded into one unified whole both paraphrase and quotation:

Black matriarchy, a sociological concept with origins in slavery, is a family situation, according to E. Earl Baughman, in which no husband is present or, if he is present, in which the wife and/or mother exercises the main influence over family affairs.[1]

For years the typical attitude toward this phenomenon has been the one expressed by E. Franklin Frazier, who argues that "because of conditions imposed by the slave system, the mother was the most dependable and the most important member of the Negro family."[2] This traditional view, defended by sociologists and historians, is based on Frazier's theory that the black family was matriarchal because of slavery, the move from rural to urban environments, and racial prejudice.[3]

[1]E. Earl Baughman, *Black Americans: A Psychological Analysis* (New York: Academic Press, 1971), pp. 80–81.

[2]*The Negro in the United States* (New York: Macmillan, 1957), p. 309.

[3]For additional information on Frazier's views see *The Negro Family in the United States* (Chicago: Univ. of Chicago Press, 1939), esp.

You cannot paraphrase and synthesize such material into the desired context without intelligent, thoughtful effort.

REPRODUCING QUOTED MATERIAL

In general, you should reproduce quoted material exactly; but one exception is permitted for logical reasons: if the quotation forms a grammatical part of the sentence in which it occurs, you need not capitalize the first word of the quotation, even though it is capitalized in the original, as in:

> For years the typical attitude toward this phenomenon has been the one expressed by E. Franklin Frazier, who argues that "because of conditions imposed by the slave system, the mother was the most dependable and the most important member of the Negro family."[2]

However, if the quotation follows a formal introduction, you should capitalize the first word as in the original:

> For years the typical attitude toward this phenomenon has been the one expressed by E. Franklin Frazier, who says, "Because of conditions imposed by the slave system, the mother was the most dependable and the most important member of the the Negro family."[2]

Other possible methods are as follows:

> . . . the one expressed by E. Franklin Frazier: "Because of conditions imposed. . . ."

> . . . the one expressed by E. Franklin Frazier, who argues that the slave system established a situation in which "the mother was the most dependable and the most. . . ."

Thus, a few rules for quoted material of four lines or less are:

1. Reproduce the quotation exactly as it appears in the original with the one exception noted above.

2. Place the material within quotation marks.

3. Insert a footnote numeral after the last word of the material.

4. Use the name of the authority, usually, to introduce the material. Items 3 and 4 apply with equal force to your paraphrases.

Should your original source contain an error, or what might appear on first reading to be an error, you are permitted to insert the term "sic" within brackets, as in the following:

```
Mama: I wish you say something, son . . . I wish

you'd say how deep inside you you [sic] think I

done the right thing-- (p. 87)
```

Placed in brackets in this manner, "sic" indicates an error or apparent error has been made in the quoted passage and you are quoting accurately.

If your paper is based solely on a single work (novel, drama, short story, or long poem) and if there is an initial footnote identifying the edition, you may employ a simpler method of documentation for citations of the primary source; that is, place the page numbers in parentheses after the prose quotations, followed by the terminal mark of punctuation, as in the examples that follow:

```
Hansberry describes Mama as a "full-bodied and

strong" woman who "has adjusted to many things

in life and overcome many more. . . ."10  We

can assume that for years she has been the dom-

inant figure in the lives of her children.

     10Lorraine Hansberry, A Raisin in the Sun
(New York:  Random House, 1959), p. 15. Subse-
quent documentation of quotations from the drama
will be intext notes within parentheses.
```

After a note that identifies your primary source, you may document page numbers in the following manner:

```
When Beneatha denies the existence of God, Mama

slaps her in the face and forces her to repeat

after her, "In my mother's house there is still

God" (p. 37).  Then Mama adds, "There are some

ideas we ain't going to have in this house.  Not

long as I am at the head of this family" (p. 37,

underlining is mine).  Thus Mama meets Beneatha's

challenge head on. . . .
```

For additional examples of intext documentation, see the sample research paper, pp. 84-91.

LONGER QUOTATIONS

Quotations that exceed four lines should be indented and single-spaced.[1] But do not overuse long quotations. The obvious fact is that most readers tend to skip over long single-spaced material unless it is strongly introduced and unless such quotations occur infrequently. The proper method for such quotations is shown below:

```
When Walter Lee mentions that the money is com—

ing, Beneatha defends Mama's position:
        That money belongs to Mama, Walter, and
        it's for her to decide how she wants to
        use it.  I don't care if she wants to buy
        a house or a rocket ship or just nail it
        up somewhere and look at it.  It's hers.
        Not ours—hers.  (p. 19)

Yet Beneatha, unlike her sister—in—law Ruth, is

a rivaling matriarch.  Apparently inheriting

many. . . .
```

As indicated in this example, you should observe the following rules:

1. Make certain that the quotation is properly introduced. Use a colon to link the quotation with its introduction.

2. Do not employ quotation marks with a long quotation that is indented.

3. Place the footnote index numeral or documentation, as always, after the last word of the quotation. With long, single-spaced, and indented materials the documentation follows the terminal mark of punctuation. In all other cases the documentation precedes the period (compare pp. 84 and 85).

4. Indent the material at least five spaces from the left margin and provide at least one line space both above and below the material.

5. If quoted matter begins with the opening of a paragraph, indent the first line at least ten spaces from the left margin; the quotation, that is, carries its own paragraph indentation (see the sample research paper, p. 86). Otherwise there is no extra indentation of the first line.

---

[1] In this instance, your instructor may request that you follow strictly the stipulations of the *MLA Style Sheet* for articles to be published: that is, set off only quotations of one hundred words or more and double space all quotations.

POETRY QUOTATIONS

Short passages of quoted poetry are included in the text in the following manner:

> In <u>Antony and Cleopatra</u> Shakespeare states his
> theme at once through the indignant, hard-
> natured Roman soldier Philo, who labels Antony
> "the triple pillar of the world transformed/
> Into a strumpet's fool" (<u>Antony</u> I.i.12–13).
> Philo thereby heralds the traditional moral
> attitude of the Roman mind as opposed by the
> senuous nature of Egypt and its queen.

As this example indicates, you should again follow certain rules:

1. Set off the quotation by quotation marks.

2. Indicate two separate lines of the poetry text by the use of a virgule (/).

3. Place the documentation in parentheses immediately following the quotation.

4. Insert the documentation inside the period because the reference, like the quotation, is a part of the larger context of the sentence.

5. Omit the footnote. But be certain that the quotation is properly introduced.

6. Good scholarship requires that the edition of Shakespeare's plays, or any similar anthology, be listed in an early footnote, for example:

[1]Citations from Shakespeare in the text are to
<u>Shakespeare</u>: <u>Twenty-Three Plays and the Sonnets</u>, ed.
Thomas M. Parrott (New York: Scribner's, 1953).

Longer passages of poetry are handled differently, as shown by the following passage from Shakespeare's *Hamlet*.

> In a famous soliloquy Hamlet declares:
>
> To be, or not to be: that is the question:
> Whether 't is nobler in the mind to suffer
> The slings and arrows of outrageous fortune,
> Or to take arms against a sea of troubles,
> And by opposing end them? To die, to sleep—
> No more; and by a sleep to say we end
> The heart-ache and the thousand natural shocks
> That flesh is heir to. . . . (<u>Ham</u>. III.i.56–63)

Also notice the form of documentation for the following:

```
In his poem "Among School Children," W. B. Yeats

asks two profound questions:

        Are you the leaf, the blossom or the
            bole?
        O body swayed to music, O brightening
            glance,
        How can we know the dancer from the
            dance?                    (11. 62-64)
```

Again, you should follow certain rules:

1. Center the quotation on the page and type with single-spacing and with quotation marks omitted.

2. Use this method whenever poetry quotations run longer than two lines.

3. Place the documentation outside the final period because the reference is not a contextual part of the quoted sentence of poetry.

4. Use a colon to link the quotation with its introduction.

5. Omit the footnote. But, again, good scholarship requires an early footnote that lists the edition or anthology in which the poem is found (see item 6, p. 66).

ELLIPSIS

In a situation where less than an entire sentence of the quoted material is needed, you should use ellipsis dots to indicate omissions in the quoted material. This mark is three spaced periods, as (. . .). When the ellipsis ends a quoted passage, you should add a fourth period (with no space before the first) to indicate the termination of thought. Note the following:

```
R. W. B. Lewis declares that "if Hester has sinned, she
has done so as an affirmation of life, and her sin is the
source of life. . . ."1

One critic insists that it is possible "to read The Scar-
let Letter . . . as an indorsement of hopefulness. . . ."1
```

If the omission is significant (one or more lines of verse or one or more paragraphs of prose), indicate the ellipsis by a single typed line of spaced periods. Use introductions to avoid opening with ellipsis periods.

BRACKETS

You may find it necessary, on occasion, to insert personal comment within a quotation. You should enclose such an interpolation within brackets. Note the following:

"The black flower [of society] is shown in striking contrast to the wild rose of Nature."

One critic indicates that "we must avoid the temptation
to read it [The Scarlet Letter] heretically."

"John F. Kennedy, assassinated in November of 1964 [sic],
became overnight an immortal figure of courage and dignity in the hearts of most Americans."

"John F. Kennedy, . . . [was] an immortal figure of courage and dignity in the hearts of most Americans."

PUNCTUATION OF QUOTATIONS

In every instance, place commas and periods *inside* the quotation marks
but semicolons and colons *outside* the quotation marks. Place the question
mark and the exclamation mark inside the quotation marks if the mark is
part of the quoted material; otherwise, place it outside the quotation marks:

The philosopher asks, "How should we order our lives?"

How should we order our lives when we face "hostility
from every quarter"?

Handling Problems of Format

In its basic organization the research paper consists of the following
parts:
1. One blank sheet
2. Title page
3. Outline (if required)
4. The text of the paper
5. Bibliography
6. One blank sheet

TITLE PAGE

The title page contains three main divisions: the title of the work, the
author, and the course information. Note the following guidelines for title
pages (see the title page of the sample research paper, p. 76, for an example):

1. If the title requires two or more lines, position the extra line(s) in
such a manner as to form an inverted pyramid.

2. Do not underline your title or capitalize it in full. Underline only
published works if they appear in your title. Also, do not use a period after
a centered heading.

3. Enter your own name with the word "by" centered above it.

4. Provide the class and section information and the date. Entry of the
instructor's name is usually optional.

5. Employ separate lines for each item.

6. Provide balanced, two-inch margins for all sides of the title page.

OUTLINE

The outline follows the title page in the finished manuscript, its pages being numbered with small Roman numerals (for example, "iii," "iv," "v") at the top right-hand corner of the page. For full information on outlining, see pp. 36-38 as well as 52-55.

THE TEXT OF THE PAPER

The heart of your paper, of course, is the text itself. Three dominant parts of the text are the opening, body, and conclusion. Each is discussed below.

The Opening

The opening of a research paper should clearly establish your subject and set limits upon the scope of your examination. The conventional opening for a research paper has three parts: identification or definition of the subject, a brief history of prior work in this subject area, and the expression of your thesis. The opening of the sample research paper (see p. 79) follows this form.

Certain papers, especially those in the sciences, may require additional information in the opening, such as methods of investigation, tools and instruments employed, or special problems encountered.

The Body of Your Paper

The body of your paper should feature a logical development of the subdivisions of your thesis. These subdivisions will be suggested by your outline. Your primary concern should be clarification and amplification of your topic as you defend your thesis with well-reasoned statements, documented wherever necessary.

Normal paragraphing for the body is adequate. You need not label separate sections of your text with subtitles, centered headings, or Roman numerals. Such division markers are reserved for much longer works.

The Closing

Sometimes a final summarizing paragraph of text will be sufficient for the end of the paper, but usually circumstances will demand a separate conclusion. You will have expressed your thesis early and then presented your findings, properly documented. A conclusion that affirms something demonstrable about the subject would now be in order. For example, the research paper about *A Raisin in the Sun* has this thesis: "Hansberry uses the sociological concept of black matriarchy to create dramatic conflict among the members of the Younger family." The conclusion should reaffirm that thesis as shown below:

> By her characterization of Walter, Lor-
> raine Hansberry has raised the black male above
> the typical stereotype. Walter is not a social
> problem, a mere victim of matriarchy. Rather,
> Hansberry creates a character who breaks out of
> the traditional sociological image that dehu-
> manizes the black male. Creating a character
> who struggles with his fate and rises above
> it, Hansberry has elevated the black male. As
> James Baldwin puts it, "Time has made some
> changes in the Negro face."[15]

For the entire conclusion, see the sample research paper, p. 91.

THE BIBLIOGRAPHY PAGE

Your bibliography should appear on a separately typed sheet at the end of the paper. See the bibliography page of the sample research paper, p. 92, for an example. Also study Chapter 6, "The Bibliography," for details about form and style of the bibliographical entries.

Handling Technicalities of Preparing the Manuscript

As you write your first draft (and even when typing the final version), you will have questions about such diverse matters as margins, numbering, type of paper, and so on. The following material, in alphabetical order, explains many of the immediate problems facing you. Other matters of a more specialized nature are explained in the "Glossary of Additional Research Terms," pp. 144-54.

ARABIC NUMERALS

Generally, spell out numbers of less than three digits (for example, "four," "sixteen," "seventy-five"), but use figures for *all* numbers in a paragraph that contains both types. Always spell out numbers that begin sentences. Use the small "l," not a capital "I," when typing the numeral "one." Samples of correct usage:

```
A.D. 200 but 200 B.C.
Art. 3
Col. 5
Fig. 6
in 1974-75 or from 1974 to 1975, but not from 1974-75
11. 32-34
March 5, 1935 or 5 March 1935, but not both styles
1960's but the sixties
one-fifth but 153½ (for three or more digits)
pp.121-22
pp. 1151-53 but pp. 1193-1215
Sec. 3
6 percent
six o'clock or 6:00 p.m.
6.213
twentieth century
```

DATES

You should follow these examples:

```
14 March or March 14, not the fourteenth of March
14 March 1975 or March 14, 1975, but consistently use one
    style
March 1975 or March, 1975, but consistently use one style
1970's or the seventies
in 1974-75 or from 1974 to 1975, but not from 1974-75
150 B.C. but A.D. 150
fourteenth century but 14th century in footnotes
```

FOOTNOTE NUMERALS

Place footnote numerals within the text of the paper by turning the roller of the typewriter so that the Arabic numeral strikes about half a space above the line. Each numeral immediately follows the quotation or material to which it refers with no space between a word or a mark of punctuation. (See also "Placing Footnote Numbers Within the Text," p. 95).

FOOTNOTES

Footnotes appear on the same page as do the footnote index numerals in your text. Separate the footnotes from the text by triple spacing (that is, leave two lines of space). Single space the footnotes, indent each as a paragraph, and double space between each note. However, your instructor may ask that you follow strictly the stipulations of the *MLA Style Sheet;* that is, double space your footnotes and place them, not at the bottom of each page, but all together on a separate page or two at the end of your paper. (For examples and a complete discussion of footnotes, see Chapter 5, "Footnoting.")

ITALICS

Indicate italics in a typed manuscript by underlining, see p. 74.

LENGTH OF THE RESEARCH PAPER

Generally speaking, plan a paper of 2000 or 3000 words, about ten typewritten pages, excluding the title page, outline, and bibliography. However, your instructor may set definite restrictions concerning the length of the paper. Various factors make it difficult to set an arbitrary length, which may well vary with the topic, the reference material available, the time allotted to the project, and the initiative of the student.

MARGINS

The following margin requirements are recommended:

Left margin:	1½ inches
Right margin:	1 inch
Bottom margin:	1 inch
Top margin:	1½ inches

Establish the top margin nine spaces below the top of a typewritten page. Place the page number seven spaces below the top of the page and in line with the right margin.

NUMBERING

Assign a number to each page of the paper, except the blank pages. Number the paper in Arabic numerals in the upper right-hand corner of the page, seven spaces down from the top edge of the page and one inch from the right edge. Number these pages consecutively from the first page of the text through the bibliography. However, do not place a number on your first page—though this page is of course counted. Number the pages before the first page of the text, except the title page, with small Roman numerals, e.g., iii, iv, v, and so on, at the top, right side of the page.

PAPER

Type on one side of white bond paper, sixteen- or twenty-pound weight, eight and one-half by eleven inches. If your final manuscript is in longhand, use ruled theme paper.

REVISING AND PROOFREADING

After you complete your first draft, begin revising and rewriting in a critical and exacting mood—there is no place for any complacent pride of accomplishment at this point. Conscientiously delete unnecessary material, add supporting statements and evidence, relate facts to one another, rearrange data, and rewrite for clarity. Follow this cycle until the paper meets your full approval. Check for errors in sentence structure, spelling, and punctuation; read each quotation for accuracy. Finally, check each footnote and bibliographic entry for correctness of content and form.

After your final copy is finished, you should proofread carefully, remembering that you, and you alone, are responsible for everything within the paper. Failure to proofread is an act of carelessness that may seriously lower your final grade. Typing a paper, of course, does not remove the requirement of proofreading; if anything, it doubles your responsibility, whether you have done the typing yourself or had it done. Typographical errors will often count against the paper just as heavily as other shortcomings. Should you find errors but have no time for retyping, you should make the necessary corrections neatly in ink. It is far better to mar a page with a few handwritten corrections than to leave damaging errors in the paper.

SHORT TITLES IN THE TEXT

Shorten titles of books and articles mentioned often in the text after a first, full reference. For example, *English as Language: Backgrounds, Developments, Usage* should be shortened, after initial usage, to *English as Language* both in the text and footnotes (see pp. 115-17). In the sample research paper the title *A Raisin in the Sun* could be shortened to *Raisin* except for the fact that a musical adaptation of the play has been produced using *Raisin* as its title.

SPACING

Double space the body of the paper. However, single space both the footnotes and bibliography, with double spacing between each entry. Also, indent and single space long quotations, omitting quotation marks. On the first page, triple space between your title and your first line of text. (However, your instructor may request that you double space everything—text, indented quotations, footnotes, and bibliography entries.)

SPELLING

Spell accurately. When in doubt, always consult a dictionary. If the dictionary says a word may be spelled in two separate ways, be consistent in the form employed, as with *theater* and *theatre,* unless the variant form occurs in quoted materials. Use American (as opposed to English) spelling throughout. In addition, proofread carefully for errors of hyphenation.

TYPING

Preferably, you should submit the paper in typed form, although some instructors will accept handwritten manuscripts, if neat and legible. Also, use pica type, though the small elite face may be used if necessary. Clean the type carefully and insert a new ribbon if necessary before starting the final copy.

UNDERLINING

Underlining takes the place of italics in a typed manuscript. The *MLA Style Sheet* stipulates that each word be underlined separately, but with your instructor's permission you may use a continuous line. Always underline the title of a book, journal, or periodical, whether it appears in the text, in a footnote, or in the bibliography. Also underline the titles of pamphlets, newspapers, plays, movies, radio and television programs, long poems, and operas. In addition, underline foreign words (except proper names, quotations in a foreign language, titles of articles in a foreign language, and other foreign words anglicized through usage). However, enclose within quotation marks titles of articles, essays, chapters, sections, short poems, stories, and songs.

On occasion underlining is also used to emphasize certain words or phrases in a typed paper, such as in this sentence from the sample research paper:

```
Yet Beneatha, unlike her sister-in-law Ruth, is a
rivaling matriarch.
```

There may be occasions when you wish to emphasize certain words within quoted materials. Handle such underlining as in the following example:

```
When Beneatha denies the existence of God, Mama
slaps her in the face and forces her to repeat
after her, "In my mother's house there is still
God" (p. 37).  Then Mama adds, "There are some
ideas we ain't going to have in this house.  Not
long as I am at the head of this family" (p. 37,
underlining is mine).  Thus Mama meets. . . .
```

Follow this rule: You may underline another person's words only if you stipulate within parentheses that you have done so.

Remember that a little underlining goes a long way. Like too many neon signs, too much underlining for emphasis (and too many exclamation marks, for that matter) distracts your reader and gives the impression that nearly everything in your paper is of the utmost importance, a practice the reader will quickly grow tired of.

SAMPLE RESEARCH PAPER

The Theme of Black Matriarchy

in A Raisin in the Sun

The comments which follow in the margins will serve to clarify the form of the research paper and to explain specific problems you may encounter.

by

Glenda Durdin

Freshman English 102b

Dr. Rimsky

April 23, 1975

The Theme of Black Matriarchy

in <u>A</u> <u>Raisin</u> <u>in</u> <u>the</u> <u>Sun</u>

Thesis sentence: Hansberry uses the sociological concept
of black matriarchy to create dramatic conflict among
the members of the Younger family.

  I. Black matriarchy as a sociological concept in <u>A</u>
     <u>Raisin</u> <u>in</u> <u>the</u> <u>Sun</u>

    A. Two views of the drama
      1. A problem play about escape from the ghetto
      2. A sociological drama about black matriarchy
    B. The history of black matriarchy
      1. Matriarchy defined
      2. The traditional views of matriarchy
    C. Reasons for today's matriarchy
      1. Women less discriminated against than men
      2. Women better educated than men
      3. Men crippled psychologically by self-reliant
        women

 II. The women in <u>A</u> <u>Raisin</u> <u>in</u> <u>the</u> <u>Sun</u> as matriarchs

    A. Mama Younger as black matriarch
      1. Her direction of all activities
      2. Her control of the finances
      3. Her development of family guidelines
    B. Beneatha as a rivaling matriarch
      1. Beneatha's education and its importance to
        her
      2. Beneatha's dominant features that make her a
        leader
      3. Beneatha's challenge to Mama
    C. Ruth in the role of mediator
      1. Ruth's patience and self-control
      2. Ruth's unifying force
      3. Ruth's reactions to Mama's meddling

III. The effects of matriarchy upon the black male

    A. Walter Lee's emasculation under the matriarchy
       system
       1. Walter's challenge to Mama's authority
       2. Walter's restlessness and insecurity
    B. Mama's desire to help Walter Lee
       1. Keeping his best interest at heart
       2. Curbing his male aggressiveness

IV. The search for family harmony

    A. Mama Younger's faith in Walter
       1. Her recognition of Walter's struggle to at-
          tain manhood
       2. Her trust of $6,500 into Walter's hands
       3. Walter's failure and loss of the money
    B. Continued faith and love of Walter by the women
       1. New hope for the family in a new home
       2. Walter's true emergence as a patriarch of the
          family
    C. Hansberry's accomplishments with the drama
       1. Raising the black male above his traditional
          stereotype
       2. Elevating the black male to a man with pride
       3. Showing Mama as an inspirational figure

There is no need to index the various references placed in the outline. The student obviously has the note cards arranged to fit the outline.

You may need to check hyphens to be certain the word is divided properly.

The Theme of Black Matriarchy

in A Raisin in the Sun

Lorraine Hansberry's popular and successful A
Raisin in the Sun, which first appeared on Broadway in
1959, is a problem play that tells the story of a
black family's determination to move out of the ghetto
to a better life. Most critics have said that this
escape theme explains the drama's forceful dramatic
conflict and its importance to the black movement in
general. Yet another issue lies at the heart of the
drama. Hansberry develops a modern view of the sociological aspects of black matriarchy in order to examine the cohesive and, more importantly, the conflict-
producing effects it has on the individual members of
the Younger family.

Black matriarchy, a sociological concept with
origins in slavery, is a family situation, according
to E. Earl Baughman, in which no husband is present
or, if he is present, in which the wife and/or mother
exercises the main influence over family affairs.[1]

[1]E. Earl Baughman, Black Americans: A Psychological
Analysis (New York: Academic Press, 1971), pp. 80–81.

For years the typical attitude toward this phenomenon has been the one expressed by E. Franklin Frazier, who argues that "because of conditions imposed
by the slave system, the mother was the most depend-
able and the most important member of the Negro family."[2] This traditional view, defended by sociologists
and historians, is based on Frazier's theory that the
black family was matriarchal because of slavery, the
move from rural to urban environments, and racial
prejudice.[3] Robert Penn Warren echoes that traditional view in a more recent statement:

> The matriarchy is, of course, a heritage of
> slavery, the result of the fact that the
> Negro was not regarded as a person. The
> father was merely a biological father; he
> had no rights, dignity, or authority, and
> therefore had no role in the family. In
> many cases he was not even present, and if
> he was present he might be sold off, or the
> family broken, at the whim of the owner.
> But even now, since the Negro woman, gener-
> ally speaking, has a less precarious eco-
> nomic value than the man, his role may be
> unstable. He may be in the family, ulti-
> mately, on sufferance.[4]

[2]_The Negro in the United States_ (New York: Macmillan, 1957), p. 309.

[3]For additional information on Frazier's views
see _The Negro Family in the United States_ (Chicago:
Univ. of Chicago Press, 1939), esp. pp. 125–45, and
The Negro in the United States, esp. pp. 306–33.

[4]_Who Speaks for the Negro_ (New York: Random
House, 1965), p. 36.

The student uses effectively both quotation and paraphrase from the note cards on Frazier's ideas.

Longer quotations are introduced with a colon. They are indented and single spaced without quotation marks and with the index numeral at the end of the quotation.

Your instructor may request that you double space indented quotations.

Footnote 2 requires no name because Frazier's name is mentioned in the text.

Footnote 3 is comprehensive and may be an aid to other scholars on this subject.

Footnotes run consecutively; they are not numbered anew on each page.

Even recent opponents of Frazier's views, like Robert Staples, admit that black women were not passive because "if they had been contented to accept the passive role ascribed to the female gender, then the travail of the past four centuries might have found the black race as extinct as the dinosaur."[5]

After slavery, the trials of emancipation had a disruptive effect on the black family as a unit because blacks were suddenly expected to change many of the social values taken on when they were slaves. One of these was the idea that the male should be the family head and chief provider. But, as with all new social values in any culture, this idea was slow in gaining acceptance by blacks; thus matriarchy is still an essential feature of today's black family.

There are several reasons for the staying power of black matriarchy. First, black women have usually been less discriminated against than black males. Dara Abubakari (Virginia E. Y. Collins) observes, "At one time the black woman was the only one that could say something and not get her head chopped off.

A change in a person's name or a pseudonym may be noted as an aid to your reader.

[5]Robert Staples, "The Myth of Black Matriarchy," The Black Scholar, 1 (Jan.-Feb. 1970), 8.

You could say certain things, you could raise the banner high. But the law was strictly against the black man."[6] Also, Marjorie Barnes states that "black women have been able to find work when their husbands couldn't and have often been the head of the family not because they wanted to be but out of economic necessity."[7] Second, black women have traditionally been better educated than black men. Once again, the dominant white society appears to be less threatened by an educated black woman than an educated black man. Even when slaves, black women were more likely to be taught to read and write than black males. Two critics note that black females today still complete more years of school than black males and are more represented in high status.[8] The third and probably

[6]Taped interview of Dara Abubakari by Gerda Lerner, New Orleans, Louisiana, 11 Oct. 1970; rpt. in Black Women in White America, ed. Gerda Lerner (New York: Pantheon, 1972), pp. 585-86.

[7]Marjorie Barnes as quoted by Renee Ferguson, Washington Post, 3 Oct. 1970; rpt. in Black Women in White America, p. 589.

[8]Eli Ginzberg and Dale L. Hiestand, "Employment Patterns of Negro Men and Women," in John P. Davis, ed., The American Negro Reference Book (Englewood Cliffs, N.J.: Prentice-Hall, 1966), pp. 79-87.

Even paraphrases should be introduced so that the reader knows exactly what you are saying and what you are borrowing.

The student cites both the original source and the source from which the quotation was actually taken.

Footnotes 7 and 8 both demonstrate proper citation of original material that has been reprinted in another text.

5

most important reason for the survival of black matriarchy is that the assertiveness and self-reliance
developed through necessity by the black female has
had a crippling effect on many black males. For example, two sociologists point out:

> Those Negro males who perceive themselves
> as relative failures, i.e., low achievers,
> with little hope of success, are also more
> prone to feel that they are failing in
> their family role performance. . . . The
> problems encountered by the Negro male in
> the areas of employment, housing, and
> general social discrimination result in
> feelings of failure and inadequacy and an
> inability to perform his family role
> adequately.[9]

A Raisin in the Sun presents a realistic view of
the differing aspects of black matriarchy and the con-
flicts it can produce. The character of Lena (Mama)
exhibits most of the characteristics of the traditional black matriarch. She directs family activities in
her apartment. She controls the family wealth, a
$10,000 insurance inheritance. She establishes guide-
lines on how the money will be spent. Hansberry de-
scribes Mama as a "full-bodied and strong" woman who
"has adjusted to many things in life and overcome many

---

[9]Peter M. Blau and Otis D. Duncan, The American
Occupational Structure (New York: Wiley, 1967), p.
250.

Ellipsis dots indicate omission, three dots for the omission and one as the mark of punctuation.

The writer now shifts her attention to the primary source after completing the introductory history of matriarchy.

more. . . ."[10] We can assume that for years she has been the dominant figure in the lives of her children. Now, however, each member is challenging her authority to some extent.

One of these challenges comes from her daughter Beneatha, an intense young woman, determined to get a good education because she sees that as her only escape from poverty. She desires to better her own situation and the situations of others, but her sacrifices and contributions are few. She, like Ruth and Walter, respects Mama's position in the family, but challenges it at times. She believes the insurance money to be Mama's and never questions Mama's use of the finances. When Walter mentions that the money is coming, Beneatha defends Mama's position:

> That money belongs to Mama, Walter, and it's for her to decide how she wants to use it. I don't care if she wants to buy a house or a rocket ship or just nail it up somewhere and look at it. It's hers. Not ours--hers. (p. 19)

Yet Beneatha, unlike her sister-in-law Ruth, is a rivaling matriarch. Apparently inheriting many of her mother's strong qualities of leadership, she often

[10]Lorraine Hansberry, A Raisin in the Sun (New York: Random House, 1959), p. 15. Subsequent documentation of quotations from the drama will be intext notes within parentheses.

This first usage of the primary source requires a footnote. Thereafter documentation may be made by placing page numbers within parentheses after each quotation from the primary source.

The brief documentation at the end of this quotation is made possible by the notation within footnote 10.

Since the quotation is part of the sentence, the documentation goes inside the period. With indented and single-spaced quotations the documentation goes outside the period.

challenges Mama's authority, especially in the area of religion. When Beneatha denies the existence of God, Mama slaps her in the face and forces her to repeat after her, "In my mother's house there is still God" (p.37). Then Mama adds, "There are some ideas we ain't going to have in this house. Not long as I am at the head of this family" (p. 37; underlining is mine). Thus Mama meets Beneatha's challenge head on and at this point in the play reaffirms her position as sole matriarch.

The other mother in the Younger household is Ruth, Walter's wife, who has one son and is now pregnant again. Quiet and patient, she holds together the threads of the family, just as Mama does in a more forceful way. This characteristic is well illustrated in the scene between Ruth and Walter when he is in a drunken rage. Ruth does not lose her temper, but through kindness wins over her husband (pp. 79–80).

Even paraphrases from the original source are noted by documentation.

Like Beneatha, Ruth respects Mama's position as matriarch in some instances, and not in others. She refuses her husband's plea to use her influence in order to convince Mama to use the money to buy a liquor store, saying, "Walter, that ain't none of our money" (p. 15). While Ruth can respect Mama's position of decision maker for most matters, the young mother resents Mama's meddling in her child's affairs (p. 23).

The most serious conflict in the play occurs between Walter and Mama. She wants her son, now thirty years old, to be strong and self-reliant. Yet she mothers and dominates him because she feels that he cannot stand alone when faced with certain situations. She exerts her strong authority over Walter when he tries to break the maternal bond by attempting to buy a liquor store with her insurance money:

> Mama: I don't 'low no yellin' in this
> house, Walter Lee, and you know it—-And
> there ain't going to be no investing in
> no liquor stores. I don't aim to have to
> speak on that again. (pp. 57-58)

Walter's desire to gain voice in the family's decision-making process is strong enough so that he can at least verbally challenge her, even though he knows his protest will fall on deaf ears:

> Oh—-so you don't aim to have to speak on
> that again? So you have decided . . .
> Well, you tell that to my boy tonight when
> you put him to sleep on the livingroom
> couch . . . Yeah—-and tell it to my wife,
> Mama, tomorrow when she has to go out of
> here to look after somebody else's kids.
> And tell it to me, Mama, every time we need
> a new pair of curtains and I have to watch
> you go out and work in somebody's kitchen.
> Yeah, you tell me then! (p. 58)

The effect of such thwarting of Walter's quest for manhood, in addition to the hostility he feels from the outside world, is one of resignation and despair:

> Sometimes it's like I can see the future
> stretched out in front of me—just plain as
> day. The future, Mama. Hanging over there
> at the edge of my days. Just waiting for
> me—a big, looming blank space—full of
> <u>nothing</u>.

Walter has expressed the common plight of the modern black male in our society. Black psychiatrists William Grier and Price Cobbs make this observation:

> For the black man in this country, it
> is not so much a matter of acquiring man-
> hood as it is a struggle to feel it his
> own. Whereas the white man regards his
> manhood as an ordained right, the black man
> is engaged in a never-ending battle for its
> possession. For the black man, attaining
> any portion of manhood is an active pro-
> cess. He must penetrate barriers and over-
> come opposition in order to assume a mascu-
> line posture. For the inner psychological
> obstacles to manhood are never so formida-
> ble as the impediments woven into American
> society.[11]

It should be noted, however, that Mama usually has Walter's best interests at heart and sincerely wants him to be self-reliant, even though, in his frustration and anger, he frequently misinterprets her actions and motivations:

> Mama: I wish you say something, son . . . I
> wish you'd say how deep inside you you
> [sic] think I done the right thing—

[11]William H. Grier and Price M. Cobbs, <u>Black</u> <u>Rage</u>
(New York: Basic Books, 1968), p. 59.

Margin notes:

It is best to avoid long quotations like this one by the use of paraphrase, but this one is well phrased and important to the student's argument.

The usage of *sic* indicates that an error or apparent error appears in the original material and that you are quoting accurately.

Walter: What you need me to say you done
right for? You the head of this family.
You run our lives like you want to.
It was your money and you did what you
wanted with it. So what you need for me
to say it was all right for? So you
butchered up a dream of mine—you—who
always talking 'bout your children's
dreams. . . . (p. 87)

In a touching scene, Mama tries to define the cause of
her need to protect her son, admitting that her actions might have been wrong at times, but they were
motivated by good intentions:

Listen to me, now. I say I been wrong,
son. That I been doing to you what the
rest of the world doing to you. Walter—
what you ain't never understood is that I
ain't got nothing, don't own nothing, ain't
never really wanted nothing that wasn't for
you. There ain't nothing as precious to me
. . . There ain't nothing worth holding on
to, money, dreams, nothing else—if it
means—if it means it's going to destroy
my boy. (pp. 93-94)

Here she realizes that her frequent opposition to Walter's ambitions have frustrated him, but that her ov-
erprotection was justified. Indirectly she has expressed a feeling common among black matriarchs—that
they need to curb the natural tendencies of masculine
aggression lest their sons place their own and the family's safety in jeopardy.[12] True to her role as matriarch, Mama has placed the well-being of the entire
family ahead of her concern for any one member.

[12]Grier and Cobbs, p. 62.

Walter Lee's desire to be head of the family and his struggle to attain manhood are the primary areas of trouble within the family. As Grier and Cobbs point out, the black family is often in serious trouble:

> It is coming apart and it is failing to provide the nurturing that black children need. In its failure the resulting isolated men and women fail generally to make a whole life for themselves in a nation designed for families. . . .[13]

Mama finally recognizes this danger and instructs Walter to put $3,000 of the insurance money in a savings account for Beneatha's education, and for him to put the remaining $3,500 in a checking account of his own. She has already spent $3,500 as a deposit for a house in a white neighborhood:

> Mama: And from now on any penny that come out of it or that go in it is for you to decide. It ain't much, but it's all I got in the world and I'm putting it in your hands. I'm telling you to be the head of this family from now on like you supposed to be.
>
> Walter (Stares at the money): You trust me like that, Mama?
>
> Mama: I ain't never stop trusting you. Like I ain't never stop loving you.
> (p. 94)

Walter Lee, with the money in his possession, believes himself to be a real man. Unknown to the others, he foolishly invests in a liquor store scheme. As the

---

[13]Grier and Cobbs, p. 83.

family prepares to move into its new house, elation
overwhelms every member. All are happy with their
patriarchal figurehead. Even a visit from Lindner,
the representative of the Clybourne Park Improvement
Association, who offers them a profit on their house
in order to keep blacks from moving into the neighbor-
hood, fails to dampen their spirits. Then comes news
of the loss of Walter's liquor store investment, and
the news is more devastating than the family knows:

> Mama: Son--Son . . . Is it gone? Son, I
> gave you sixty-five hundred dollars. Is
> it gone? All of it? Beneatha's money
> too?
>
> Walter: Mama . . . I never . . . went to
> the bank at all . . .
>
> Mama: You mean . . . your sister's school
> money . . . you used that too . . . Wal-
> ter? . . .
>
> Walter: Yesss! . . . All of it . . . It's
> all gone . . . (pp. 116-17)

Mama, in a trance of dissolution, resumes her role as
matriarch and beats Walter senselessly in the face
until she is restrained.

However, the family had been very happy with Walter in charge. Consequently, despite Walter Lee's
terrible mistake, Mama loves him and searches for a
way to help him. "The true worth of a race must be
measured by the character of its womanhood," argues
Mary McLeod Bethune, who adds: "Both before and since

A brief summary
paragraph like this
one is often
necessary. Better
this than a paper
that retells the plot
throughout the
entire research
paper.

emancipation, by some rare gift, she has been able . . . to hold onto the fibres of family unity and keep the home one unimpaired whole."[14] In an act of ultimate faith, Mama allows Walter to decide their next course of action. She tells Beneatha:

> There is always something left to love. And if you ain't learned that, you ain't learned nothing. Have you cried for that boy today? . . . When you start measuring somebody, measure him right, child, measure him right. Make sure you done taken into account what hills and valleys he come through before he got to whatever he is. (pp. 135-36)

Walter calls Lindner and has every intention of selling the new house at a profit to make up for some of the lost money. The others watch in despair as he prepares to sell out to the white man. When the time comes, however, and Walter confronts Lindner, he becomes a man for the first time in the drama's most touching scene:

> Walter: What I am telling you is that we called you here to tell you that we are very proud and that this is—this is my son, who makes the sixth generation of our family in this country, and that we have all thought about your offer and we have decided to move into our house because my father—my father—he earned it. We don't want to make no trouble for nobody or fight no causes—but we will try to be good neighbors. That's all we

[14]"A Century of Progress of Negro Women," Address delivered before the Chicago Women's Federation, June 30, 1933; rpt. in Black Women in White America, p. 583.

Three ellipsis dots indicate omission from within a single sentence.

Three ellipsis dots with a terminal mark, a period or question mark, indicate omission of one or more sentences from within the quoted material.

The modern trend toward collections of essays makes this sort of footnote rather common.

got to say. We don't want your money.
(p. 138)

The family is thus once again united with Walter Lee,
not Mama, as its head.

By her characterization of Walter, Lorraine Hansberry has raised the black male above the typical
stereotype. Walter is not a social problem, a mere
victim of matriarchy. Rather, Hansberry creates a
character who breaks out of the traditional sociological image that dehumanizes the black male. Creating a
character who struggles with his fate and rises above
it, Hansberry has elevated the black male. As James
Baldwin puts it, "Time has made some changes in the
Negro face."[15]

Additionally, Hansberry's women are pleased that
their black man has assumed his new role with authority and dignity. Mama says to Ruth, "He finally come
into his manhood today, didn't he? Kind of like a
rainbow after the rain . . ." (p. 141). Mama is a
black matriarch, but she is also a noble and inspira-
tional figure in freely relinquishing control of the
family to Walter so that he can grow more fully into
manhood. The departure for their new home takes place
and, despite the loss of their money, the family holds
new hope for its future.

[15]Notes of a Native Son (New York: Dial Press,
1963), p. 24.

Intext documentation goes immediately after the material, but when necessary, put it on a line immediately below the quotation.

Rather than a summary, the student now reaches some demonstrable conclusions about the drama.

Note the three dots for ellipsis and the period after the documentation.

A Selected Bibliography

Baldwin, James. <u>Notes</u> <u>of</u> <u>a</u> <u>Native</u> <u>Son</u>. New York: Dial Press, 1963.

Baughman, E. Earl. <u>Black</u> <u>Americans</u>: <u>A</u> <u>Psychological</u> <u>Analysis</u>. New York: Academic Press, 1971.

Blau, Peter M., and Otis Dudley Duncan. <u>The</u> <u>American</u> <u>Occupational</u> <u>Structure</u>. New York: Wiley, 1967.

Bracey, John H., August Meier, and Elliott Rudwick, eds. <u>Black</u> <u>Matriarchy</u>: <u>Myth</u> <u>or</u> <u>Reality</u>? Belmont, Cal.: Wadsworth, 1970.

Frazier, E. Franklin. <u>The</u> <u>Negro</u> <u>Family</u> <u>in</u> <u>the</u> <u>United</u> <u>States</u>. Chicago: Univ. of Chicago Press, 1939.

————————. <u>The</u> <u>Negro</u> <u>in</u> <u>the</u> <u>United</u> <u>States</u>. New York: Macmillan, 1957.

Ginzberg, Eli, and Dale L. Hiestand. "Employment Patterns of Negro Men and Women." In <u>The</u> <u>American</u> <u>Negro</u> <u>Reference</u> <u>Book</u>. Ed. John P. Davis. Englewood Cliffs, N.J.: Prentice–Hall, 1966.

Grier, William H., and Price M. Cobbs. <u>Black</u> <u>Rage</u>. New York: Basic Books, 1968.

Hansberry, Lorraine. <u>A</u> <u>Raisin</u> <u>in</u> <u>the</u> <u>Sun</u>. New York: Random House, 1959.

Lerner, Gerda, ed. <u>Black</u> <u>Woman</u> <u>in</u> <u>White</u> <u>America</u>. New York: Pantheon, 1972.

Staples, Robert. "The Myth of Black Matriarchy," <u>The</u> <u>Black</u> <u>Scholar</u>, 1 (Jan.–Feb. 1970), 8–16.

Warren, Robert Penn. <u>Who</u> <u>Speaks</u> <u>for</u> <u>the</u> <u>Negro</u>. New York: Random House, 1965.

Your instructor may request that you double space entries within the bibliography.

You may employ this form or a blanket entry for the book in hand, as with the Lerner citation below.

This blanket entry for *Black Women in White America* covers citations to material by Dara Abubakari, Marjorie Barnes, and Mary Bethune, footnotes 6, 7, and 14. A separate entry for each of the three would also be acceptable.

■ With as much effort as you have already exercised in organizing the body of your paper, you will now want to note your sources with complete accuracy. Consequently, you must credit in a footnote the source of every quotation, paraphrase, fact, or idea, specifying the exact location of each item so that the reader may investigate further if he or she so desires. Therefore, you should fully understand, perhaps even memorize, the basic forms of documentation—that is, both footnote and bibliography entries for a book and for a periodical article. (For a fuller discussion of bibliography entries, see pp. 119-35.)

The basic forms for a book are:

Footnote

[1]Carl Wellman, <u>Morals</u> <u>and</u> <u>Ethics</u> (Glenview, Ill.: Scott, Foresman, 1975), p. 203.

Bibliography

Wellman, Carl. <u>Morals</u> <u>and</u> <u>Ethics</u>. Glenview, Ill.: Scott, Foresman, 1975.

In other words, a footnote for a book differs from the bibliography entry for that book in six ways: (1) indentation of the first line; (2) raised index numeral, (3) author's given name first, (4) a comma following the author's name, (5) publication data within parentheses, and (6) a specific page reference.

The basic forms for periodical articles are:

Footnote

[2]Daniel Stempel, "Angels of Reason: Science and Myth in the Enlightenment," <u>Journal</u> <u>of</u> <u>the</u> <u>History</u> <u>of</u> <u>Ideas</u>, 36 (Jan.–March 1975), 63–64.

Bibliography

Stempel, Daniel. "Angels of Reason: Science and Myth in the Enlightenment." <u>Journal</u> <u>of</u> <u>the</u> <u>History</u> <u>of</u> <u>Ideas</u>, 36 (Jan.–March 1975), 63–78.

That is, a footnote for a periodical article differs from the bibliography entry for that article in six ways: (1) indentation of the first line, (2) raised index numeral, (3) author's given name first, (4) a comma following the author's name, (5) a comma rather than a ·period following the title of the article, and (6) a specific page reference rather than complete pagination.

You must keep your footnotes correct, clear, and concise. By recording data *carefully* and by double-checking each entry *before* typing the final manuscript, you can ensure accuracy. (Imagine the reaction of your reader, or instructor, if your reference directs him or her to page 568 of a book that contains only 465 pages!) Also, you must maintain clarity. Remember, for example, that "Ibid." should not appear as the first note on a page (thereby forcing the reader to turn back to the preceding page) and that "Smith, op. cit., p. 16" may confuse the reader more than a simple reference to "Smith, p. 16." More information on when to use these forms is provided on pp. 115-17. Finally, you should not interrupt the reader with an overabundance of footnotes at the bottom of the page. In fact, when you are citing a primary source many times in the paper, you can insert a brief note, within parentheses, in the text itself. Clearly, you will not seriously interrupt the reader's attention with such references in your text as (p. 35), (XI.357), or (*Ham*.III.i.56-63). Remember, however, in such cases to write a first full reference to a work that you cite often, putting it in proper footnote position at the bottom of the page, and informing your reader that subsequent references to this edition appear in your text (see pp. 64-66).

When to Footnote

Sometimes the decision to document or not to document certain information with a footnote becomes troublesome. If in doubt, you should ask yourself, "Would a mature reader be likely to know this information?" If you believe he or she would not, you should provide a footnote that locates the source for the reader. For example, the fact that Richard M. Nixon was president of the United States would not usually require a footnote entry. Nor would you probably need to indicate a source for the fact that Nixon's foreign policy resulted in détente with Russia and the renewal of diplomatic relations with China. For that matter, his decision to resign as a result of the Watergate scandal is common knowledge. However, you should credit, by means of a footnote, the source of specific decisions and statements by Nixon—for example, his communications with Russian and Chinese leaders, his cabinet decisions, or his public proclamations and statements.

Do *not* footnote a common dictionary definition, but *do* footnote a special or extended definition from, for example, the *Oxford English Dictionary* or an encyclopedia. Do *not* footnote an item of common knowledge, such as: "Faulkner created a mythic community within his novels that he labeled Yoknapatawpha county"; "Faulkner wrote *The Sound and the Fury*"; "Faulkner was preoccupied with the South's heritage." But *do* footnote any paraphrase of highly specific information or commentary so original that it goes beyond what an average young scholar might know. Do *not* footnote an idea of your own, though the idea may result from your reading and the combination of ideas suggested by your sources, but *do* footnote any idea that you can credit to a specific source.

Therefore, a good rule of thumb might well be the following: You should footnote when borrowing directly from your notes, but you may omit the footnote when you compose sentences not directly derived from reference material. Of course, you must always footnote a quotation, précis, summary, or paraphrased sentence. (See pp. 43-48, and the discussion of plagiarism, pp. 48-51.)

In addition, resist the tendency to construct each paragraph so that a footnote at the end of it would blanket the entire unit. This method results in ambiguous references. Rather, you should consider each sentence you write as a separate unit, using the rule of thumb mentioned above to assess the general nature of the material contained in it. You should not find it necessary to footnote a complete paragraph if you synthesize and develop all the material as your own. (See "Handling Reference Material," pp. 59-68.)

Placing Footnote Numbers Within the Text

The rules for inserting footnote numbers into your text are:

1. Use Arabic numerals typed slightly above the line.

2. Always place the number at the *end* of your quotation, paraphrase, idea, and so on—not after introductory words or punctuation.

3. The footnote number comes immediately after the final word or punctuation—there is no space between a word or a mark of punctuation and the index numeral:

```
     . . . the mother was the most dependable and

the most important member of the Negro fami-

ly."2  This traditional view, defended by soci-

ologists and historians, is based on Frazier's

theory that the black family was matriarchal

because of slavery, the migration from rural to

urban environments, and racial prejudice.3

Robert Penn Warren echoes. . . .
```

Arranging the Footnotes

When writing your footnotes, be sure to:

1. Number the footnotes consecutively throughout the entire paper (but by chapters in longer works such as a graduate thesis).

2. Collect at the bottom of each page all footnotes for citations made on that page. (However, your instructor may request that you place all notes together on separate sheets at the end of your paper.)

3. Separate the footnotes from your text by triple spacing (that is, leave two lines of space). Also, single space each footnote, but double space between the notes:

Even recent opponents of Frazier's views, like Robert Staples, admit that black women were not passive because "if they had been contented to

[2]The Negro in the United States (New York: Macmillan, 1957), p. 309.

[3]For additional information on Frazier's views see The Negro Family in the United States (Chicago: Univ. of Chicago Press, 1939), esp. pp. 125–45, and The Negro in the United States, esp. pp. 306–33.

[4]Who Speaks for the Negro (New York: Random House, 1965), p. 36.

(However, your instructor may request that you double space *all* materials, even the footnotes.)

4. Do not start a footnote on one page and complete it on the next. In order to prevent your footnotes from running over to the next page or descending below your bottom margin, you can estimate the amount of space you will need by inserting each footnote, with the proper spacing, etc., in the *rough* draft of the text in this fashion:

```
But the law was strictly against the black man."6


    6Taped interview of Dara Abubakari by Gerda
Lerner, New Orleans, Louisiana, Oct. 11, 1970;
rpt. in Black Women in White America, ed. Gerda
Lerner (New York: Pantheon, 1972), pp. 585-96.



Marjorie Barnes states that "black women have
```

This is done in the rough draft only. At the retyping stage, then, the exact number of lines and spaces needed can be calculated and enough room left at the bottom for footnotes.

5. Employ a separate line for each footnote unless you have numerous short notes. The following form is acceptable:

```
4Johnson, p. 3.        6Thomas, p. 456.

5Ibid., p. 9.          7Johnson, p. 9.
```

Also acceptable:

```
4Johnson, p. 3.

5Ibid., p. 9.

6Thomas, p. 456.

7Johnson, p. 9.
```

Footnote Form—Books

You should use the following order when placing data for books within the first, full footnote, omitting any unnecessary items:

1. The author's or authors' name(s), in normal order, followed by a comma:

¹Elizabeth Bowen, <u>Pictures</u> <u>and</u> <u>Conversations</u> (New York: Knopf, 1975), p. 17.

Avoid abbreviations by providing the name in the fullest form known to you. Imagine the dilemma of a reader searching the card catalog for "L. Lewis" or "J. H. Smith"! However, if you supply missing ingredients—that is, ones not given on the title page of the book—place them within square brackets (for example, "L[awrence] Lewis"). In the case of well-known authors, give the name in its most usual form (for example, "T. S. Eliot" and "Dante").

2. The title of the chapter or part of the book, within quotation marks, followed by a comma inside the final quotes:

²Lonne Elder, "Ceremonies in Dark Old Men," in <u>New</u> <u>Black</u> <u>Playwrights</u>: <u>An</u> <u>Anthology</u>, ed. William Couch, Jr. (Baton Rouge: Louisiana State Univ. Press, 1968), p. 80.

This entry is usually necessary only with separate works in collections or specific chapters of long works. See below, "Component part of a book," p. 102.

3. The title of the book, underlined, followed by a comma unless the next item is enclosed within parentheses. Use the full title as shown on the title page of the book, including any subtitle (which you distinguish by a colon):

³Arthur O. Lovejoy, <u>The</u> <u>Great</u> <u>Chain</u> <u>of</u> <u>Being</u>: <u>A</u> <u>Study</u> <u>in</u> <u>the</u> <u>History</u> <u>of</u> <u>an</u> <u>Idea</u> (Cambridge, Mass.: Harvard Univ. Press, 1936), p. 118.

4. The name of the editor, translator, or compiler, in normal order, preceded by "ed.," "trans.," or "comp.," followed by a comma unless the next item is enclosed within parentheses:

⁴Aleksandr Solzhenitsyn, <u>August</u> <u>1914</u>, trans. Michael Glenny (New York: Farrar, Straus and Giroux, 1972), p. 17.

⁵N. Scott Momaday, "A Vision Beyond Time and Place," in <u>Speaking</u> <u>for</u> <u>Ourselves</u>: <u>American</u> <u>Ethnic</u> <u>Writing</u>, ed. Lillian Faderman and Barbara Bradshaw, 2nd ed. (Glenview, Ill.: Scott, Foresman, 1975), p. 15.

Note that this text is *edited by* the two authors (compare with note 6 below).

If you are discussing the editor's or translator's work rather than the text, provide his or her name first, followed by a comma, followed by "ed.," eds.," or "trans.," and another comma. Place the author's name, if any, preceded with a comma and "by," after the title:

> 6Lillian Faderman and Barbara Bradshaw, eds., <u>Speaking for Ourselves</u>: <u>American Ethnic Writing</u>, 2nd ed. (Glenview, Ill.: Scott, Foresman, 1975), p. iv.

> 7Richmond Lattimore, trans., <u>The Iliad</u>, by Homer (Chicago: Univ. of Chicago Press, 1962), p. iii.

5. The edition number, if it is not the first, in Arabic numerals, followed by a comma unless the next item is enclosed within parentheses:

> 8William Bloom and Don W. Fawcett, <u>A Textbook of Histology</u>, 9th ed. (Philadelphia: Saunders, 1968), p. 342.

Reprints of old editions, paperback reprints especially, require notation of the original date and edition as well as publication facts of the reprint:

> 9John Livingston Lowes, <u>The Road to Xanadu</u>: <u>A Study in the Ways of the Imagination</u>, 2nd ed. (1930; rpt. New York: Vintage-Knopf, 1959), p. 76.

6. The series name, without quotation marks and not underlined, followed by a comma, followed by the number of this book in the series, followed by a comma unless the next item is enclosed within parentheses:

> 10David Fowler, <u>Piers the Plowman</u>, Univ. of Washington Publications in Lang. and Lit., 16 (Seattle: Univ. of Washington Press, 1961), p. 89.

7. The number of volumes with this title, in Arabic numerals (for example, "5 vols."). Use only if there is more than one volume and the information is pertinent—that is, if your reference is to the work as a whole, not to a specific passage:

> 11Vernon L. Parrington, <u>Main Currents in American Thought</u>, 3 vols. (New York: Harcourt Brace, 1927-32).

> Note that the page number is omitted in this footnote because the reference is to the entire work.

8. The place, publisher, and date of publication within parentheses and with a colon between the place and publisher and commas after the publisher and the second parenthesis:

> ¹²Andrew Wright, A Reader's Guide to English and American Literature (Glenview, Ill.: Scott, Foresman, 1970), p. xix.

If more than one city appears on the title page, use only the first. Include the name of the state if necessary for clarity (for example, "Springfield, Mass." or "Springfield, Ill."). Provide the publisher's name in an abbreviated form (for example, "Macmillan," "Norton," "McGraw-Hill," etc.). But list university presses in full to distinguish between a publication of the university and that of a university press (for example, "Louisiana State Univ." or "Univ. of Oklahoma Press"). If the title page does not carry the publication date, use the most recent copyright date as shown on the reverse side of the title page.

9. The volume number, if the book is one of two or more volumes with the same title, in Roman numerals, followed by a comma:

> ¹³Ivan Turgenev, Virgin Soil, trans. Constance Garnett (New York: Macmillan, 1951), I, 81.

If the volumes were published in different years, show this fact by placing the volume number *before* the place and date of publication:

> ¹⁴Vernon L. Parrington, "Roger Williams," Main Currents in American Thought, I (New York: Harcourt Brace, 1927), 62.

10. Page number(s), preceded by a comma, in Arabic numerals unless the text has small Roman numerals (for example, "p. iv."). Use "p." and "pp." only for works of a single volume. Also note the following common usage: "pp. 92-93," not "pp. 92-3"; but "pp. 215-18," not "pp. 215-8" or "pp. 215-218." Page numbers are followed by a period unless some additional information must be included (for example, "p. 12, n. 2.").

SPECIMEN FOOTNOTES—BOOKS

Author, *first full reference*

> ¹E. Earl Baughman, Black Americans: A Psychological Analysis (New York: Academic Press, 1971), pp. 80–81.

Subsequent reference:

²Baughman, p. 75.

Here and elsewhere below, the inclusion of "subsequent references" will indicate how to set up footnotes for sources that have been cited previously in the text of the paper.

Author's name already given in text

¹<u>Black Americans</u>: <u>A Psychological Analysis</u> (New York: Academic Press, 1971), pp. 80–81.

Use this form even if both author and title are given in your text.

Subsequent reference:

²Baughman, <u>Black American: A Psychological Analysis</u>, p. 75.

Since you did not name Baughman in the first note, you must connect him with the title in the second note. Thereafter, "Baughman, p. 7." will suffice.

Author, *anonymous*

³<u>The Song of Roland</u>, trans. Frederick Bliss Luquines (New York: Macmillan, 1960), p. 22.

Subsequent reference:

⁴<u>Roland</u>, p. 23.

Author, *anonymous but name supplied*

⁵[James Madison], <u>All Impressments Unlawful and Inadmissible</u> (Boston: William Pelham, 1804), p. 10.

Subsequent reference:

⁶[Madison], p. 12.

Author, *pseudonymous but name supplied*

⁷Robert Slender [Philip Freneau], <u>Letters on Various and Important Subjects</u> (Philadelphia: D. Hogan, 1799), p. 140.

Subsequent reference:

⁸Slender [Freneau], p. 141.

Authors, *two*

⁹Nena O'Neill and George O'Neill, <u>Shifting Gears: Finding Security in a Changing World</u> (New York: M. Evans, 1974), pp. 31–33.

Subsequent reference:

¹⁰O'Neill and O'Neill, p. 32.

Authors, *three*

[11]Wilbur O. Sypherd, A. M. Fountain, and V. E. Gibbens, <u>Manual of Technical Writing</u> (Glenview, Ill.: Scott, Foresman, 1957), p. 60.

Subsequent reference:

[12]Sypherd et al., p. 61.

Authors, *more than three*

[13]Albert C. Baugh et al., <u>A Literary History of England</u>, 2nd ed. (New York: Appleton, 1967), p. 797.

The use of "and others" is also acceptable (see p. 118).

Subsequent reference:

[14]Baugh et al., p. 798.

Biblical references

[15]Psalms 14:4–5.

[16]II Peter 2:17 (The Interpreter's Bible, XII).

Editions of the Bible other than the King James version should be noted within parentheses.

Classical works

[17]Homer, <u>The Iliad</u>, trans. Richmond Lattimore (Chicago: Univ. of Chicago Press, 1951), p. 101 (Bk. III, ll. 38–45).

[18]Plato, <u>The Republic</u>, trans. Paul Shorey (Cambridge, Mass.: Harvard Univ. Press, 1937), p. 225 (III, vi).

You should give the reader more information than the page number for classics that appear in several editions. However, do not use this form if you make numerous citations to one work. Rather, you should provide an initial full reference and thereafter place the documentation in your text (see pp. 64-66).

Component part of a book

[19]Lewis Thomas, "The Music of This Sphere," <u>The Lives of a Cell</u> (New York: Viking, 1974), pp. 20–25.

[20]Dante, "Purgatorio," <u>The Divine Comedy</u>, trans. Lawrence Grant White (New York: Pantheon, 1948), p. 74.

Use this form (notes 19 and 20) for citation to one chapter or section of a complete work by an author.

[21]Robert Penn Warren, "Holly and Hickory," in <u>You Emperors, and Others</u>: <u>Poems 1957–1960</u>, by Robert Penn Warren (New York: Random House, 1960), p. 38.

[22]Flannery O'Connor, "The Nature and Aim of Fiction," in <u>Mystery and Manner</u>, by Flannery O'Connor, ed. Sally and Robert Fitzgerald (New York: Noonday, 1970), pp. 76–77.

Use this form (notes 21 and 22) for citation to one piece in a collection of different pieces all by the same author.

^{23}Nathan Scott, Jr., "Society and Self in Recent American Literature," The Broken Center (New Haven: Yale Univ. Press, 1966), pp. 539–54, rpt. in Dark Symphony: Negro Literature in America, ed. James A. Emanuel and Theodore L. Gross (New York: Free Press, 1968), p. 540.

> Collections of articles are highly useful, but you must take care that you inform your reader about the original source as well as the collection from which you quote or paraphrase. You cannot usually check a reprint against the original, so caution dictates that citations be made to the text actually in hand.

^{24}Robert Browning, "My Last Duchess," in Better Reading Two: Literature, ed. Walter Blair, John Gerber, and Eugene Garber, 4th ed. (Glenview, Ill.: Scott, Foresman, 1966), pp. 55–56.

> Use this form (note 24) for a festschrift or collection of many pieces by different authors.

Subsequent reference:

^{25}Browning, pp. 55–56.

Consolidation of several references in one note

^{26}For additional commentary on this point see Lionel Trilling, "F. Scott Fitzgerald," The Liberal Imagination: Essays on Literature and Society, by Lionel Trilling (New York: Viking, 1951); William Troy, "Scott Fitzgerald, the Authority of Failure," Accent (Autumn 1945); and John Aldridge, "Fitzgerald: The Horror and the Vision of Paradise," in After the Lost Generation, by John W. Aldridge (New York: McGraw-Hill, 1951).

Corporate authorship

^{27}Committee on Telecommunications, Reports on Selected Topics in Telecommunications (New York: National Academy of Sciences, National Research Council, 1970), p. 4.

Subsequent reference:

^{28}Committee on Telecommunications, p. 5.

Double reference

^{29}Stuart Symington as quoted in Victor Marchetti and John D. Marks, The CIA and the Cult of Intelligence (New York: Knopf, 1974), p. 321.

Subsequent reference:

^{30}Symington, p. 321.

Edition

^{31}Oscar Thompson, The International Cyclopedia of Music and Musicians, rev. Robert Sabin, 9th ed. (New York: Dodd, Mead, 1964), p. 81.

Editor

^{32}Hugh Henry Brackenridge, <u>Modern Chivalry</u>, ed.
Claude M. Newlin (New York: American Book, 1962), p.
18.

The writer is citing Brackenridge, the author.

^{33}Hardin Craig and David Bevington, eds., <u>The
Complete Works of Shakespeare</u>, rev. ed. (Glenview,
Ill.: Scott, Foresman, 1973), p. 22.

The writer is citing Craig and Bevington, the editors.

Encyclopedia

^{34}Basil D. Henning, "Norman Conquest," <u>The World
Book Encyclopedia</u>, 1969.

References alphabetically arranged need not be identified by volume and page. Footnotes to unsigned articles begin with the title of the article.

Subsequent reference:

^{35}Henning.

^{36}A[rne] D. N[aess], "Martin Heidegger," <u>Encyclo-
paedia Britannica</u>, Macropaedia 8, 1974.

Authors of articles in the 15th edition of the *Encyclopaedia Britannica* are identified by initials at the end of the article, and their full names are given in a separate volume called the "Propaedia." Brackets are required because you are adding full information to the "A.D.N."

Subsequent reference:

^{37}N[aess].

Footnote citation

^{38}Fawn M. Brodie, <u>Thomas Jefferson</u>: An Intimate
History (New York: Norton, 1974), p. 543, n. 61.

Foreword, *or introduction*

^{39}Robert Lowell, "Foreword," <u>Ariel</u>, by Sylvia
Plath (New York: Harper & Row, 1966), pp. ix–xi.

Manuscript collections

^{40}British Museum, <u>Cotton Vitellius</u>, A. XV.

Subsequent reference:

^{41}<u>Cotton Vitellius</u>.

^{42}Corpus Christi College, Cambridge, MS CCCC 201.

Play, *classical*

^{43}William Shakespeare, <u>Macbeth</u>, in <u>Shakespeare</u>:
<u>Twenty-Three Plays and the Sonnets</u>, ed. T. M. Parrott
(New York: Scribner's, 1953), p. 835 (II.i.33–34).

Since your reader may not have the same edition of Shakespeare's plays, you offer a courtesy by providing act, scene, and lines within parentheses at the end of the footnote.

Subsequent reference:

Should be placed within the text (see pp. 64-66).

Play, *modern*

[44]Tom Stoppard, <u>Rosencrantz and Guildenstern Are</u> <u>Dead</u> (New York: Grove Press, 1967), p. 16.

Poem, *classical*

[45]Dante, ""Purgatorio," <u>The Divine Comedy</u>, trans. Lawrence Grant White (New York: Pantheon, 1948), p. 74 (vii.1–12).

Again, your reader may not have the same edition as you, therefore you offer a courtesy by providing the canto and lines within parentheses at the end of the footnote.

[46]Edmund Spenser, <u>The Faerie Queene</u>, ed. Ernest Rhys (London: Dutton, 1910), I, 58–59 (I.iv.21).

Note that this edition of *The Faerie Queene* is published in two volumes.

Poem, *modern*

[47]Gary Snyder, "Burning the Small Dead," in <u>The</u> <u>Back Country</u>, by Gary Snyder (New York: New Directions, 1968), p. 13.

[48]John Keats, "Ode to a Nightingale," in <u>Beginnings in Poetry</u>, ed. William J. Martz, 2nd ed. (Glenview, Ill.: Scott, Foresman, 1973), pp. 302–4.

Reprint

[49]Raymond M. Weaver, "Introduction," <u>The Shorter Novels of Herman Melville</u> (1928; rpt. New York: Premier–Fawcett, 1960), p. 56.

Series, *numbered*

[50]David Fowler, <u>Piers the Plowman</u>, Univ. of Washington Publications in Lang. and Lit., 16 (Seattle: Univ. of Washington Press, 1961), p. 89.

Since a series number rather than a volume number is given, use the abbreviation "p." with the page number.

Series, *unnumbered*

[51]Lawrence Henry Gibson, <u>The Coming of the Revolution: 1762–1775</u>, ed. Henry Steele Commager and Richard B. Morris, The New American Nation Series (New York: Harper & Row, 1954), pp. 1–10.

[52]Howard E. Wilson, "Education, Foreign Policy, and International Affairs," in <u>Cultural Affairs and Foreign Relations</u>, ed. Robert Blum, The American Assembly Series (Englewood Cliffs, N.J.: Prentice–Hall, 1963), p. 22.

Source books

[53]Cleanth Brooks, "The Formalist Critics," _Kenyon Review_, 13 (1951), 73, rpt. in H. G. Duffield and Manuel Bilsky, eds., _Tolstoy and the Critics: Literature and Aesthetics_ (Glenview, Ill.: Scott, Foresman, 1965), p. 13.

> Source books contain articles gathered from other publications and compiled into one book. If possible, you should find the original material, cite from it, and document accordingly. But when you cannot locate the primary source, cite from your source book and use the method demonstrated above and below, that is, provide an exact reference to both sources, including page numbers if available.

[54]Richard Ellmann, "Reality," _Yeats: The Man and the Masks_ (New York: Macmillan, 1948), rpt. in John Unterecker, ed., _Yeats: A Collection of Critical Essays_, Twentieth Century Views (Englewood Cliffs, N.J.: Prentice-Hall, 1963), p. 165.

Translator

[55]Yukio Mishima, _The Decay of the Angel_, trans. Edward G. Seidensticker (New York: Knopf, 1974), Part 4 of _The Sea of Fertility_, p. 7.

[56]Benedictus de Spinoza, _Spinoza's Short Treatise on God, Man and His Well Being_, trans. and ed. A. Wolf (New York: Russell and Russell, 1963), p. 3.

> In instances where the author's name is included in the title, you must show the name twice, as above.

Volumes, _one of several_

[57]Edgar Allan Poe, "MS. Found in a Bottle," in _The Works of Edgar Allan Poe_ (New York: Crowell, 1902), II, 1–15. Hereafter cited as _Works_.

> When all volumes are published in the same year, place the volume number after the facts of publication. Cf. note 61 below.

Subsequent reference:

[58]Poe, _Works_, 13.

[59]Constance Garnett, trans., "Introduction," _Virgin Soil_, by Ivan Turgenev (New York: Macmillan, 1951), I, v.

[60]Aleksandr Pushkin, _Eugene Onegin_, trans. Vladimir Nabokov, Bollingen Series 72 (New York: Bollingen, 1964), I, 186.

[61]Harold Child, "Jane Austen," in _The Cambridge History of English Literature_, ed. A. W. Ward and A. R. Waller, XII (London: Cambridge Univ. Press, 1914), 231–33. Hereafter cited as _CHEL_.

> When the separate volumes of a work are published in different years, the volume number precedes the facts of publication. Cf. note 57 above.

⁶²Child, <u>CHEL</u>, 232.

⁶³Christopher Marlowe, <u>The Tragical History of Doctor Faustus</u>, in <u>The Literature of England</u>, ed. George K. Anderson and William E. Buckler, 5th ed. (Glenview, Ill.: Scott, Foresman, 1968), I, 711.

⁶⁴Bliss Perry, <u>The American Spirit in Literature</u>, in The Chronicles of America Series, ed. Allen Johnson, XXXIV (New Haven: Yale Univ. Press, 1918), 35.

Works alphabetically arranged

⁶⁵E[dmund] K. A[lden], "Alden, John," <u>DAB</u> (1928).

There is no need to give publishing data on the *Dictionary of American Biography* in an ordinary footnote. However, give that data in the bibliography entry.

Subsequent reference:

⁶⁶A[lden].

Footnote Form—Periodicals

You should use the following order when placing data within the first, full footnote, omitting any items that are unnecessary:

1. The author's name in normal order, followed by a comma:

¹Herbert Aptheker, "The History of Anti-Racism in the United States," <u>The Black Scholar</u>, 6 (1975), 17.

2. The complete title of the article, enclosed within quotation marks, followed by a comma inside the second quotation mark (see footnote 1 above).

3. The name of the periodical, underlined, followed by a comma (see footnote 1 above).

4. The volume number (without the abbreviation "Vol." preceding), in Arabic numerals, followed by a comma unless the next item is enclosed within parentheses (see footnote 1 above). However, omit the volume number for weekly or monthly periodicals which are paged anew in each issue. Give instead the complete date, set off by commas, not parentheses:

²"Labor's Grand Old Godfather," <u>Time</u>, 3 March 1975, p. 11.

5. The issue number when pagination of the issue is separate and the month of publication is not given:

³William R. Elkins, "Thoreau's <u>Cape Cod</u>: The Violent Pond," <u>Oklahoma English Bulletin</u>, 2, No. 2 (1965), 15.

Without the issue number the reader could find the article only by looking on page 15 of every issue of 1965.

6. The month (if needed) and year, enclosed in parentheses, followed by a comma. If you can quickly determine that all issues of a journal fall within a calendar year, use only the year. However, you must always precede the year with the month or season (Spring 1970) when pagination is separate in the issue of a periodical. When in doubt, include the month.

[4]Hans Joachim Marx, "Some Corelli Attributions Assessed," Musical Quarterly, 56 (1970), 89.

Because all 1970 issues are bound together in one volume that is paged continuously, there is no need to include the month.

[5]Jerrald Ranta, "Palindromes, Poems, and Geometric Form," College English, 36 (Oct. 1974), 161–72.

This journal has a volume number that does not coincide with the calendar year (i.e., its first issue is published in October of each year). Adding the month is an aid to a reader who may wish to locate this article.

7. The page number(s), in Arabic numerals, followed by a period, except when additional information follows (for example, "17, n. 3."). Use abbreviations "p." or "pp." only when a volume number is *not* included in the reference:

[6]Curtis J. Sitomer, "Baby Black Market Charged in California," Christian Science Monitor, 5 March 1975, p. 1.

Since a volume number is *not* included, use the abbreviation "p."

[7]Robert M. Jordan, "The Non–Dramatic Disunity of the Merchant's Tale," PMLA, 78 (1963), 293–94.

Since a volume number is provided, do *not* use the abbreviation "pp."

SPECIMEN FOOTNOTES—PERIODICALS

Address

[1]President's Address to Veterans of Foreign Wars, 19 Aug. 1974; rpt. in Weekly Compilation of Presidential Documents, 10 (26 Aug. 1974), 1045–46.

Author, *anonymous*

[2]"Commodities: Sweet and Sour," Time, 16 Dec. 1974, p. 32.

Subsequent reference:

[3]"Commodities," p. 32.

Authors, *multiple*

[4]Roger W. Libby, Alan C. Acock, and David C. Payne, "Configurations of Parental Preferences Concerning Sources of Sex Education of Adolescents," Adolescence, 9 (Spring 1974), 76–77.

Subsequent reference:

[5]Libby et al., 77.

Bulletin

6"Spotlight on Crime," <u>World of Politics Monthly</u>, Nov. 1974, pp. 10–11.

Monthly bulletin for subscribers to *Taylor's Encyclopedia of Government Officials.*

Subsequent reference:

7"Spotlight on Crime," p. 10.

8Economic Research Service, "Demand and Price Situation," (Washington, D.C.: Dept. of Agriculture, Aug. 1974), DPS–141, p. 7.

Critical review

9Brom Weber, rev. of <u>The World of Flannery O'Connor</u>, by Josephine Hendin, <u>Saturday Review</u>, 18 July 1970, p. 29.

Information above is sufficient, but if additional publication information is readily available include it also, as in footnotes 10 and 12.

10Review of <u>Sexual Suicide</u>, by George F. Gilder (New York: Quadrangle, 1973), <u>Adolescence</u>, 9 (Spring 1974), 151.

Subsequent reference:

11Rev. of <u>Sexual Suicide</u>, 151.

12Remi Clignet, rev. of <u>Urban Poverty in a Cross-cultural Context</u>, by Edwin Eames and Judith Granich Goode (New York: Free Press, 1973), <u>American Journal of Sociology</u>, 80 (Sept. 1974), 589–90.

Subsequent reference:

13Clignet, 590.

14Irving Dolodin, "Verdi for Openers," rev. of <u>Simone Boccanegra</u>, <u>Saturday Review World</u>, 2 Nov. 1974, pp. 54–55.

Interview

15"For an 'Uncultured' America, World Leadership in Arts," Interview with Nancy Hanks, Chairman, National Endowment for the Arts, <u>U.S. News and World Report</u>, 7 Oct. 1974, p. 59.

Journal, *with continuous pagination*

16Vernon Van Dyke, "Human Rights and the Rights of Groups," <u>American Journal of Political Science</u>, 81 (1974), 729.

There will be only one page "729" in a volume numbered consecutively through all issues.

17John A. Dussinger, "Conscience and the Pattern of Christian Perfection in <u>Clarissa</u>," <u>PMLA</u>, 81 (1960), 238–39.

Adding the month is not necessary.

Journal, *with separate pagination*

[18]Doreen Mangan, "Henry Casselli: Superb Contradictions," American Artist, 38 (Dec. 1974), 39.

Because each issue of this journal is paged separately, you should include the month; i.e., page "39" will prove inadequate because a researcher will find a page "39" in each of the twelve issues of volume 38.

[19]Jesse Stuart, "Love Affair at the Pasture Gate," Ball State University Forum, 15 (Winter 1974), 3-6.

Adding the season, rather than month or issue number, is sometimes necessary.

[20]Raven I. McDavid, "Sense and Nonsense About American Dialects," PMLA, 81, No. 2 (1966), 9-11.

PMLA normally pages continuously, but this issue is paged separately, necessitating the issue number. Compare note 17 above.

Journal, *volume number embracing two years*

[21]Douglas J. Kramer, "Protecting the Urban Environment from the Federal Government," Urban Affairs Quarterly, 9 (March 1974), 359-60.

Again, adding the month will locate the article more specifically for your reader. Any time you have doubts, put the month into your footnote.

Magazine, *monthly*

[22]Alex Poinsett, "The 'Whys' Behind the Black Lawyer Shortage," Ebony, Dec. 1974, p. 95.

The volume number is now omitted and "p." is added before the page number.

[23]Leonard Cottrell, "How Egypt Lived and Died," Réalités, March 1970, pp. 52-53.

[24]Karen Lingo, "The Merchants of Veracruz," Southern Living, Feb. 1975, pp. 38 and 42.

This page reference is necessary with magazine articles that often skip from an opening page or two to the back of the magazine where the article is finished.

Magazine, *weekly*

[25]"Labor's Grand Old Godfather," Time, 3 March 1975, pp. 11-12.

Use the above form for those articles that do not list an author.

[26]Harry T. Moore, "Motes in the Eye of a Mountainous Man," Saturday Review, 7 March 1970, pp. 23-24.

[27]"United Nation's Unfinished Task in Enforcing the Rights of Man," The Bulletin: Weekly Survey of German Affairs, 18 Dec. 1973, p. 349.

Quotation, *within the article's title*

[28]Warren Bennett, "Character, Irony, and Resolution in 'A Clean, Well-Lighted Place,'" American Literature, 62 (March 1970), 70-71, 74.

This page reference is clearer to the reader than "70 et passim."

Footnote Form—Public Documents

Since the nature of public documents is so varied, the form of the entry cannot be standardized. Therefore, you should provide sufficient information so that the reader can easily locate the reference. As a general rule, arrange information in the footnote in this order: government, body, subsidiary body, title of document, identifying numbers.

Congressional papers

[1]U.S., Congress, Senate, <u>A Bill to Protect the Individual's Right to Privacy by Prohibiting the Sale or Distribution of Certain Information</u>, S3116, 93rd Cong., 2nd sess., 1974, p. 2.

[2]U.S., Congress, Senate, <u>Senate Joint Resolution 1</u>, 89th Cong., 1st sess., 1965, pp. 2–3.

[3]U.S., Congress, Senate, <u>The Constitution of the United States of America</u>: <u>Analysis and Interpretation</u>, Senate Document 170, 82nd Cong., 2nd sess., 1952, pp. 512–13.

[4]U.S., Congress, Senate, Committee on Foreign Relations, <u>Hearings on S. 2793, Supplemental Foreign Assistance Fiscal Year 1966--Vietnam</u>, 89th Cong., 2nd sess., 1966, p. 8.

[5]U.S., Congress, House, Committee on Interstate and Foreign Commerce, <u>Federal Cigarette Labeling and Advertising Act</u>, 89th Cong., 1st sess., 1965, H. Rept. 449 to accompany H.R. 3014, pp. 9–12.

[6]U.S., Congress, Senate, Senator Barry Goldwater, Speech on the Fuel Crisis, 93rd Cong., 2nd sess., 6 March 1974, <u>Congressional Record</u>, CXX, No. 28, pp. S2916–17.

[7]U.S., Congress, House, Select Committee on Crime, <u>Drugs in Our Schools</u>, H. Rept. 357, 93rd Cong., 1st sess., 1973, pp. 5–6.

Executive branch documents

[8]U.S., President, "John F. Kennedy: 1963," <u>Public Papers of the Presidents of the United States</u> (Washington, D.C.: Office of the Federal Registrar, 1964), pp. 454–55.

[9]U.S., Bureau of the Budget, <u>Special Analysis</u>: <u>Budget of the United States, Fiscal Year 1967</u> (Washington, D.C.: GPO, 1966), p. 2.

[10]U.S., Department of State, <u>Foreign Relations of the United States</u>: <u>Diplomatic Papers, 1943</u>, II. 175–77.

Compare footnote 11 below. Since the date is part of the title above, it precedes the volume number.

[11]U.S., Department of State, <u>United States Treaties and Other International Agreements</u>, XV, Part 1, 1964, 556.

[12]U.S., President, <u>Alternative to Drugs</u>: <u>A New Approach to Drug Education</u> (Washington, D.C.: GPO) Pr Ex 13.2:D84/3/1972.

"Pr Ex" is a code for Executive Office of the President.

[13]U.S., Department of Health, Education, and Welfare, <u>Growing Up in America</u>: <u>A Background to Contemporary Drug Abuse</u> (Washington, D.C.: GPO) HE 20.2402: G91/1973.

Legal citations

[14]U.S., <u>Constitution</u>, Art. II, sec. 1.

[15]California, <u>Constitution</u>, Art. II, sec. 4.

[16]<u>Noise Control Act of 1972</u>, <u>Statutes at Large</u>, LXXXVI, Public Law 92–574, 1234–1250 (1972).

Laws enacted by Congress are printed in *Statutes at Large* as public laws, private laws, and proclamations. Later they are printed in the *U.S. Code.* Compare note 19 below.

[17]<u>An Act for the Relief of Appalachian Regional Hospitals, Inc.</u>, <u>Statutes at Large</u>, LXXXVI, Private Law 92–161, 1568 (1972).

[18]U.S. President, <u>A Proclamation Modifying Proclamation 3279, Relating to Imports of Petroleum and Petroleum Products</u>, <u>Statutes at Large</u>, LXXXVI, 1667–68 (1972).

[19]<u>Gold Coin and Gold Bullion Act</u>, <u>U.S. Code</u>, 1970 ed., Supp. III, Title 31, sec. 442 (1970).

[20]<u>Environmental Protection Agency et al</u>. v. <u>Mink et al</u>., <u>U.S. Reports</u>, CDX (1972).

Footnote Form—Other Sources

The sample entries below will enable you to formulate a suitable footnote for miscellaneous types of reference material:

Bulletin

[1]"Financial Operation of Government Agencies and Funds," <u>Treasury Bulletin</u> (Washington, D.C.: Dept. of Treasury, June 1974), p. 135.

[2]Earl French, "Personal Problems in Industrial Research and Development," Bulletin of N.Y. State School of Industrial and Labor Relations, No. 51 (Oct. 1963), p. 22.

Dissertation, *published*

[3]Per Nykrog, <u>Les Fabliaux</u>: <u>Etude d'histoire littéraire et de stylistique médiévale</u>, Diss. Aarhus 1957 (Copenhagen: Munksgaard, 1957), p. 62.

Dissertation, *unpublished*

⁴Emmett Loy Phillips, "A Study of Aesthetic Distance in Thoreau's <u>Walden</u>," Diss. Univ. of Oklahoma 1970, p. 42.

⁵Emmett Loy Phillips, "A Study of Aesthetic Distance in Thoreau's <u>Walden</u>," <u>Dissertation Abstracts International</u>, 30 (1970), 3953–A (Univ. of Oklahoma).

This footnote refers to the abstract, not the dissertation itself.

Film

⁶<u>The World of the Weed</u> (Bloomington, Ind.: National Educational TV, Inc.), 16 mm., 21 min., black/white.

⁷Bernard Wilets, <u>Environment</u> (Santa Monica, Calif.: BFA Educational Media, 1971), 16 mm., 29 min., color.

Interview

⁸Interview with Robert Turrentine, President, Acme Boot Co., Clarksville, Tenn., 11 Feb. 1975.

Letter, *personal*

⁹Information in a letter to the author from Professor Winston Weathers of the University of Tulsa, 5 March 1975.

Mimeographed material

¹⁰Jane L. Smith, "Terms for the Study of Fiction" (mimeographed paper, Cleveland, 1975), p. 2.

Monograph

¹¹NEA Research Division, <u>Kindergarten Practices, 1961</u> (monograph 1962–M2, Washington, D.C., 1962), p. 3.

¹²William R. Veeder, <u>W. B. Yeats: The Rhetoric of Repetition</u>, Univ. of California English Studies, 34 (Berkeley: Univ. of California Press, 1968), p. 12.

Newspaper

¹³Jane E. Brody, "Harvard Backs Genetic Study," <u>New York Times</u>, 14 Dec. 1974, p. 20, col. 1.

Locate the article on the page whenever possible with notations such as "col. 1."

¹⁴Richard Holbrooke, "Kissinger: A Study in Contradictions," Editorial, <u>Washington Post</u>, 15 Sept. 1974, pp. B1–B2.

Use this form for special newspaper articles, such as editorials, letters to the editor, cartoons, and so on.

¹⁵Alice Franklin Bryant, "U.N. Role," Letter to the Editor, <u>Chattanooga Times</u>, 15 Dec. 1974, p. B7.

[16]Elizabeth Mooney, "The Unreal Real Estate Game," Potomac, Washington Post magazine, 15 Sept. 1974, p. 12.

> Most newspapers publish a magazine with their Sunday edition. This citation requires the name of the magazine as well as the newspaper.

[17]"Egypt Demands That Israel Put Limit on Population Growth," Los Angeles Times, 14 Dec. 1974, p. 1, col. 4.

> When an item is unsigned, the title comes first and all the subsequent information remains the same.

Subsequent reference:

[18]"Egypt Demands," p. 1.

Pamphlet

[19]U.S. Civil Service Commission, The Human Equation: Working in Personnel for the Federal Government, Pamphlet 76 (Washington, D.C.: GPO, May 1970), pp. 2–4.

Public address or lecture

[20]David Sarnoff, "Television: A Channel for Freedom," Address presented at the University of Detroit Academic Convocation, Detroit, 1961.

Recording

[21]"Chaucer: The Nun's Priest's Tale," Caedmon recording, No. E8C40, narrated in Middle English by Robert Ross.

[22]Elton John, "This Song Has No Title," in Goodbye Yellow Brick Road, MCA Record, MCA2-10003.

Report

[23]Fabian Linden, "Women: A Demographic, Social and Economic Presentation," Report by The Conference Board (New York: CBS/Broadcast Group, 1973), pp. 24–25.

[24]Panama Canal Company, Annual Report: Fiscal Year Ended June 30, 1968 (Panama: Canal Zone Government, 1968), pp. 7–9.

[25]Womanpower (Brookline, Mass.: Betsy Hogan Associates, Nov. 1974), p. 1.

> If you cannot quickly determine the author of the report, begin with the title. Reports in book or pamphlet form require underlining.

Reproductions and photographs

[26]Blake's Comus, Plate 4, as reproduced in Irene Tayler, "Blake's Comus Designs," Blake Studies, 4 (Spring 1972), 61.

[27]James A. Michener, "Structure of Earth at Centennial, Colorado," Centennial (New York: Random House, 1974), p. 26.

Table or illustration

^{28}Donald L. Helmich, "Organizational Growth and Succession Patterns," Academy of Management Journal, 17 (Dec. 1974), 773, Table 2.

^{29}Edward P. J. Corbett, Syllogism graph, Classical Rhetoric for the Modern Student (New York: Oxford Univ. Press, 1965), p. 46.

Because the graph has no title, the descriptive heading should not be placed within quotation marks.

Television or radio program

^{30}Eric Sevareid, CBS News (New York: CBS-TV, 11 March 1975).

^{31}William Shakespeare, As You Like It (Nashville: Nashville Theatre Academy, 11 March 1975), WDCN-TV.

Local productions should include the local broadcasting station; national programs require only the network.

^{32}The Commanders: Douglas MacArthur (New York: NBC-TV, 13 March 1975).

Thesis, *published*

See "Dissertation, published," p. 112.

Thesis, *unpublished*

See "Dissertation, unpublished," p. 113.

Unpublished paper

^{33}William R. Elkins, "The Dream World and the Dream Vision: Meaning and Structure in Poe's Art," an unpublished paper.

Subsequent References

To repeat, after you once provide full reference data for a primary citation, your subsequent notes for the same source should be brief but clear. Normally, the author's last name and the page number will suffice (for example, "Johnson, p. 12."). However, if the first full reference is not found in a recent note or if you are citing more than one book by this author, you should add the title, preferably in the shortest possible form (for example, "Johnson, *Experiences*, p. 12."). If another author has an identical surname, you must add the given name to each reference (for example, "James Johnson, p. 12.").

As an alternative to repeating the title or author's name, you may use the Latinate abbreviation "Ibid." ("in the same place") *if* it refers to the source in the immediately preceding footnote and *if* it appears on the same page.[1] For example, when you refer to the identical page(s) of the preced-

---

[1]The *MLA Style Sheet* considers "Ibid." and other Latinate words as Americanized, thereby negating the need for underlining. Your professor, however, may desire that you underline the Latinate words.

ing note, insert only "Ibid.," capitalized and followed by a period ("Ibid."). If your reference is to the same book as the preceding note but to a different page, insert "Ibid.," followed by a comma, followed by the page number ("Ibid., p. 16.").

You should find it unnecessary to employ the Latinate abbreviations "op. cit." and "loc. cit." "Op. cit." is an abbreviation for *opere citato*, which means "in the work cited." It is sometimes employed when nonconsecutive references are made to the same work (for example, "Jones, op. cit., p. 65."). But a simple reference to "Jones, p. 65" serves the same purpose and is less confusing. "Loc. cit." is an abbreviation for *loco citato*, which means "in the place cited." Since this footnote names the exact source listed immediately preceding it, the author's name and a page reference are omitted (for example, "Loc. cit."). But the use of "Ibid." without a page reference serves the same purpose (see above).

Note the following sequence of specimen footnotes:

[1]Lionel Stevenson, " 'My Last Duchess' and <u>Parisina</u>," <u>Modern Language Notes</u>, 74 (1959), 490.

[2]Ibid., 491.

But do not use this form if the note occurs on a different page.

[3]William C. DeVane, <u>A Browning Handbook</u> (New York: Appleton, 1955), pp. 98–99.

[4]Robert F. Fleissner, "Browning's Last Lost Duchess: A Purview," <u>Victorian Poetry</u>, 5 (1967), 218.

[5]Stevenson, 492.

[6]DeVane, p. 98.

[7]Ibid.

But use only on the same page with footnote 6. Otherwise, write "[7]DeVane, p. 98."

[8]Ibid., p. 99.

But use only on the same page with footnotes 6 and 7.

[9]Robert F. Fleissner, "My Last Duchess," <u>Times Literary Supplement</u>, No. 3, 536 (4 Dec. 1959), p. 1405.

Although it has continuous pagination, this journal does not employ a volume number; therefore you do the reader a service by providing issue number and exact date.

[10]Stevenson, 492.

[11]Fleissner, "My Last Duchess," p. 1405.

Since two separate articles by Fleissner appear above, you must add a title to this note.

[12]"Browning's Shrewd Duke," <u>PMLA</u>, 74 (1959), 157–59.

Use this form when the author's name and even the title have been given in the text.

¹³DeVane, p. 98; cf. B. E. Jerman, "Browning's Witless Duke," <u>PMLA</u>, 72 (1957), 488–93.

¹⁴Laurence Perrine, "Browning's Shrewd Duke," 158.

¹⁵Fleissner, "My Last Duchess," p. 1405.

¹⁶Ibid.

But use only on the same page with footnote 15.

Content Footnotes

As shown on the preceding pages, reference footnotes perform the basic function of documenting the original source. But you may have occasion to write other types of notes, classified as content footnotes, offering further information that the average reader might need or profit by. Rather than distract the reader with an incidentally related item within the text, you should place it within a footnote, using one of the following types of brief content footnotes:

Definition

¹Briefly, existentialism expounds the theory that man lives in a purposeless universe in which he must exercise freedom of will to combat his environment.

This type of note defines or amplifies a term or phrase you have used in the text.

Explanation and elaboration

²Jean–Paul Sartre became the chief spokesman for existentialism in France after World War II. (Smith, p. 6.)

This note offers additional information that is not pertinent to textual matters. The entry at the end is necessary if the information is borrowed from an authority.

Evaluation and comparison of authorities

³Cf. Edmund Wilson, <u>Axel's Castle</u>, p. 114: "As a critic, Eliot occupies today a position of distinction and influence equal in importance to his position as a poet."

The writer is asking the reader to compare textual analysis with Wilson's statement.

Cross reference to another part of the paper

⁴The importance of Emerson as a poet, however, is questioned by some authorities. See above, p. 3.

The writer is asking the reader to refer to an earlier portion of the paper for the discussion of Emerson.

Reference to a special source

     [5]A thorough analysis of <u>anomie</u> as it relates to Durkheim may be found in Stephen R. Marks, "Durkheim's Theory of Anomie," <u>American Journal of Sociology</u>, 80 (Sept. 1974), 329–63.

Abbreviations in Footnotes

You should employ abbreviations often and consistently in the footnotes, though in your text you should avoid them (except "Dr.," "Esq.," "Hon.," "Jr.," "Mr.," "Ms.," "Rev.," and "St."). In footnotes you should abbreviate dates (for example, "Jan.," "Feb.") and institutions (for example "Univ.," "Assn."). Finally, you may use or encounter the following common abbreviations and reference words:

A.D. *anno Domini* 'in the year of the Lord'; *precedes* numerals with no space between letters, as in "A.D. 350"

anon. anonymous

art., arts. article(s)

B.C. 'Before Christ'; *follows* numerals with no space between letters, as in "500 B.C."

bk., bks. book(s)

ca. (*or* c.) *circa* 'about,' used to indicate an approximate date, as in "ca. 1812"

cf. *confer* 'compare' (one source with another); not, however, to be used in place of "see"

ch., chs. (*or* chap., chaps.) chapter(s)

col., cols. column(s)

comp. compiled (by) or compiler

diss. dissertation

ed., eds. editor(s), edition, or edited (by)

e.g. *exempli gratia* 'for example,' preceded and followed by a comma

enl. enlarged, as in "enl. ed."

esp. especially, as in "pp. 312-15, esp. p. 313"

et al. *et alii* 'and others'; "John Smith et al." means John Smith and other authors

et pas. *et passim* 'and here and there' (see "passim")

et seq. *et sequens* 'and the following'; "pp. 9 et seq." means page nine and the following page; compare "f." and "ff."

f., ff. page or pages following a given page; "pp. 8f." means page eight and the following page; but exact references are preferable, for example, "pp. 45-51, 55, 58" instead of "pp. 45 ff."

ibid. *ibidem* 'in the same place,' i.e., in the immediately preceding title (see p. 115)

i.e. *id est* 'that is,' preceded and followed by a comma

illus. illustrated by, illustrations, or illustrator

infra 'below,' refers to a succeeding portion of the text; compare "supra." Generally, it is best to write "see below"

intro. (*or* introd.) introduction (by)

l., ll. line(s)

loc. cit. *loco citato* 'in the place (passage) cited' (see p. 116)

MS, MSS manuscript(s); but followed by a period ("MS.") when referring to a specific manuscript

n., nn. note(s), as "p. 23, n. 2" or "p. 51 n."

n.d. no date (in a book's title or copyright pages)

no., nos. number(s)

n.p. no place (of publication)

op. cit. *opere citato* 'in the work cited' (see p. 116)

p., pp. page(s); use "Pages" instead of "Pp."

passim 'here and there throughout the work,' e.g., "pp. 67, 72, et passim"

pseud. pseudonym

pt., pts. part(s)

rev. revised (by), revision, review, or reviewed (by)

rpt. reprint, reprinted

sec., secs. section(s)

sic 'thus,' placed in brackets to indicate an error has been made in the quoted passage and the writer is quoting accurately

st., sts. stanza(s)

sup. (*or* supra) 'above,' refers to a preceding portion of the text; it is just as easy to write "above"

s.v. *sub voce (verbo)* 'under the word or heading'

trans. (*or* tr.) translator, translated (by), or translation

vol., vols. volume(s), as in "Vol. III"

THE BIBLIOGRAPHY 6

■ After writing your paper, you should prepare a selected bibliography, listing the source material actually used in the writing of your manuscript. That is, you should provide publication data for each reference. Some instructors may request that you label the bibliography "List of References Cited" or "Selected Bibliography" because the bibliography will offer the reader a limited indication of the scholarship related to your subject, not a comprehensive or exhaustive list.

If you have carefully developed your working bibliography (pp. 11-15), you will find that preparation of the final one is a relatively simple process. The final bibliography is really not a new assignment at all because your bibliography cards, arranged alphabetically, already provide the necessary information. However, this will be true only if you have kept the bibliography cards up-to-date during note-taking by adding new sources and by disposing of cards that you have found to be irrelevant.

To repeat: you should include in the bibliography all works actually used in your study. And you must, without exception, include a bibliography entry for all first references in the footnotes. You may also insert other works pertinent to the paper, such as an article that strongly influenced your thinking, although you did not quote or paraphrase it and therefore had no footnote reference to it.

Bibliography Form

You should arrange the items of the bibliography in alphabetical order by the surname of the author. Place the first line of each entry flush with the left margin and indent succeeding lines approximately five spaces. Single space each entry, but double space between each reference. (However, your instructor may request that you double space all materials, even the individual bibliography entries.) Study carefully the examples given in the following sample "Selected Bibliography":

A Selected Bibliography

The Bible. Revised Standard Version.

Bulfinch, Thomas. Bulfinch's Mythology. 2 vols. New
        York: Mentor, 1962.

Campbell, Joseph. The Hero With a Thousand Faces.
        Cleveland: Meridian Books, 1956.

————————. The Masks of God. 4 vols. New York:
        Viking-Compass, 1970.

Henderson, Joseph L., and Maud Oakes. The Wisdom of
        the Serpent: The Myths of Death, Rebirth, and
        Resurrection. New York: Collier, 1971.

Homer. The Iliad. Trans. Richmond Lattimore.
        Chicago: Univ. of Chicago Press, 1951.

Laird, Charlton. "A Nonhuman Being Can Learn Lan-
        guage." College Composition and Communication,
        23 (May 1972), 142-54.

Levi-Strauss, Claude. "The Structural Study of
        Myth." In Myth: A Symposium. Ed. A. Sebeok.
        Bloomington: Indiana Univ. Press, 1958.

McFadden, George. " 'Life Studies'—Robert Lowell's
        Comic Breakthrough." PMLA, 90 (1975), 96-106.

Robinson, Lillian S. "Criticism—and Self-Criti-
        cism." College English, 36 (Dec. 1974), 436-45.

BIBLIOGRAPHY FORM—BOOKS

When entering references to books, you should use the following order, omitting unnecessary items:

1. The author's name, surname first, followed by given name or initials, followed by a period:

Wellman, Carl. Morals and Ethics. Glenview, Ill.:
        Scott, Foresman, 1975.

Always give authors' names in the fullest possible form; for example, "Cosbey, Robert C." rather than "Cosbey, R. C." unless, as indicated on the title page of the book, the author's preference is for initials.

However, if an author has two or more works in the bibliography, do not repeat his or her name with each work. Rather, insert a continuous, twelve-space line flush with the left margin, followed by a period:

Hansberry, Lorraine. A Raisin in the Sun. New York:
    Random House, 1959.

————————. To Be Young, Gifted and Black. Ed. Rob-
    ert Nemiroff. Englewood Cliffs, N.J.: Prentice-
    Hall, 1969.
    An alternative is that of extending the line of dashes the length of the au-
    thor's name.

2. A chapter or a part of a book, placed before the title, within quotation marks or underlined, followed by a period (the word "In" may follow
this period to specify the anthology or collection in which this piece appears):

Elder, Lonne. "Ceremonies in Dark Old Men." In New
    Black Playwrights: An Anthology. Ed. William
    Couch, Jr. Baton Rouge: Louisiana State Univ.
    Press, 1968.

Aristophanes. The Birds. In Five Comedies of Aristo-
    phanes. Trans. Benjamin B. Rogers. Garden
    City, N.Y.: Doubleday, 1955.

Usually the listing of chapter or part of a book is made in bibliographies
only when the work is separately edited, translated, or written. For
example, note the following:

Thomas, Lewis. "The Music of This Sphere." The Lives
    of a Cell. New York: Viking, 1974.

                but preferably

Thomas, Lewis. The Lives of a Cell. New York: Viking,
    1974.
    Since "The Music of This Sphere" is not separately published, it need not
    be mentioned in the bibliography (but the footnote should contain that
    information).

In some instances the name of the primary author of an article may be
omitted:

Child, Harold. "Jane Austen." The Cambridge History of
    English Literature. Ed. A. W. Ward and A. R. Wal-
    ler. London: Cambridge Univ. Press, 1927, XII,
    231–44.

                but preferably

Ward, A. W., and A. R. Waller, eds. The Cambridge Histo-
    ry of English Literature. 15 vols. London: Cam-
    bridge Univ. Press, 1927.

3. The title of the work, underlined, followed by a period:

Lagercrantz, Olof. From Hell to Paradise: Dante and
    His Comedy. Trans. Alan Blair. New York:
    Washington Square Press, 1966.
    Separate the subtitle from the primary title by a colon, even though the ti-
    tle page may have no mark of punctuation or the card catalog entry may
    have a semicolon.

4. The name of the editor or translator, preceded by "Ed." or "Trans.":

Mishima, Yukio. The Decay of the Angel. Trans. Edward
    G. Seidensticker. New York: Knopf, 1974.

However, if the work is a collection or if the editor's or translator's work rather than the text is under discussion, place the editor's or translator's name first, followed by a comma, followed by "ed." or "eds." or "trans." without further punctuation:

> Craig, Hardin, and David Bevington, eds. The Complete Works of Shakespeare. Rev. ed. Glenview, Ill.: Scott, Foresman, 1973.

> Ciardi, John, trans. The Purgatorio, by Dante. New York: New American Library, 1961.

5. Edition used, whenever it is not the first, in Arabic numerals (for example, "2nd ed."), without further punctuation:

> Bloom, William, and Don W. Fawcett. A Textbook of Histology. 9th ed. Philadelphia: Saunders, 1968.

6. The name of the series, without quotation marks and not underlined, followed by a comma, followed by the number of this work in the series in Arabic numerals (for example, "vol. 3," "No. 3," or simply "3"), followed by a period:

> Fowler, David. Piers the Plowman. Univ. of Washington Publications in Lang. and Lit., 16. Seattle: Univ. of Washington Press, 1961.

7. The number of volumes with this particular title, if more than one, in Arabic numerals (for example, "6 vols."):

> Parrington, Vernon L. Main Currents in American Thought. 3 vols. New York: Harcourt, Brace, 1927-32.

> Note that the volumes were not published in the same year.

8. The place, publisher, and date of publication, followed by a period (for example, "New York: Macmillan, 1967."). If more than one place of publication appears on the title page, the first city mentioned is usually sufficient. Also, if successive dates of copyright are given, the most recent is usually sufficient (unless your study is specifically concerned with an earlier, perhaps definitive, edition):

> Steinbeck, John. The Grapes of Wrath. New York: Viking, 1939.

A new printing does not constitute a new edition nor demand usage of its corresponding date. If the text has a 1940 copyright date but a 1975 third printing, use 1940 unless you have other information, such as: "1975 Diamond Printing," "1975 third printing rev.," or "1975 reprint of original 1940 edition" (see immediately below).

> Weaver, Raymond. "Introduction." The Shorter Novels of Herman Melville. 1928; rpt. New York: Premier-Fawcett, 1960.

Include the name of the state if necessary for clarity:

> Blum, Robert, ed. <u>Cultural Affairs and Foreign Rela-</u>
> <u>tions</u>. The American Assembly Series. Englewood
> Cliffs, N.J.: Prentice-Hall, 1963.

If the place or date of publication is not provided, insert either "n.p." or "n.d.":

> Bouret, Jean. <u>The Life and Work of Toulouse Lautrec</u>.
> Trans. Daphne Woodward. New York: Abrams, n.d.

> Lowell, James Russell. <u>Democracy</u>. N.p., 1886.

Provide the publisher's name in a slightly shortened form whenever possible, for example: Macmillan; Doubleday; Free Press; Scott, Foresman; Norton; Dell; Little, Brown; William Brown; Wiley; Knopf.

But list university presses in full to distinguish between a publication of the university and that of a university press: Harvard Univ. Press, Louisiana State Univ. Press, Yale Univ. Press, Oxford Univ. Press.

9. The volume number, in capital Roman numerals, preceded and followed by a comma, only if you find it necessary to specify such information (and the occasions are rare because you will normally insert only the total number of volumes, for example, "5 vols."). Remember that your footnote, not the bibliography, contains the specific location of the material:

> Child, Harold. "Jane Austen." <u>The Cambridge History of</u>
> <u>English Literature</u>. Ed. A. W. Ward and A. R.
> Waller. London: Cambridge Univ. Press, 1927. XII,
> 231-44.

10. Page numbers of the entire selection, in Arabic numerals, preceded by a comma and followed by a period. Again, supply this information only upon rare occasions (see item 9 above and item 2, p.121).

Sample Bibliography Entries—Books
Author

> Wellman, Carl. <u>Morals and Ethics</u>. Glenview, Ill.:
> Scott, Foresman, 1975.

Author, *anonymous*

> <u>The Song of Roland</u>. Trans. Frederick Bliss Luq-
> uines. New York: Macmillan, 1960.
>> Usually you should alphabetize this entry by the "S" of the first important
>> word of the title, but alphabetizing by the "T" is also acceptable.

Author, *anonymous but name supplied*

> [Madison, James.] <u>All Impressments Unlawful and Inadmis-</u>
> <u>sible</u>. Boston: William Pelham, 1804.

Author, *pseudonymous but name supplied*

> Slender, Robert [Freneau, Philip]. <u>Letters on Various</u>
> <u>and Important Subjects</u>. Philadelphia: D. Hogan,
> 1799.

Author, *more than one work by the same author*

Hansberry, Lorraine. <u>A Raisin in the Sun</u>. New York: Random House, 1959.

——————————. <u>To Be Young, Gifted and Black</u>. Ed. Robert Nemiroff. Englewood Cliffs, N.J.: Prentice-Hall, 1969.

Rather than repeat the author's name in succeeding entries, insert twelve continuous typewriter dashes above the line, or extend a line of dashes the length of the author's name.

Authors, *two*

O'Neill, Nena, and George O'Neill. <u>Shifting Gears: Finding Security in a Changing World</u>. New York: M. Evans, 1974.

Authors, *three*

Richardson, Charles E., Fred V. Hein, and Dana L. Farnsworth. <u>Living: Health, Behavior, and Environment</u>. 6th ed. Glenview, Ill.: Scott, Foresman, 1975.

Authors, *more than three*

Baugh, Albert C., Tucker Brooke, Samuel C. Chew, Kemp Malone, and George Sherburn. <u>A Literary History of England</u>. 2nd ed. New York: Appleton, 1967.

An alternative to this form is the use of "et al." or "and others," as follows:

Baugh, Albert C., et al. <u>A Literary History of England</u>. 2nd ed. New York: Appleton, 1967.

Bibles

The Bible.

The Bible. Revised Standard Version.

The King James Version is assumed unless you specify another version.

Classical works

Homer. <u>The Iliad</u>. Trans. Richmond Lattimore. Chicago: Univ. of Chicago Press, 1951.

Shorey, Paul, trans. <u>The Republic</u>, by Plato. Cambridge, Mass.: Harvard Univ. Press, 1937.

Use the translator's name first only if his or her work rather than the text is the focus of your study (see p. 122).

Component part of a book

Thomas, Lewis. "The Music of This Sphere." <u>The Lives of a Cell</u>. New York: Viking, 1974.

but preferably

Thomas, Lewis. The Lives of a Cell. New York: Viking, 1974.

> Citation to a specific piece in a collection or a longer work is seldom necessary in bibliography entries. Remember that your footnote will offer specific information.

Scott, Nathan, Jr. "Society and Self in Recent American Literature." In The Broken Center. New Haven: Univ. Press, 1966. Rpt. in Dark Symphony: Negro Literature in America. Ed. James A. Emanuel and Theodore L. Gross. New York: Free Press, 1968.

but preferably

Emanuel, James A., and Theodore L. Gross, eds. Dark Symphony: Negro Literature in America. New York: Free Press, 1968.

Corporate authorship

Committee on Telecommunications. Reports on Selected Topics in Telecommunications. New York: National Academy of Sciences, National Research Council, 1970.

Double reference

Symington, Stuart. As quoted in Victor Marchetti and John D. Marks. The CIA and the Cult of Intelligence. New York: Knopf, 1974.

but preferably

Marchetti, Victor, and John D. Marks. The CIA and the Cult of Intelligence. New York: Knopf, 1974.

> As with the "Component part of a book" (above), you may offer specific information, but the main purpose of a bibliography is the listing of books used, not parts of books.

Edition

Bloom, William, and Don W. Fawcett. A Textbook of Histology. 9th ed. Philadelphia: Saunders, 1968.

Editor

Craig, Hardin, and David Bevington, eds. The Complete Works of Shakespeare. Rev. ed. Glenview, Ill.: Scott, Foresman, 1973.

> If the work is a collection or if the editor's work rather than the text is under discussion, place the editor's name first. Otherwise, place the editor's name after the title, as follows:

Brackenridge, Hugh Henry. Modern Chivalry. Ed. Claude M. Newlin. New York: American Book, 1962.

Encyclopedia

The World Book Encyclopedia. Chicago: Field Enterprises, 1969.

> If you feel a necessity for specific information, which you should have located within a footnote, employ the following form.

Henning, Basil D. "Norman Conquest." The World Book
Encyclopedia. Chicago: Field Enterprises, 1969.

N[aess], A[rne] D. "Martin Heidegger." Encyclopaedia
Britannica. Macropaedia 8, 1974.

Illustrations

Venturi, Lionello. Botticelli. With 50
Plates. Greenwich, Conn.: Fawcett, n.d.

Honoré Daumier: Drawings and Watercolors. Selected and
with introduction by Jean Adhemar. With 58 Illustrations. New York: Macmillan, 1954.

Introduction

Webb, Walter Prescott. The Great Frontier. Introduction
by Arnold J. Toynbee. Austin, Texas: Univ. of
Texas Press, 1964.

Lowell, Robert. "Foreword." Ariel, by Sylvia Plath.
New York: Harper & Row, 1966.

Use the above form only if your subject is Lowell's work, not the poetry of
Plath.

Manuscript collections

British Museum. Cotton Vitellius. A. XV.

Corpus Christi College, Cambridge. MS CCCC 201.

Play, *classical*

Parrott, T. M., ed. Shakespeare: Twenty-Three Plays
and the Sonnets. New York: Scribner's, 1953.

but also

Shakespeare, William. Macbeth. In Shakespeare:
Twenty-Three Plays and the Sonnets. Ed. T. M.
Parrott. New York: Scribner's, 1953.

See item 2, p. 121, and item 4, pp. 121-22.

Play, *modern*

Greene, Graham. The Complaisant Lover. New York:
Viking, 1959.

Poem, *classical*

Dante. The Divine Comedy. Trans. Lawrence Grant
White. New. York: Pantheon, 1948.

Ciardi, John, trans. The Purgatorio, by Dante. New
York: New American Library, 1961.

Use the translator's or editor's name first only if his or her work rather
than the primary text is under discussion (see p. 122).

Poem, *modern*

Warren, Robert Penn. <u>You</u>, <u>Emperors</u>, <u>and</u> <u>Others</u>: <u>Poems</u>
<u>1957–1960</u>. New York: Random House, 1960.

Keats, John. "Ode to a Nightingale." In <u>Beginnings</u> <u>in</u>
<u>Poetry</u>. Ed. William J. Martz. 2nd ed. Glenview,
Ill.: Scott, Foresman, 1973.

but preferably

Martz, William J., ed. <u>Beginnings</u> <u>in</u> <u>Poetry</u>. 2nd ed.
Glenview, Ill.: Scott, Foresman, 1973.

Reprint

Lowes, John Livingston. <u>The</u> <u>Road</u> <u>to</u> <u>Xanadu</u>: <u>A</u> <u>Study</u> <u>in</u>
<u>the</u> <u>Ways</u> <u>of</u> <u>the</u> <u>Imagination</u>. 2nd ed., 1930; rpt.
New York: Vintage–Knopf, 1959.

Weaver, Raymond. "Introduction." <u>The</u> <u>Shorter</u> <u>Novels</u> <u>of</u>
<u>Herman</u> <u>Melville</u>. 1928; rpt. New York: Premier–
Fawcett, 1960.

Series, *numbered and unnumbered*

Fowler, David. <u>Piers</u> <u>the</u> <u>Plowman</u>. Univ. of Washington
Publications in Lang. and Lit., 16. Seattle: Univ.
of Washington Press, 1961.

Gibson, Lawrence Henry. <u>The</u> <u>Coming</u> <u>of</u> <u>the</u> <u>Revolution</u>:
<u>1762–1775</u>. Ed. Henry Steele Commager and
Richard B. Morris. The New American Nation Series.
New York: Harper & Row, 1954.

Series, *paperback*

Commager, Henry Steele. <u>The</u> <u>Nature</u> <u>and</u> <u>the</u> <u>Study</u> <u>of</u>
<u>History</u>. Social Science Seminar Series. Columbus,
Ohio: Merrill, 1965.

Wilson, Howard E. "Education, Foreign Policy, and In-
ternational Relations." In <u>Cultural</u> <u>Affairs</u> <u>and</u>
<u>Foreign</u> <u>Relations</u>. Ed. Robert Blum. The American
Assembly Series. Englewood Cliffs, N.J.:
Prentice–Hall, 1963.

but preferably

Blum, Robert, ed. <u>Cultural</u> <u>Affairs</u> <u>and</u> <u>Foreign</u> <u>Rela-</u>
<u>tions</u>. The American Assembly Series. Englewood
Cliffs, N.J.: Prentice–Hall, 1963.

Source books

Unterecker, John, ed. <u>Yeats</u>: <u>A</u> <u>Collection</u> <u>of</u> <u>Critical</u>
<u>Essays</u>. Twentieth Century Views. Englewood Cliffs,
N.J.: Prentice–Hall, 1963.

Walker, Warren S., ed. <u>Leatherstocking</u> <u>and</u> <u>the</u> <u>Crit-</u>
<u>ics</u>. Glenview, Ill.: Scott, Foresman, 1965.

but also

Wasserstrom, William. "Cooper, Freud, and the Origins
of Culture." The American Image, 17 (Winter 1960),
423–37. Rpt. in Warren S. Walker, ed. Leather-
stocking and the Critics. Glenview, Ill.: Scott,
Foresman, 1965.

Use this last form if a footnote does not include specific details of both
sources.

Translator

Lagercrantz, Olof. From Hell to Paradise: Dante and
His Comedy. Trans. Alan Blair. New York:
Washington Square Press, 1966.

Homer. Iliad. Trans. Robert Fitzgerald. Garden City,
N.Y.: Anchor, 1974.

Ciardi, John, trans. The Purgatorio, by Dante. New
York: New American Library, 1961.

If the translator's work rather than the text is under discussion, place the
translator's name first (see item 4, pp. 121-22).

Volumes, *a work of several volumes*

Parrington, Vernon L. Main Currents in American
Thought. 3 vols. New York: Harcourt, Brace,
1927–32.

Volumes, *one of several volumes*

Perry, Bliss. The American Spirit in Literature. In The
Chronicles of America Series. Ed. Allen Johnson, 48
vols. New Haven: Yale Univ. Press, 1918.

It is seldom necessary to include a specific volume number in the bibliography entry (see below).

Volumes, *component part of one of several volumes*

Child, Harold. "Jane Austen." The Cambridge History of
English Literature. Ed. A. W. Ward and A. R. Waller. London: Cambridge Univ. Press, 1927. XII,
231–44.

but also

Ward, A. W., and A. R. Waller, eds. The Cambridge History of English Literature. 15 vols. London:
Cambridge Univ. Press, 1927.

For a discussion of these entries, see p. 121.

Works alphabetically arranged

Dictionary of American Biography. Ed. Allen Johnson and
Dumas Malone. 20 vols. New York: Scribner's,
1928–37.

but also

A[lden], E[dmund] K. "Alden, John." Dictionary of American
Biography. Ed. Allen Johnson and Dumas Malone. New
York: Scribner's, 1928–37.

For a discussion of these entries, see p. 107 and item 2, p. 121.

BIBLIOGRAPHY FORM—PERIODICALS

As you recall, the footnote entry for a periodical article employs the following form:

    [1]Daniel Stempel, "Angels of Reason: Science and
    Myth in the Enlightenment," Journal of the History of
    Ideas, 36 (1975), 63–78.

The bibliography entry for this same reference differs in only three ways:

1. The author's name is flush with the left margin, without a numeral, and with succeeding lines indented approximately five spaces. Enter the surname first, followed by a comma, followed by a given name or initials, followed by a period:

    Stempel, Daniel. "Angels of Reason: Science and Myth
        in the Enlightenment." Journal of the History of
        Ideas, 36 (1975), 63–78.

2. Place a period after the title of the article (see example above).

3. Provide page numbers for the entire article, not for specific pages cited (see example above). If the article is paged here and there throughout the issue (for example, pages 46, 48, 50, and 81), the following are possible methods of page citation:

pp. 46 et passim.   which means page 46 and several pages here and there throughout the work

pp. 46,48,50,81.   which designates each page; use this method if only three or four pages are involved

In other circumstances the following forms might be appropriate:

pp. 46ff.   which means page 46 and several immediately following pages

pp. 46 et seq.   which means page 46 and the following page

pp. 46f.   which means page 46 and the following page (same as "pp. 46 et seq.")

Sample Bibliography Entries—Periodicals
Address

    President's Address to Veterans of Foreign Wars, 19 Aug.
        1974. Rpt. in Weekly Compilation of Presidential
        Documents, 10 (26 Aug. 1974), 1045–50.

Author, *anonymous*

    "Commodities: Sweet and Sour." Time, 16 Dec. 1974, p.
        32.

Authors, *multiple*

Libby, Roger W., Alan C. Acock, and David C. Payne. "Configurations of Parental Preferences Concerning Sources of Sex Education of Adolescents." <u>Adolescence</u>, 9 (Spring 1974), 73–80.

Bulletin

"Financial Operations of Government Agencies and Funds." <u>Treasury Bulletin</u>. Washington, D.C.: Dept. of Treasury, June 1974, pp. 134–41.

"Spotlight on Crime." <u>World of Politics Monthly</u>, Nov. 1974, pp. 10–11.

For examples of bulletins published separately, see p. 133.

Critical review

Clignet, Remi. Rev. of <u>Urban Poverty in a Cross–cultural Context</u>, by Edwin Eames and Judith Granich Goode (New York: Free Press, 1973). In <u>American Journal of Sociology</u>, 80 (Sept. 1974), 589-90.

Kolodin, Irving. "Verdi for Openers." Rev. of <u>Simone Boccanegra</u>. <u>Saturday Review World</u>, 2 Nov. 1974, pp. 54–55.

Rev. of <u>Sexual Suicide</u>, by George F. Gilder (New York: Quadrangle, 1973). In <u>Adolescence</u>, 9 (Spring 1974), 151.

Weber, Brom. Rev. of <u>The World of Flannery O'Connor</u>, by Josephine Hendin. <u>Saturday Review</u>, 18 July 1970, pp. 29–30.

Interview

"For an 'Uncultured' America, World Leadership in Arts." Interview with Nancy Hanks, Chairman, National Endowment for the Arts. <u>U.S. News and World Report</u>, 7 Oct. 1974, pp. 58–60.

Journal, *with continuous pagination*

Dyke, Vernon Van. "Human Rights and the Rights of Groups." <u>American Journal of Political Science</u>, 18 (1974), 725–41.

Kilchenmann, Ruth. "Traum und Wirklichkeit in den Werken Friedrich Schnacks." <u>German Quarterly</u>, 34 (May 1961), 257–63.

The month may be added for clarity but is not necessary.

Journal, *with separate pagination*

Mangan, Doreen. "Henry Casselli: Superb Contradictions." <u>American Artist</u>, 38 (Dec. 1974), 39–43.

Because each issue of the journal is paged separately, you should include the month, season, or issue number. Page numbers alone will not locate the article within a volume of twelve issues with each issue having separate pagination.

McDavid, Raven I. "Sense and Nonsense About American
Dialects." PMLA, 81, No. 2 (1966), 9–11.

*PMLA normally pages continuously, but this issue is paged separately,
necessitating the issue number.*

Stuart, Jesse. "Love Affair at the Pasture Gate." Ball
State University Forum, 15 (Winter 1974), 3–6.

Journal, *volume number embracing two years*

Ranta, Jerrald. "Palindromes, Poems, and Geometric
Form." College English, 36 (Oct. 1974), 161–72.

Magazine, *monthly*

Cottrell, Leonard. "How Egypt Lived and Died." Réalités, March 1970, pp. 52–59.

Poinsett, Alex. "The 'Whys' Behind the Black Lawyer
Shortage." Ebony, Dec. 1974, pp. 95 et passim.

Sontag, Susan. "Baby." Playboy, Feb. 1974, pp. 74 et
passim.

*Note that monthly magazine citations often require the "et passim" desig-
nation for page numbers, which means page 74 and several following
pages here and there throughout the issue.*

Magazine, *weekly*

"Commodities: Sweet and Sour." Time, 16 Dec. 1974,
p. 32.

DeMott, Benjamin. "Saul Bellow and the Dogmas of
Possibility." Saturday Review, 7 Feb. 1970,
pp. 25–29, 37.

Quotation, *within the article's title*

Morgan, William W. "Form, Tradition, and Consolation
in Hardy's 'Poems of 1911–13.'" PMLA, 89 (1974),
496–505.

Skulsky, Harold. "'I Know My Course': Hamlet's Confi-
dence." PMLA, 89 (1974), 477–86.

BIBLIOGRAPHY FORM—PUBLIC DOCUMENTS

Since the nature of public documents is so varied, the form of the entry
cannot be standardized. Therefore, you should provide sufficient information so that the reader can easily locate the reference. As a general rule,
place information in the bibliography entry in this order: Government.
Body. Subsidiary body. Title of document. Identifying numbers.

Congressional papers

U.S. Congress. Senate. A Bill to Protect the Individu-
al's Right to Privacy by Prohibiting the Sale or
Distribution of Certain Information. S. 3116, 93rd
Cong., 2nd sess., 1974.

U.S. Congress. Senate. Senate Joint Resolution 1. 89th Cong., 1st sess., 1965.

U.S. Congress. Senate. The Constitution of the United States of America: Analysis and Interpretation. Senate Document 170, 82nd Cong., 2nd sess., 1952.

U.S. Congress. Senate. Committee on Foreign Relations. Hearings on S. 2793, Supplemental Foreign Assistance Fiscal Year 1966--Vietnam. 89th Cong., 2nd sess., 1966.

U.S. Congress. House. Committee on Interstate and Foreign Commerce. Federal Cigarette Labeling and Advertising Act. H. Rept. 449 to accompany H. R. 3014, 89th Cong., 1st sess., 1965.

U.S. Congress. Senate. Senator Barry Goldwater. Speech on the Fuel Crisis. 93rd Cong., 2nd sess., 1974. Congressional Record, CXX, No. 28, S2916-17.

U.S. Congress. House. Select Committee on Crime. Drugs in Our Schools. H. Rept. 357, 93rd Cong., 1st sess., 1973.

Executive branch documents

U.S. President. Public Papers of the Presidents of the United States. Washington, D.C.: Office of the Federal Registrar, 1974.

U.S. President. Alternative to Drugs: A New Approach to Drug Education. Washington, D.C.: GPO, Pr Ex 13.2:D84/3/1972.

U.S. Bureau of the Budget. Special Analysis: Budget of the United States, Fiscal Year 1967. Washington, D.C.: GPO, 1966.

U.S. Department of State. Foreign Relations of the United States: Diplomatic Papers, 1943. Washington, D.C.: GPO, 1944.

U.S. Department of State. United States Treaties and Other International Agreements. XV, Part 1, 1964.

U.S. Department of Health, Education, and Welfare. Growing Up in America: A Background to Contemporary Drug Abuse. Washington, D.C.: GPO, HE 20.2402:G91/1973.

Legal citations

U.S. Constitution. Art. II, sec. 1.

California. Constitution. Art. II, sec. 4.

Noise Control Act of 1972. Statutes at Large, LXXXVI, Public Law 92-574 (1972).

An Act for the Relief of Appalachian Regional Hospitals, Inc. Statutes at Large, LXXXVI, Private Law 92-161 (1972).

U.S. President. <u>A</u> <u>Proclamation</u> <u>Modifying</u> <u>Proclamation</u>
<u>3279</u>, <u>Relating</u> <u>to</u> <u>Imports</u> <u>of</u> <u>Petroleum</u> <u>and</u> <u>Pe-</u>
<u>troleum</u> <u>Products</u>. <u>Statutes</u> <u>at</u> <u>Large</u>, LXXXVI
(1972).

<u>Gold</u> <u>Coin</u> <u>and</u> <u>Gold</u> <u>Bullion</u> <u>Act</u>. <u>U</u>.<u>S</u>. <u>Code</u>, Supp. III,
Title 31, sec. 442 (1970).

<u>Environmental</u> <u>Protection</u> <u>Agency</u> <u>et</u> <u>al</u>. v. <u>Mink</u> <u>et</u> <u>al</u>.
<u>U</u>.<u>S</u>. <u>Reports</u>, CDX (1972).

BIBLIOGRAPHY FORM—OTHER SOURCES

Bulletin

Economic Research Service. "Demand and Price Situation." Washington, D.C.: Dept. of Agriculture,
Aug. 1974, DPS-141, 14 pp.

French, Earl. "Personal Problems in Industrial Research and Development." Ithaca, N.Y., 1963.
(Bulletin of the New York State School of Industrial and Labor Relations, No. 51.)

For examples of bulletins published within periodicals, see p. 130.

Dissertation, *published*

Nykrog, Per. <u>Les</u> <u>Fabliaux</u>: <u>Etude</u> <u>d'histoire</u> <u>littér-</u>
<u>aire</u> <u>et</u> <u>de</u> <u>stylistique</u> <u>médiévale</u>. Diss. Aarhus,
1957. Copenhagen: Munksgaard, 1957.

Dissertation, *unpublished*

Phillips, Emmett Loy. "A Study of Aesthetic Distance
in Thoreau's <u>Walden</u>." Diss. Univ. of Oklahoma
1970.

Film

Wilets, Bernard. <u>Environment</u>. 16 mm., 29 min.,
color. Santa Monica, Calif.: BFA Educational
Media, 1971.

<u>The</u> <u>World</u> <u>of</u> <u>the</u> <u>Weed</u>. 16 mm., 21 min., black/white.
Bloomington, Ind.: National Education TV, Inc.,
n.d.

Interview

Interview with Robert Turrentine, President, Acme Boot
Co. Clarksville, Tenn., 11 Feb. 1975.

Letter, *personal*

Information in a letter to the author from Professor
Winston Weathers of the University of Tulsa, 5
March 1975.

Mimeographed material

Smith, Jane L. "Terms for the Study of Fiction."
Cleveland, 1975. (Mimeographed.)

Monograph

NEA Research Division. <u>Kindergarten Practices, 1961</u>.
　　Washington, D.C., 1962. (Monograph 1962-M2.)

Veeder, William R. <u>W. B. Yeats</u>: <u>The Rhetoric of Repe-
　　tition</u>. Univ. of California English Studies, 34.
　　Berkeley: Univ. of California Press, 1968.

Newspaper

Bryant, Alice Franklin. "U.N. Role." Letter to the
　　Editor. <u>Chattanooga Times</u>, 15 Dec. 1974, p. B7,
　　cols. 6-7.

> Use this form for special newspaper articles, such as editorials, letters to
> the editor, cartoons, and so on.

"Egypt Demands That Israel Put Limit on Population
　　Growth." <u>Los Angeles Times</u>, 14 Dec. 1974, p. 1.

> When an item is unsigned, the title comes first and all subsequent infor-
> mation remains the same.

Sperling, Godfrey, Jr. "Ford's Plan to Spur Republi-
　　can Revival." <u>Christian Science Monitor</u>, 29
　　Nov. 1974, p. 20.

> The basic form for signed newspaper articles.

Pamphlet

U.S. Civil Service Commission. <u>The Human Equation</u>:
　　<u>Working in Personnel for the Federal Government</u>.
　　Pamphlet 76. Washington, D.C.: GPO, May 1970.

Public address or lecture

Sarnoff, David. "Television: A Channel for Freedom."
　　Detroit, 1961. (Address presented at the Uni-
　　versity of Detroit Academic Convocation.)

Recording

"Chaucer: The Nun's Priest's Tale." Narrated in Mid-
　　dle English by Robert Ross. Caedmon Recording,
　　No. E8C40.

"I Can Hear It Now: Winston Churchill." Ed. Edward R.
　　Murrow and Fred W. Friendly. Narrator, Edward
　　R. Murrow. Columbia Masterworks Recording, No.
　　E9C10.

John, Elton. "This Song Has No Title." In <u>Goodbye
　　Yellow Brick Road</u>. MCA Records, MCA 2-10003,
　　1974.

Report

Linden, Fabian. "Women: A Demographic, Social and
　　Economic Presentation." Report by The Confer-
　　ence Board. New York: CBS/Broadcast Group,
　　1973.

Panama Canal Company. <u>Annual Report</u>: <u>Fiscal Year End-
　　ed June 30, 1968</u>. Panama: Canal Zone Govern-
　　ment, 1968.

> Reports in the form of books or pamphlets require underlining.

<u>Womanpower</u>. Brookline, Mass.: Betsy Hogan Associates, 1974.

Reproductions and photographs

Blake's <u>Comus</u>, Plate 4. As reproduced in Irene Tayler. "Blake's <u>Comus</u> Designs." <u>Blake Studies</u>, 4 (Spring 1972), 61.

Michener, James A. "Structure of Earth at Centennial, Colorado." <u>Centennial</u>. New York: Random House, 1974.

Table or illustration

Corbett, Edward P. J. Syllogism graph. <u>Classical Rhetoric for the Modern Student</u>. New York: Oxford Univ. Press, 1965.

Because the graph has no title, the descriptive heading should not be placed within quotation marks.

Helmich, Donald L. "Organizational Growth and Succession Patterns." <u>Academy of Management Journal</u>, 17 (Dec. 1974), 773, Table 2.

Television or radio program

The <u>Commanders: Douglas MacArthur</u>. New York: NBC–TV, 17 March 1975.

Sevareid, Eric. <u>CBS News</u>. New York: CBS–TV, 11 March 1975.

There is a tendency in documentation to omit periods in abbreviations of well-known societies and associations.

Shakespeare, William. <u>As You Like It</u>. Nashville: Nashville Theatre Academy, 11 March 1975, WDCN–TV.

Thesis

See "Dissertation, unpublished," p. 133.

Unpublished paper

Elkins, William R. "The Dream World and the Dream Vision: Meaning and Structure in Poe's Art." (Unpublished paper.)

DOCUMENTATION OF SCIENCE PAPERS   7

■ You may discover that your science instructor requires a system of documentation quite different from that described in the preceding two chapters. Accordingly, when you write a research paper in the fields of biological science, physical science, mathematics, or psychology, you should consult this chapter, which is intended to supply a brief but adequate description of science-paper documentation. However, you should keep in mind at the start that modifications of style exist from field to field, and agreement does not always exist within a given field. Nevertheless, after consultation with your instructor, you should find one of the two systems outlined below satisfactory for your needs.

As a general rule, science papers, excluding those dealing with physics (see p. 142), require no footnotes except content footnotes (see p. 117). Instead you insert within your text reference numbers (1) or reference dates (1975). Then at the end of your paper you list, numerically or alphabetically, only those references actually mentioned in your text. You may label the list as "List of References" or "Literature Cited." The title "Bibliography" seldom appears in science papers.

In addition, you should be aware of other characteristics of the scientific reference entries. First, you will usually capitalize only the first word of titles of books and articles (for example, "The biology of the algae"). But some fields (for example, chemistry and physics) omit completely the title of a periodical article. Second, you will usually abbreviate and seldom underline the name of the periodical (for example, "Amer. J. Bot."; see pp. 156-60, 162-63 for listings of science journals and their standard abbreviations). But you should note that the field of psychology, since 1963, spells in full the names of periodicals. Third, you will usually write the volume numbers in Arabic numerals, although placement and form will vary (for example, "vol. 70" or "70").

Name and Year System

When employing the name and year system, you should place within your text, in parentheses or brackets, the year of publication of the authority's book or journal article. Furthermore, note the following:

1. Place the entry immediately after the authority's name:

```
Smith (1965) ascribes no species-specific be-

havior to man.  However, Adams (1967) presents

data that tend to be contradictory.
```

2. If your sentence construction does not require the use of the authority's name, insert both the name and date in parentheses:

```
Hopkins (1966) found some supporting evidence

for a portion of the Marr data (Marr and Brown,

1957) through point bi-serial correlation tech-

niques.
```

3. For two authors, employ both names: "(Torgerson and Andrews, 1975)." For three authors, name them all in the first entry, as "(Torgerson, Andrews, and Dunlap, 1975)," but thereafter use "(Torgerson et al., 1975)." For four or more authors, employ "(Fredericks et al., 1975)" in the first and all subsequent instances.

4. Use small letters (a, b, c) to identify two or more works published in the same year by the same author, for example, "Thompson (1966a)" and "Thompson (1966b)."

5. If necessary, specify additional information; for example, "Thompson (1967, III)," "(Wallace, 1948, 1967)," and "White and Thurston (1975, 211-14)":

```
Horton (1966; cf. Thomas, 1962, p. 89) suggests

an intercorrelation of these testing devices.

But after multiple-group analysis, Welston

(1967, p. 211) reached an opposite conclusion.
```

6. Alphabetize the "List of References" at the end of your paper. List chronologically two or more works by the same author (for example, Fitzgerald's 1964 publication would precede his 1967 publication). Main parts for a periodical reference entry are: name(s) of author(s); year of publication; title of the article; name of the journal; volume number; and inclusive page numbers. Main parts for a book reference entry are: name(s) of author(s); year of publication; title of the book; name and city of publisher; number of pages in the book.

A sample "List of References"[1] follows:

Fig. 33: Sample List of References

List of References

Klein, R. M., and D. T. Klein. 1970. Research methods in plant science. Natural History Press, Garden City, New York. 796 p.

Muller, W. H. 1974. Botany: A functional discharge. Macmillan, Riverside, N.J. 601 p.

Olive, L. S., 1962. The genus *Protostelium*. Amer. J. Bot. 49: 297–303.

————. 1964a. Spore discharge mechanism in basidiomycetes. Science 146: 542–543.

————. 1964b. A new member of the Mycetozoa. Mycologia 61: 885–896.

Thomson, W. W., and R. DeTournett. 1970. Studies on the ultrastructure of the guard cells of Opuntia. Amer. J. Bot. 57: 309–316.

The Number System

After completing your "List of References," you should assign a number to each entry. Then, to designate your source of information, you should employ the appropriate number within your text. Furthermore, note the following:

[1]The form of these botany entries conforms to the *CBE Style Manual,* 3rd ed. (Washington, D.C.: American Institute of Biological Sciences, 1972).

1. Place the entry, enclosed within parentheses (or brackets), immediately after the authority's name:

```
In particular the recent paper by Hershel,

Hobbs, and Thomason (1) raises many interesting

questions related to photosynthesis, some of

which were answered by Skelton (2), (3).
```

2. If the sentence construction does not require the use of the authority's name, employ one of the following three methods:
- Insert both name and number within parentheses:

```
Additional observations include alterations in

carbohydrate metabolism (Evans, 3), changes in

ascorbic acid incorporation into the cell (Dodd

and Williams, 11) and adjoining membranes (Holt

and Zimmer, 7).
```

- Insert both name and number within parentheses and enclose the number within brackets (few journals, however, use this method):

```
The subject of the cytochrome oxidase system in

cell metabolism has received a great deal of

attention (Singleton [4]).
```

- Insert the number only, enclosing it within parentheses (or brackets):

```
It is known (1) that the DNA concentration of a

nucleus doubles during interphase.
```

3. If necessary, add specific data to the entry (for example, "[3, Proposition 8]" or "[6, p. 76]"):

> The results of the respiration experiment published by Jones (3, p. 412) had been predicted earlier by Smith (5).

Arrange your references in alphabetical order and number them consecutively (in which case, of course, the numbers will not appear in consecutive order in your text), *or* forego an alphabetical arrangement and number the references consecutively as they appear in the text, interrupting that order in your text when entering an earlier reference. An entry for the number system is usually similar to that for the name-and-year system (see p. 137) except that it is preceded by a numeral on the line (not a superscript, as in text citation) and a period.

A numbered, alphabetized list follows: [2]

Fig. 34: Literature Cited

Literature Cited

1. Griffeth, T., K. P. Hellman, and R. V. Byerrum. 1960. Studies on the biogenesis of the ring systems of nicotine. J. Biol. Chem. 235: 800–804.

2. Hodson, P. H., and J. W. Foster. 1966. Dipicolinic acid synthesis in *Penicillium citreoviride*. J. Bacteriol. 91: 562–569.

3. Kaminskas, Edvardas, and B. Magasanik. 1970. Sequential synthesis of histidine-degrading enzymes in *Bacillus sybtilis*. J. Biol. Chem. 245: 3549–3555.

4. McClintic, J. Robert. 1975. Basic anatomy and physiology of the human body. John Wiley and Sons, New York. 528 p.

5. Meister, A. 1965. Biochemistry of the amino acids, 2nd ed., vol. 2. Academic Press, Inc., New York.

6. Smith. I. [ed.] 1960. Chromatographic and electrophoretic techniques, vol. 1. Chromatography. Interscience Publishers, Inc., New York.

---

[2]The form of these biology entries conforms to the *CBE Style Manual*, 3rd ed. (Washington, D.C.: American Institute of Biological Sciences, 1972). See also "List of References" p. 138.

SAMPLE FORMS OF ENTRIES FOR THE VARIOUS SCIENCE DISCIPLINES

Biology

See above, "Literature Cited," p. 140.

Botany

See above, "List of References," p. 138.

Chemistry[3]

(1) L. W. Fine, "Chemistry Decoded," Oxford Univ. Press, Oxford, England, 1975, pp. 23-41.

(2) J. D. Corbett in "Fused Salts," B. R. Sundheim, Ed., McGraw-Hill Book Co., Inc., New York, 1964, p. 341.

(3) W. H. Baddley, Ph.D. Dissertation, Northwestern University, Evanston, Ill., 1964.

(4) P. J. Lewi and W. W. Braet, J. Chem. Doc., 10, 95-97 (1970).

(5) G. C. Berry and T. G. Fox, J. Am. Chem. Soc., 86, 3540 (1964).

(6) J. R. Morton, Chem. Rev., 64, 452 (1964).

Geology[4]

Donath, F. A., 1963, Strength variation and deformational behavior in anisotropic rock, p. 281-297 in Judd, Wm. R., Editor, State of stress in the earth's crust: New York, American Elsevier Publishing Co., Inc., 732 p.

Friedlander, G., Kennedy, J. W., and Miller, J. M., 1964, Nuclear and radiochemistry: New York, John Wiley and Sons, 585 p.

Harker, Alfred, 1965, The natural history of igneous rocks: New York, Hafner, 384 p.

Heard, H. C., Turner, F. J., and Weiss, L. E., 1965, Studies of heterogeneous strain in experimentally deformed calcite, marble, and phyllite: Univ. Calif. Pub. Geol. Sci., v. 46, p. 81-152.

Hill, M. L., and Troxel, B. W., 1966, Tectonics of Death Valley region, California: Geol. Soc. America Bull., v. 77, p. 435-438.

Thorpe, R. S., 1974, Aspects of Magmatism and Plate Tectonics in the Precambrian of England and Wales: Geol. J., v. 9, p. 115-136.

[3] The form of these chemistry entries conforms to the *Handbook for Authors* (Washington, D.C.: American Chemical Society, 1967).
[4] The form of these geology entries conforms to *Suggestions to Authors of the Reports of the United States Geological Survey*, 5th ed. (Washington, D.C.: Dept. of the Interior, 1958).

Mathematics[5]

1. R. Artzy, <u>Linear geometry</u>, Addison—Wesley, Reading, Mass., 1965.

2. H. Halpern, <u>Quasi—Equivalence classes of normal representations for a separable C*—algebra</u>, Trans. Am. Math. Soc. <u>203</u> (1975), 129—140.

3. I. M. Isaacs and D. S. Passman, <u>Groups with representations of bounded degree</u>, Canad. J. Math. <u>16</u> (1964), 299—309.

4. ------, <u>Characterization of groups in terms of the degrees of their characters</u>, Pacific J. Math. <u>15</u> (1965), 877—903.

5. C. E. Rickart, <u>General theory of Banach algebras</u>, Van Nostrand, Princeton, N.J., 1960.

6. O. Solbrig, <u>Evolution and systematics</u>, The Macmillan Co., New York, 1966.

Physics[6]

[1]F. Riesz and Bela Nagy, <u>Functional Analysis</u> (Frederick Ungar Publishing Company, New York, 1955), Secs. 121 and 123.

[2]S. Bergia and L. Brown, in <u>Proceedings of the International Conference on Nucleon Structure</u>, edited by R. Hofstadter and L. I. Schiff (Stanford University Press, Stanford, California, 1963), p. 320.

[3]Oswald H. Blackwood, William C. Kelly, Raymond M. Bell, <u>General Physics</u> (John Wiley and Sons, Inc., New York, 1963), p. 510.

[4]S. Hess, Phys. Rev. A, <u>11</u>, 1086 (1975).

[5]K. Gottfried and J. D. Jackson, Nuovo Cimento <u>22</u>, 309 (1964).

[6]E. T. Jaynes, Am. J. Phys. <u>33</u>, 391 (1965).

Psychology[7]

Anderson, J. R., and Bower, G. H. Recognition and retrieval processes in free recall. <u>Psychological Review</u>, 1972, <u>79</u>, 97—123.

Gaito, John (Ed.) <u>Macromolecules and behavior</u>. New York: Appleton—Century—Crofts, 1966.

Harvey, O. J., Hunt, D. E., & Schroder, H. M. <u>Conceptual systems of personality organization</u>. New York: Wiley, 1961.

[5]The form of these math entries conforms to *A Manual for Authors of Mathematical Papers*, 4th ed. (Providence: American Mathematical Society, 1971).

[6]The form of these entries conforms to *Style Manual for Guidance in the Preparation of Journals Published by the American Institute of Physics*, rev. ed. (New York: American Institute of Physics, 1970).

[7]The form of these psychology entries conforms generally to *Publication Manual*, rev. ed. (Washington, D.C.: American Psychological Association, 1967).

Herman, Louis M. Information encoding and decision time as variables in human choice behavior. _Journal of Experimental Psychology_, 1966, _71_ (5), 718–724.

Keniston, Kenneth. _The uncommitted_: _alienated youth in American society_. New York: Harcourt Brace Jovanovich, Inc., 1966.

Winett, Richard A. Attribution of attitude and behavior change and its relevance to behavior therapy. _The Psychological Record_, 1970, _20_, 17–32.

Zoology

See forms for biology, p. 140, and for botany, p. 138.

APPENDIX I

A GLOSSARY OF ADDITIONAL RESEARCH TERMS

Acknowledgments Place necessary acknowledgments or explanations in a footnote to your first sentence:

> [1]I wish here to express my thanks to Mrs. Horace A. Humphrey for permission to examine the manuscripts of her late husband.

Usually there is no need for a preface in a research paper.

Ampersand Avoid using the ampersand symbol "&." Instead, spell out the "and" in the name of a company or organization, unless custom demands it, e.g., "A&P."

Annotated Bibliography Write descriptive notes for each entry.

Appendix Place additional material in an appendix at the end of your paper. It is a logical location for numerous tables and illustrations or other accumulated data.

Apostrophe Add an apostrophe and *s* to form the possessive of one-syllable proper names that end in *s* or another sibilant (for example, "Keats's poem," "Rice's story," "Bates's *The Kinds of Man*"). In words of more than one syllable ending in a sibilant, add the apostrophe only (for example, "Rawlings' novel," "Evans' essay," "Daiches' criticism"), except for names ending in a sibilant and a final *e* (for example, "Lovelace's enduring appeal").

Asterisks Use Arabic numerals for footnote numbers and asterisks only for footnoting illustrations or tables (see Fig. 40, p. 151).

Bible Use parenthetical documentation for biblical references in your text — that is, place the entry within parentheses immediately after the quotation, for example, "(II Kings xviii.13)." Do not underline titles of books of the Bible. Abbreviations of most books of the Bible follow (but do not abbreviate one-syllable titles, for example, "Mark" or "Acts"):

I and II Chron.	I and II Chronicles	Lev.	Leviticus
Col.	Colossians	Mal.	Malachi
I and II Cor.	I and II Corinthians	Matt.	Matthew
Dan.	Daniel	Mic.	Micah
Deut.	Deuteronomy	Nah.	Nahum
Eccles.	Ecclesiastes	Neh.	Nehemiah
Eph.	Ephesians	Num.	Numbers
Exod.	Exodus	Obad.	Obadiah
Ezek.	Ezekiel	I and II Pet.	I and II Peter
Gal.	Galatians	Phil.	Philippians
Gen.	Genesis	Prov.	Proverbs
Hab.	Habakkuk	Ps. (Pss.)	Psalm (s)
Hag.	Haggai	Rev.	Revelation
Heb.	Hebrews	Rom.	Romans
Hos.	Hosea	I and II Sam.	I and II Samuel
Isa.	Isaiah	Song of Sol.	Song of Solomon
Jas.	James	I and II Thess.	I and II Thessalonians
Jer.	Jeremiah	I and II Tim.	I and II Timothy
Josh.	Joshua	Zech.	Zechariah
Judg.	Judges	Zeph.	Zephaniah
Lam.	Lamentations		

Capitalization Titles of books: capitalize the first word and all principal words, but not articles, prepositions, and conjunctions (for example, *The Last of the Mohicans*).

Titles of magazines and newspapers: as above, except do not treat an initial definite article as part of the title except when the title is entered separately in a list:

```
"He was referring to the Kansas City Star and. . . ."
    10Editorial, Kansas City Star, March 18, 1966, p.
43D.
```

Titles of parts of a specific work: capitalize as for books (for example, "Thompson's Appendix II," "Jones's Preface," "Writing the Final Draft").

Abbreviations: capitalize a noun followed by a numeral indicating place in a sequence (for example, "Act II," "Ch. iv," "No. 14," "Vol. III"). Do not capitalize "1.," "n.," "p.," or "sig."

Titles of French, Italian, and Spanish works: capitalize the first word, the proper nouns, but not adjectives derived from proper nouns.

Titles of German works: capitalize the first word, all nouns, and all adjectives derived from names of persons.

Definitions For definitions within your text, use single quotation marks without intervening punctuation (for example, *"et alii* and others' ").

Enumeration of Items Incorporate short items into the text, as follows.

```
College instructors are usually divided into four ranks:
(1) instructors, (2) assistant professors, (3) associate
professors, and (4) full professors.
```

Present longer items in a tabular form, as follows:

```
College instructors are usually divided into four ranks:

    1. Instructors, at the bottom of the scale, are usu-
       ally beginning teachers with little or no experi-
       ence.
    2. Assistant professors. . . .
```

Etc. *Et cetera* "and so forth": avoid using in the text by listing at least four items, as follows:

```
Images of color occur frequently in Crane's writing,
especially blue, gold, red, and grey.
```

Foreign Languages Underline foreign words used in an English text:

```
Like his friend Olaf, he is aut Caesar, aut nihil, ei-
ther overpowering perfection or ruin and destruction.
```

Do not underline quotations:

```
Obviously, he uses it to exploit, in the words of Jean
Laumon, "une admirable mine de themes poetiques."
```

Do not underline titles of magazine articles:

```
     3Von Thomas O. Brandt, "Brecht und die Bibel,"
PMLA, 79 (March 1964), 171.
```

Do not underline places, institutions, proper names, or titles that precede proper names:

```
Of course, Racine became extremely fond of Mlle Champ-
meslé, who interpreted his works at the Hotel de Bour-
gogne
```

Illustrations and Tables A table is a systematic arrangement of statistical materials, usually in columns. An illustration is any item that is not a table: blueprint, chart, diagram, drawing, graph, photograph, photostat, map, and so on. Note the following samples:

Fig. 35: Illustration

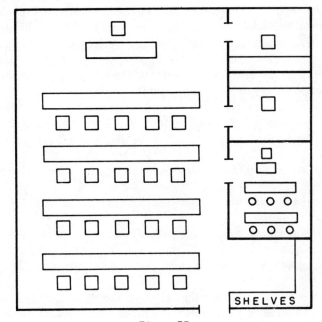

Fig. 35

Audio Laboratory With Private Listening Rooms and a
Small Group Room

Fig. 36: Table

TABLE I

RESPONSE BY CLASS ON VIETNAM POLICY

	Freshmen	Sophomores	Juniors	Seniors
1. Holding action	2	7	19	0
2. Withdrawal	150	137	111	78
3. Escalation	296	301	229	187

When presenting an illustration or table in your research paper, conform to
the following stipulations:

1. Present only one kind of information in each illustration, making it
as simple and as brief as possible; frills and fancy art work may distract
rather than attract the reader.

2. Place small illustrations within your text. Large illustrations should
go on a separate page. If you have numerous illustrations or long, complex
tables, these should be placed in an appendix at the end of your paper.

3. Place the illustration as near to your textual discussion as possible, although the illustration should not precede your first mention of it.

4. Make certain that your textual discussion adequately explains the significance of the illustration. Follow two rules: (1) write the illustration so that your reader can understand it without reference to your discussion; and (2) write your discussion of the illustration so that your reader may understand your observations without reference to the illustration. But avoid giving too many numbers and figures in your text.

5. In your textual discussion refer to illustrations by number (for example, "Figure 5" or "Table IV, p. 16"), not by a vague reference (for example, "the table above," "the following illustration," or "the chart below").

6. Number illustrations consecutively throughout the paper with Arabic numbers, preceded by "Fig." or "Figure" (for example, "Figure 4"), placed one double space above the caption and centered on the page *below* the illustration.

7. Number tables consecutively throughout the paper with capital Roman numerals, preceded by "Table" (for example, "Table II"), placed one double space above the caption and centered on the page *above* the table.

8. Always insert a caption that explains the illustration, placed *above* the table and *below* the illustration, centered, in full capital letters or in capitals and lower case, but do not mix forms in the same paper. An alternative is to place the caption on the same line with the number (see Fig. 37 below).

9. Insert a caption or number for each column of a table, centered above the column or, if necessary, inserted diagonally or vertically above it.

10. When inserting an explanatory or reference footnote, place it below both a table and an illustration; then use an asterisk as the identifying superscript, not an Arabic numeral (for example, see Figs. 39 and 40, p. 151).

Note the following samples of charts and illustrations such as you might use in a research paper:

Fig. 37: Illustration

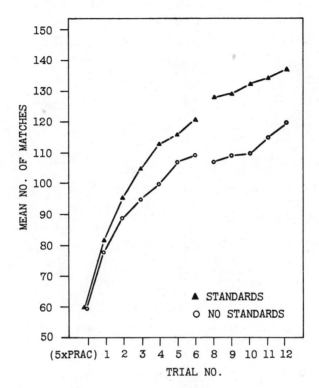

Fig. 37: Mean Number of Matches by Subjects With and Without Standards (By Trial). From Edwin A. Locke and Judith F. Bryan. Cognitive Aspects of Psychomotor Per-formance. Journal of Applied Psychology, 1966, 50, 289.

Fig. 38: Illustration

SUPRASEGMENTAL

> STRESS ╱   ⋀   ╲   ⋃
> (primary) (secondary) (tertiary) (weak)
>
> PITCH
>
>   1   2   3   4 (relatively rare)
>
> (low) (average) (high) (exceptionally high)
>
> <u>Juncture</u>
>
>   open
>
> ┼ at minor break, usually between words
>
>   terminal
>
>   │ or ⟶   "level'
>
>   at greater break within sentence, also in
>
>   apposition;
>
>   level pitch
>
> ‖ or ↗   "rising"
>
>   in "yes–no" questions, series;
>
>   pitch–rise before the pause
>
> ╫ or ↘   "falling'
>
>   at end of most sentences;
>
>   pitch–drop, voice fades off

Fig. 38: Phonemes of English. Generally, this figure
follows the Trager–Smith system, used widely in American
linguistics. From Anna H. Live, "Pattern in Language,"
<u>The Journal of General Education</u>, 18 (July 1966), 94.

Fig. 39: Table

TABLE II*

Mean Scores of Six Values Held by College

Students According to Sex

All Students		Men		Women	
Pol.	40.61	Pol.	43.22	Aesth.	43.86
Rel.	40.51	Theor.	43.09	Rel.	43.13
Aesth.	40.29	Econ.	42.05	Soc.	41.62
Theor.	39.80	Rel.	37.88	Pol.	38.00
Econ.	39.45	Soc.	37.05	Econ.	36.85
Soc.	39.34	Aesth.	36.72	Theor.	36.50

*From Carmen J. Finley, Jack M. Thompson, and Albert Cognata, "Stability of the California Short Form Test of Mental Maturity: Grades 3, 5, and 7," California Journal of Educational Research, 17 (Sept. 1966), 165.

Fig. 40: Table

TABLE III. Inhibitory effects of sugars on the growth of Clostridium histolyticum (11 strains) on nutrient agar*

Sugar added (2%)	Aerobic incubation (hr)		Anaerobic incubation (hr)	
	24	48	24	48
None	11**	11	11	11
Glucose	0	0	11	11
Maltose	0	0	11	11
Lactose	1	1	11	11
Sucrose	3	6	11	11
Arabinose	0	0	0	0
Inositol	0	0	11	11
Xylose	0	0	0	0
Sorbitol	2	7	11	11
Mamnitol	9	10	11	11
Rhamnose	0	0	11	11

*From Shoki Nishida and Masaaki Imaizumi. 1966. Toxigencity of Clostridium histolyticum. J. Bacteriol. 91: 481.
**No. of strains which gave rise to colonies in the presence of the sugar.

Names of Persons Formal titles (Mr., Mrs., Ms., Dr., Hon.) are usually omitted in textual and footnote references to distinguished persons, living or dead. As a general rule, first mention of a person requires the full name (for example, Ernest Hemingway or Margaret Mead) and thereafter requires only usage of the surname (Hemingway or Mead).

Convention suggests that certain prominent figures (Lord Byron, Dr. Johnson, Dame Edith Sitwell) require the title while others, for no apparent reason, do not (for example, use Tennyson, Browne, and Hillary rather than Lord Tennyson, Sir Thomas Browne, or Sir Edmund Hillary). Where custom dictates, you may employ simplified names of famous authors (for example, use "Dante" rather than his surname "Alighieri" and use "Michelangelo" rather than "Michelangelo Buonarroti"). You may also use pseudonyms where custom dictates (for example, George Eliot, Maxim Gorkey, Mark Twain).

Parenthetical Documentation Handle references within sentences in one of the following ways:

```
According to William C. DeVane, A Browning Handbook (New
York:  Appleton, 1955), p. 37, Browning's liberalism
follows the doctrine of Victorian laissez-faire.
```

or

```
According to William C. DeVane--A Browning Handbook (New
York:  Appleton, 1955), p. 37--Browning's liberalism
follows the doctrine of Victorian laissez-faire.
```

If these forms prove awkward, recast the sentence so that the documentation comes at the end:

```
Browning's laissez-faire liberalism is stressed by
William C. DeVane, A Browning Handbook (New York:
Appleton, 1955), p. 37.
```

Punctuation Consistency is a key to punctuation for research writing. A careful proofreading of your paper for punctuation errors will generally improve the clarity and accuracy of your writing.

1. *Commas* are used·in a series of three or more before "and" and "or." Never use a comma and a dash together. The comma follows a parenthesis (such as this), if your text requires the comma. The comma goes inside single quotation marks as well as double quotation marks (for example, "The Sources of Franklin's 'The Ephemera,' ").

2. *Dashes* are formed with your typewriter by typing two hyphens with no blank space before or after.

3. *Exclamation marks* are seldom used in research writing. A forceful declarative sentence is preferable.

4. *Hyphens* to separate words at the end of a typed line are acceptable in research papers. However, you should always double-check word division by consulting a dictionary. If possible, do not separate by a hyphen two letters at the end or beginning of a line (for example, use "depend-able," not "de-pendable"). If possible, avoid the hyphenation of proper names.

5. *Periods* end complete sentences of the text, footnotes, and all bibliography entries. The period normally follows the parenthesis. (The period is placed within the parenthesis only when the parenthetical statement is independent, as in this instance.) See also "Ellipsis," p. 67, for explanation of the period in conjunction with ellipsis dots.

6. *Brackets* should be inserted by hand if these figures are not on your typewriter. Brackets are used to enclose a parenthesis within a parenthesis, to enclose phonetic transcription, and to enclose interpolations in a quotation (See "Brackets," p. 67).

7. *Words discussed*, such as slang, words cited as words, or words purposely misused, should be enclosed within quotation marks. Also use quotation marks for English translations of foreign words. However, linguistic studies require that you underline all linguistic forms (letters, words, phrases) that are subjects of discussion and also require that you employ single quotation marks for definitions, without intervening punctuation (for example, nosu 'nose').

8. *Quotation marks* should enclose all quotations run on as part of your text. For quotations within quotations, use single marks. You should put all commas or periods inside quotation marks, whether double or single, unless a parenthetical reference intervenes. Other marks of punctuation go inside the quotation marks only when such items (question mark, dash, exclamation) are actually part of the quoted materials. Semicolons and colons generally fall outside the quotation marks.

Roman Numerals Use capital or small Roman numerals as shown below:

```
Act II        Bk. x
Vol. III      Chap. xi
Part IV       scene xii
Div. V        canto xiii
Plate VI      pp. xiv-xvii
Table VII
```

A list of Roman numerals:

	UNITS	TENS	HUNDREDS
1	i	x	c
2	ii	xx	cc
3	iii	xxx	ccc
4	iv	xl	cd
5	v	l	d
6	vi	lx	dc
7	vii	lxx	dcc
8	viii	lxxx	dccc
9	ix	xc	cm

Shakespearean Plays For use in parenthetical documentation, the editorial board of the *Shakespeare Quarterly* has approved the following abbreviations of titles of Shakespearean works: *Ado; Ant.; AWW; AYL; Cor.; Cym.; Err.; Ham.; 1H4; 2H4; H5; 1H6; 2H6; 3H6; H8; JC; Jn; LLL; Lr.; Mac.; MM; MND; MV; Oth.; Per.; R2; R3; Rom.; Shr.; TGV; Tim.; Tit.; Tmp.; TN; TNK; Tro.; Wiv.; WT; LC; Luc.; PhT; PP; Son.; Ven.*

Slang Enclose in double quotation marks any words to which you direct attention.

Underlining Underline the following: books, bulletins, pamphlets, periodicals, plays, motion pictures, newspapers, operas, ships, symphonies, and yearbooks. If separately published, underline the following: essays, lectures, poems, proceedings, reports, sermons, and stories.

Word Division When necessary, divide a word with a hyphen so that the break comes between two syllables, but avoid one-letter and two-letter division (for example, "o-ver" or "separate-ly"). When in doubt about the proper division of a word, always consult a dictionary.

APPENDIX II
LIST OF GENERAL REFERENCE BOOKS AND JOURNALS

Applied and Physical Sciences

GENERAL

Books

American Library Association. *Guide to the Selection of Computer-Based Science and Technology Reference Services in the U.S.A.* Chicago: American Library Association, 1969.

Applied Science and Technology Index. New York: H. W. Wilson, 1958-date. Before 1958, see *Industrial Arts Index.*

Besterman, Theodore. *Technology.* 2 vols. Totowa, N.J.: Littlefield, 1971.

Bolton, Henry C. *Catalogue of Scientific and Technical Periodicals, 1665-1895.* 2nd ed. 1897; rpt. New York: Johnson Reprint, 1974.

Hawkins, R. R., ed. *Scientific, Medical, and Technical Books Published in the United States of America.* 2nd ed. Washington, D.C.: National Academy of Sciences, 1958.

Industrial Arts Index. New York: H. W. Wilson, 1913-57. Superseded by *Applied Science and Technology Index.*

Lasworth, Earl J. *Reference Sources in Science and Technology.* Metuchen, N.J.: Scarecrow, 1972.

Mitcham, Carl, and Robert McKay. *Bibliography of the Philosophy of Technology.* Chicago: Univ. of Chicago Press, 1973.

McGraw-Hill Encyclopedia of Science and Technology. Rev. ed. 15 vols. New York: McGraw-Hill, 1966.

McGraw-Hill Yearbook of Science and Technology. New York: McGraw-Hill, annually.

Scientific and Technical Books in Print. New York: Bowker, 1972.

Statistical Techniques in Technological Research: An Aid to Research Productivity. New York: Halsted Press, 1968.

Susskind, Charles. *Understanding Technology.* Baltimore: Johns Hopkins, 1973.

Technical Book Review Index. New York: Special Libraries Association, 1935-date.

CHEMICAL ENGINEERING

Books

Bourton, K. *Chemical and Process Engineering: Unit Operations, a Bibliographical Guide.* New York: Plenum, 1968.

Brown, R., and G. A. Campbell. *How to Find Out About the Chemical Industry.* Elmsford, N.Y.: Pergamon, 1969.

Ernst, Richard. *Dictionary of Chemistry, Including Chemical Engineering and Fundamentals of Allied Sciences.* 2 vols. New York: International Publications Service, 1969.

Kent, James A. *Riegel's Handbook of Industrial Chemistry.* 7th ed. New York: Reinhold, 1973.

Perry, John H., and C. H. Chilton. *Chemical Engineers Handbook.* 5th ed. New York: McGraw-Hill, 1973.

Journals

Chemical and Engineering News (Chem. & Eng. N.)

Chemistry and Industry (Chem. & Ind.)

Chemical and Process Engineering (Chem. & Process Eng.)
Chemical Engineering (Chem. Eng.)
Chemical Engineering Progress (Chem. Eng. Prog.)
Chemical Technology (Chem. Tech.)
Industrial and Engineering Chemistry Fundamentals (Ind. and Eng. Chem. Fundamentals)
Industrial and Engineering Chemistry Process Design and Development (Ind. and Eng. Chem. Process Design)
Industrial and Engineering Chemistry Product Research and Development (Ind. and Eng. Chem. Product Res. and Develop.)
Industrial and Engineering Chemistry Product Research and Development (Ind. and Eng. Chem. Product Res. and Develop.)
Petro/Chem Engineer (Petro/Chem Eng.)

CHEMISTRY

Books

American Chemical Society. *Searching the Chemical Literature.* Washington, D.C.: American Chemical Society, 1961.

Bennett, Harry, ed. *Concise Chemical and Technical Dictionary.* 2nd ed. New York: Chemical Publications, 1973.

Bottle, R. T., ed. *Use of Chemical Literature.* 2nd ed. Hamden, Conn.: Shoe String, 1969.

Burman, C. R. *How to Find Out in Chemistry.* 2nd ed. Elmsford, N.Y.: Pergamon, 1966.

Clark, George L., et al. *The Encyclopedia of Chemistry.* 2nd ed. New York: Reinhold, 1966.

Cooke, Edward I. *Chemical Synonyms and Trade Names.* 7th ed. Cleveland: CRC Press, 1971.

Crane, Evan Jay, et al. *A Guide to the Literature of Chemistry.* 2nd ed. New York: Wiley, 1957.

Grant, Julius. *Hackh's Chemical Dictionary.* 4th ed. New York: McGraw-Hill, 1973.

Handbook for Authors of Papers in the Journals of the American Chemical Society. Washington, D.C.: American Chemical Society, 1967.

Hodgman, Charles D., ed. *Handbook of Chemistry and Physics.* Cleveland: CRC Press, 1913-date.

Lange, Norbert A., and Gordon M. Forker, eds. *Handbook of Chemistry.* 10th ed. New York: Wiley, 1957.

Literature Resources for Chemical Process Industries. Washington, D.C.: American Chemical Society, 1954.

Mellon, M. G. *Chemical Publications: Their Use and Nature.* 4th ed. New York: McGraw-Hill, 1965.

Merck Index of Chemicals and Drugs: An Encyclopedia of Chemists, Pharmacists, Physicians. 7th ed. Rahway, N.J.: Merck, 1960.

Singer, T. E., and Julian F. Smith. *Literature of Chemical Technology.* Washington, D.C.: American Chemical Society, 1968.

Weast, Robert C., and S. M. Selby, eds. *CRC Handbook of Chemistry and Physics.* 53rd ed. Cleveland: CRC Press, 1972.

Journals

Accounts of Chemical Research (Acc. of Chem. Res.)
Analytical Chemistry (Analyt. Chem.)
Biochemistry (Biochem.)
Chemical Abstracts (Chem. Abstracts)
Chemical News (Chem. N.)
Chemical Reviews (Chem. Rev.)
Chemical Society, Proceedings (Chem. Soc. Proc.)
Chemical Titles (Chem. Titles)
Chemistry (Chem.)
Current Contents
Inorganic Chemistry (Inorg. Chem.)
Journal of the American Chemical Society (J. Am. Chem. Soc.)
Journal of Chemical and Engineering Data (J. Chem. Eng. Data)
Journal of Chemical Documentation (J. Chem. Document.)
Journal of Chemical Education (J. Chem. Educ.)
Journal of the Chemical Society, London (J. Chem. Soc., London)
Journal of Organic Chemistry (J. Org. Chem.)
Journal of Physical Chemistry (J. Phys. Chem.)

ELECTRONICS

Books

Annotated Bibliography of Electronic Data Processing. Gainesville: Univ. of Florida Press, 1968.

Carter, Harley. *Dictionary of Electronics.* Blue Ridge Summit, Pa.: TAB Books, 1972.

Electronic Properties of Materials: A Guide to the Literature. 3 vols. New York: Plenum, 1967-71.

Goedecke, W. *Dictionary of Electrical Engineering, Telecommunications, and Electronics.* 3 vols. New York: Ungar, 1974.

Gotterer, Malcolm H. *KWIC Index: A Bibliography of Computer Management.* Philadelphia: Auerbach, 1970.

Harper, Charles A. *Handbook of Materials and Processes for Electronics.* New York: McGraw-Hill, 1969.

Markus, John. *Electronics and Nucleonics Dictionary.* 3rd ed. New York: McGraw-Hill, 1967.

Meacham, Stanley, and Donald Herrington. *Handbook of Electronic Tables and Formulas.* 4th ed. Indianapolis: Howard Sams, 1973.

Moore, C. K., and K. J. Spencer. *Electronics: A Bibliographical Guide.* New York: Plenum, 1965.

Morrill, Chester, Jr. *Computers and Data Processing Information Sources.* Detroit: Gale, 1969.

National Computing Centre Ltd. *International Computer Bibliography.* 2 vols. New York: International Publications Service, 1968-72.

Randle, Gretchen R., ed. *Electronic Industries Information Sources.* Detroit: Gale, 1968.

Shiers, George. *Bibliography of the History of Electronics.* Metuchen, N.J.: Scarecrow, 1972.

Journals

Electrical Engineer
Electrical News and Engineering
Electrical Review
Electrical World
Electronic Engineer
Electronic Engineering
Electronic News
Electronics
Electronics Abstracts Journal
Electronics World

ENGINEERING

Books

Anderson, J. C., et al. *Data and Formulae for Engineering Students.* 2nd ed. Elmsford, N.Y.: Pergamon, 1969.

Classed Subject Catalog of the Engineering Societies Library. 10th Supplement. Boston: G. K. Hall, 1974.

Engineering Index Annual. New York: Engineering Index Inc., annually.

Jones, Franklin D., and Paul B. Schubert. *Engineering Encyclopedia.* 3rd ed. New York: Industrial Press, 1963.

Malinowsky, R. H. *Science and Engineering Reference Sources.* Littleton, Colo.: Libraries Unlimited, 1967.

Oppermann, Alfred. *Dictionary of Modern Engineering.* 2 vols. 3rd ed. New York: International Publications Service, 1972-73.

Parke, Nathan G. *Guide to the Literature of Mathematics and Physics.* Rev. ed. New York: Dover, 1958.

Schenck, Hilbert. *Introduction to the Engineering Research Project.* New York: McGraw-Hill, 1969.

------------. *Theories of Engineering Experimentation.* 2nd ed. New York: McGraw-Hill, 1968.

Souders, Mott. *Engineer's Companion.* New York: Wiley, 1966.

Yakovlev, K. P., et al. *Handbook for Engineers.* 2 vols. Elmsford, N.Y.: Pergamon, 1965.

Journals

Engineer
Engineering
Engineering and Science
Engineering and Science Review
Engineering Designer
Engineering Digest
Engineering Forum
Engineering Index
Engineering Journal
Engineering Materials and Design
Engineering News
Engineering Review
International Journal of Engineering Science
Journal of Engineering Education
Professional Engineer (U.S.)

GEOLOGY

Books

Challinor, John. *A Dictionary of Geology.* New York: Oxford Univ. Press, 1974.

Corbin, John B. *Index of State Geological Survey Publications Issued in Series.* Metuchen, N.J.: Scarecrow, 1965.

Gary, Margaret, et al. *Glossary of Geology.* Boulder, Colo.: American Geological Society, 1972.

Siegrist, Marie, et al. *Bibliography and Index of Geology Exclusive of North America.* Boulder, Colo.: Geological Society of America, 1933-65.

U.S. Geological Survey Library. *Catalog of the U.S. Geological Survey Library.* Boston: G. K. Hall, 1964. Supplement.

Ward, Dederick, and Marjorie Wheeler. *Geologic Reference Sources: A Subject and Regional Bibliography to Publications and Maps in the Geological Sciences.* Metuchen, N.J.: Scarecrow, 1972.

Journals

American Journal of Science
Economic Geology
Geology Society Bulletin
Journal of Geology
Journal of Petroleum Technology
Mining Congress Journal
Mining Engineering
Petro/Chem Engineer
Petroleum Engineer International
Society of Petroleum Engineers Journal

MATHEMATICS

Books

Aaboe, Asger. *Episodes from the Early History of Mathematics.* New York: Random House, 1964.

American Mathematical Society. *Index to Translations Selected by the AMS.* Providence, R.I.: American Mathematical Society, 1966.

------------. *Mathematical Reviews Cumulative Indices.* Providence, R.I.: American Mathematical Society, 1966-date.

Baker, Cyril C. *Dictionary of Mathematics.* New York: Hart, 1970.

Bell, J. L., and A. B. Slomson. *Models and Ultraproducts.* Atlantic Highlands, N.J.: Humanities Press, 1969.

Carr, George S. *Formulas and Theorems in Pure Mathematics.* New York: Chelsea, 1970.

Dick, Elie M. *Current Information Sources in Mathematics: An Annotated Guide to Books and Periodicals, 1960-71.* Littleton, Conn.: Libraries Unlimited, 1973.

Eves, Howard. *Introduction to the History of Mathematics.* 3rd ed. New York: Holt, Rinehart, & Winston, 1969.

Fang, Joong. *Guide to the Literature of Mathematics Today.* Memphis: Paideia Press, 1972.

Fletcher, Alan, et al. *An Index of Mathematical Tables.* 2nd ed. 2 vols. Reading, Mass.: Addison-Wesley, 1962.

Herland, Leo. *Dictionary of Mathematical Sciences.* 2 vols. New York: Ungar, 1974.

International Catalogue of Scientific Literature 1901-1914. Section A: Mathematics. Metuchen, N.J.: Scarecrow, 1974.

International Dictionary of Applied Mathematics. New York: Reinhold, 1960.

Korn, G. A., and T. M. Korn. *Mathematical Handbook for Scientists and Engineers: Definitions, Theorems, and Formulas.* New York: McGraw-Hill, 1967.

Merritt, Frederick S. *Mathematics Manual.* New York: McGraw-Hill, 1962.

Millington, William, and T. Alaric Millington. *Dictionary of Mathematics.* New York: Barnes & Noble, 1971.

National Council of Teachers of Mathematics. *Cumulative Index: The Mathematics Teachers, 1908-1965.* Reston, Va.: NCTM, 1967.

National Council of Teachers of Mathematics Yearbook, New York: City College, Columbia Univ., 1926-date.

Parke, Nathan G. *Guide to the Literature of Mathematics and Physics.* Rev. ed. New York: Dover, 1958.

Pemberton, J. E. *How to Find Out in Mathematics.* 2nd ed. Elmsford, N.Y.: Pergamon, 1970.

Schaaf, William L. *The High School Mathematics Library.* Rev. ed. Reston, Va.: NCTM, 1970.

Sneddon, I. N. *Dictionary of Mathematics for Engineers.* Elmsford, N.Y.: Pergamon, 1974.

The Universal Encyclopedia of Mathematics. New York: Simon & Schuster, 1964.

Journals

ACTA Mathematica (ACTA Math.)

American Journal of Mathematics (Am. J. Math.)

American Mathematical Monthly (Am. Math. Monthly)

American Mathematical Society, Bulletin (Bull. Am. Math. Soc.)

American Mathematical Society, Proceedings (Proc. Am. Math. Soc.)

American Mathematical Society, Transactions (Trans. Am. Math. Soc.)

Annals of Mathematics (Ann. of Math.)

Arithmetic Teacher

Canadian Journal of Mathematics (Canad. J. Math.)

Canadian Mathematical Bulletin (Canad. Math. Bull.)

Duke Mathematics Journal (Duke Math. J.)

Duodecimal Bulletin (Duodecimal Bul.)

The Fibonacci Quarterly (Fibonacci Q.)

Journal of Algebra (J. Algebra)

Journal of Computer and Systems Sciences (J. Computer & Systems Sci.)

Journal of Mathematics and Physics (J. Math. & Phys.)

Journal of Research of the National Bureau of Standards (J. Res. Nat. Bur. Stand.)

Mathematical Reviews (Math. Reviews)

Mathematics Magazine (Math. Mag.)

Mathematics of Computation

Mathematics Teacher (Math Teacher)

Pacific Journal of Mathematics (Pacific J. Math.)

Philosophia Mathematica (Philos. Math.)

Proceedings of the Royal Society, Series A (Proc. Roy. Soc. Ser. A)

Quarterly Journal of Mathematics (Q. J. Math.)

Recreational Mathematics (Recreational Math.)

Scripta Mathematica

SIAM Review

SRA New Mathematics Extension Services

SRA New Mathematics for Today's Teachers (K-6)

Two-Year College Mathematics Journal

Updating Mathematics Services

PHOTOGRAPHY

Books

Abstracts of Photographic Science and Engineering Literature. New York: Columbia Univ. Department of Graphics in cooperation with the Society of Photographic Scientists and Engineers, 1962-date.

Backhouse, D., et al. *Illustrated Dictionary of Photography.* New York: International Publications Service, 1974.

Boni, Albert, *Photographic Literature.* 2 vols. New York: Morgan and Morgan, 1962-72.

Edkins, Diana. *Photography: An Information Guide.* Detroit: Gale, 1974.

Focal Encyclopedia of Photography. 2 vols. Garden City, N.Y.: American Photographic Book Pub., 1968.

Grau, Wolfgang. *Dictionary of Photography and Motion Picture Engineering and Related Topics.* New York: International Publications Service, 1968.

International Glossary of Photographic Terms. Garden City, N.Y.: American Photographic Book Pub., 1968.

Jones, Bernard E., ed. *Cassell's Cyclopaedia of Photography.* The Literature of Photography Series. 1911: rpt. New York: Arno Press, 1973.

Kirillou, N. I. *Problems in Photographic Research and Technology.* New York: Pitman, 1967.

Photographic Abstracts. London: Scientific and Technical Group of the Royal Photographic Society of Great Britain, 1921-61.

Stubbs, S. G. Glaxland, ed. *Modern Encyclopedia of Photography.* 2 vols. Boston: American Photographic Pub., 1938.

Journals

American Surveyor and Photogrammetrist
Aperture
British Journal of Photography
Image Technology
Industrial Photography
Infinity
Journal of Photographic Science
Leica Photography
Modern Photography
Photographic Journal
Photographic Science and Engineering
Photographic Society of America Journal
Popular Photography
Professional Photographer
Technical Photography
Visual

PHYSICS

Books

Annual Review of Nuclear Science. Palo Alto, Calif.: Annual Reviews, 1952-date.

Besancon, Robert M., ed. *Encyclopedia of Physics.* 2nd ed. New York: Reinhold, 1974.

Fluegge, E., ed. *Encyclopedia of Physics.* 54 vols. New York: Springer-Verlag, 1956-date.

Glazebrook, Richard T. *A Dictionary of Applied Physics.* 5 vols. New York: Macmillan, 1922-23.

> Largely replaced by *Encyclopaedic Dictionary of Physics,* ed. J. Thewlis (see below).

Isaacs, A., and H. J. Gray. *New Dictionary of Physics.* 2nd ed. New York: Longmans Green, 1974.

Mayer, Herbert. *Physik Duenner Schichten—Physics of Thin Films: Complete Bibliography.* 2 vols. New York: International Publications Service, 1972.

Michels, Walter C., et al. *International Dictionary of Physics and Electronics.* New York: Reinhold, 1956.

Parke, Nathan G. *Guide to the Literature of Mathematics and Physics.* Rev. ed. New York: Dover, 1958.

Solid State Physics Literature Guides. New York: Plenum, 1972-date.

Thewlis, J., ed. *Encyclopaedic Dictionary of Physics.* 9 vols. Elmsford, N.Y.: Pergamon, 1961-64.

United Nations Atomic Energy Commission Group. *An International Bibliography on Atomic Energy.* 2 vols. Lake Success, N.Y.: United Nations, 1949-51.

Whitford, Robert H. *Physics Literature.* 2nd ed. Metuchen, N.J.: Scarecrow, 1958.

Yates, B. *How to Find Out About Physics.* Elmsford, N.Y.: Pergamon, 1965.

Journals

Advances in Physics (Advances in Phys.)
American Institute of Physics Newsletter (AIP Newsletter)
American Journal of Physics (Am. J. Phys.)
Annals of Physics (Ann. of Phys.)
JETP Letters
Journal of Applied Physics (J. Appl. Phys.)
Journal of Chemical Physics (J. Chem. Phys.)
Journal of Physics (J. of Phys.)
Journal of Physics and Chemistry of Solids (J. of Phys. & Chem. Solids)
Nuclear Physics (Nuclear Phys.)
Physical Review Letters (Phys. Rev. Letters)
Proceedings of the Royal Society, London (Proc. Royal Soc., London)
Review of Modern Physics (Rev. Mod. Phys.)
Science Abstracts (Section A—Physics)

Art

Books

Adeline, Jules. *Adeline Art Dictionary.* New York: Ungar, 1966. Supplement.

American Federation of Arts. *American Art Directory.* New York: Bowker, 1952-date.

-----------. *Who's Who in American Art.* Washington, D.C. The American Federation of Arts, 1935-date.

The Art Index. New York: H. W. Wilson, 1929-date.

Art-Kunst: International Bibliography of Art Books. New York: International Publications Service, 1972.

Bell, David, ed. *Praeger Encyclopedia of Art.* 5 vols. New York: Praeger, 1971.

Besterman, Theodore. *Art and Architecture: Including Archaeology.* Besterman World Bibliographies Series. Totowa, N.J.: Littlefield, 1971.

Britannica Encyclopedia of American Art. New York: Simon & Schuster, 1973.

Chamberlin, Mary W. *Guide to Art Reference Books.* Chicago: American Library Association, 1959.

Columbia University. *Catalog of the Avery Memorial Architectural Library.* 19 vols. Boston: G. K. Hall, 1968.

Curry, Larry. *American West: From Catlin to Russell.* Los Angeles: Los Angeles County Museum of Art Bookshop, 1972.

Goldman, Bernard. *Reading and Writing in the Arts: A Handbook.* Detroit: Wayne State Univ. Press, 1972.

Encyclopedia of Art. 24 vols. New York: Greystone Press, n.d.

Encyclopedia of World Art. 15 vols. New York: McGraw-Hill, 1959-68.

Hammond, William A. *A Bibliography of Aesthetics and of the Philosophy of the Fine Arts from 1900 to 1932.* Rev. ed. New York: Longmans, Green, 1934.

Havlice, Patricia P. *Art in Time.* Metuchen, N.J.: Scarecrow, 1970.

The Index of Twentieth Century Artists. 4 vols. New York: College Art Association, 1933-37.

Lemke, Antje, and Ruth Fleiss. *Museum Companion: A Dictionary of Art Terms and Subjects.* New York: Hippocrene Books, 1973.

Lucas, E. Louise. *Art Books: A Basic Bibliography on the Fine Arts.* Greenwich, Conn.: New York Graphic Society, 1968.

Monro, Isabel S., and Kate M. Monro. *Index to Reproductions of American Paintings.* New York: H. W. Wilson, 1948. Supplement, 1964.

------------. *Index to Reproductions of European Paintings.* 3 vols. New York: H. W. Wilson, 1956.

Myers, Bernard S., and Shirley D. Myers, eds. *Dictionary of Art.* 5 vols. New York: McGraw-Hill, 1969.

Osborne, Harold, ed. *Oxford Companion to Art.* New York: Oxford Univ. Press, 1970.

Praeger Encyclopedia of Art. 5 vols. Chicago: Encyclopaedia Britannica, 1971.

Ryerson Library—Art Institute of Chicago. *Index to Art Periodicals.* 11 vols. Boston: G. K. Hall, n.d.

Smith, Ralph C. *A Biographical Index of American Artists.* Baltimore: Williams & Wilkins, 1930.

Sokol, David M. *American Art and Architecture: An Information Guide.* Detroit: Gale, n.d.

Sturgis, Russell. *Annotated Bibliography of Fine Art: Painting, Sculpture, Architecture, Arts of Decoration and Illustration.* Boston: American Library Association, 1897.

Journals

American Artist
Apollo
Art Bibliographies/Modern
Art Bulletin
Art Education
Art Forum
Art in America
Art International
Art Journal
Art News
Art Quarterly
Artist's Proof
Arts and Activities
Arts Magazine
Arts of Asia
Burlington Magazine
CA Magazine
Connoisseur
Craft Horizons
Design Quarterly
Eastern
Eighteenth-Century Studies
Horizon
Italix
Journal of Aesthetics and Art Criticism
Magazine of Art
Metropolitan Museum of Art

Print
School Arts Magazine
Studies in Art Education
Studio

Biological Sciences

Books

Altman, Philip L., and D. S. Sittmer, eds. *Biology Data Book.* Washington, D.C.: Federation of American Societies for Experimental Biology, 1964.

Besterman, Theodore. *Biological Sciences.* Besterman World Bibliographies Series. Totowa, N.J.: Littlefield, 1971.

Biological Abstracts. Philadelphia: Biological Abstracts, 1926-date.

Biological and Agricultural Index. New York: H. W. Wilson, 1964-date.

Blackwelder, Richard E. *Guide to the Taxonomic Literature of Vertebrates.* Ames: Iowa State Univ. Press, 1972.

Blake, Sidney F. *Geographical Guide to Floras of the World: An Annotated List With Special Reference to Useful Plants and Common Plant Names.* Washington, D.C.: GPO, 1942-61.

Blanchard, Joy Richard, and Harald Ostvold. *Literature of Agricultural Research.* Berkeley: Univ. of California Press, 1958.

Bottle, R. T., and Wyatt, H. V. *Use of Biological Literature.* 2nd ed. Hamden, Conn.: Shoe String, 1971.

Carter, John L., and Ruth C. Carter. *Bibliography and Index of North American Carboniferous Brachiopods 1898-1968.* Boulder, Colo.: Geological Society, 1970.

Cattell, Jacques. *American Men of Science: A Biographical Directory.* 10th ed. 5 vols. Tempe, Ariz.: Jacques Cattell Press, Arizona State Univ., 1960-62.

Cowgill, R. W., and A. B. Pardee. *Experiments in Biochemical Research Technique.* New York: Wiley, 1957.

Fernald, M. L. *Gray's Manual of Botany.* 8th ed. New York: American Book, 1950.

Gray, Peter, ed. *Encyclopedia of the Biological Sciences.* 2nd ed. New York: Reinhold, 1970.

------------. *Student Dictionary of Biology.* New York: Reinhold, 1973.

Henderson, Isabella F., and W. D. Henderson. *A Dictionary of Biological Terms.* 8th ed. New York: Reinhold, 1963.

International Catalogue of Scientific Literature 1901-1914. Metuchen, N.J.: Scarecrow, n.d.

Jacobs, Morris B., et al. *Dictionary of Microbiology.* New York: Reinhold, 1957.

Jenkins, Frances B. *Science Reference Sources.* 4th ed. Champaign, Ill.: Illini Union Bookstore, 1965.

Smith, R. C. *Guide to the Literature of the Zoological Sciences.* 6th ed. Minneapolis: Burgess, 1962.

Solbrig, O., and W. J. Gadella. *Contributions to a Biosystematic Literature Index.* New York: Hafner, 1970.

Swift, Lloyd H. *Botanical Bibliographies: A Guide to Bibliographic Materials Applicable to Botany.* Minneapolis: Burgess, 1970.

Tarpley, W. A. *A Glossary of Ecological and Environmental Biology.* New York: Hafner, 1973.

Van Nostrand's Scientific Encyclopedia. 4th ed. New York: Reinhold, 1968.

Willis, J. C. *A Dictionary of the Flowering Plants and Ferns.* 6th ed. New York: Cambridge Univ. Press, 1931.

Journals

Advancement of Science

Advances in Botanical Research (Advances Botan. Res.)

Advancing Frontiers of Plant Sciences

American Journal of Anatomy (Am. J. Anat.)

American Journal of Botany (Am. J. Botany)

American Journal of Physiology (Am. J. Physiol.)

American Scientist (Am. Scientist)

Animal Behavior

Annales de l'Institut Pasteur

Annals and Magazine of Natural History (Ann. & Mag. Nat. Hist.)

Annals of Botany (Ann. Botany)

Annals of the Missouri Botanical Garden (Ann. Mo. Botan. Garden)

Applied Microbiology (Appl. Microbiol.)

Archiv für Hydrobiologie

Archives of Biochemistry and Biophysics (Arch. Biochem. & Biophys.)

Audubon Field Notes

Audubon Magazine

Bacteriological Reviews (Bacteriol. Rev.)

Biochemical and Biophysical Research Commission (Biochem. & Biophys. Research Comm.)

Biochemistry (Biochem.)

Biochemistry Journal (Biochem. J.)

Biochimica et Biophysica Acta

Bioscience

Botanical Review (Botan. Rev.)

Bulletin of Aquatic Biology (Bull. Aquatic Biol.)

Bulletin of Experimental Biology and Medicine (Bull. Exptl. Biol. & Med.)

Bulletin of the Atomic Scientists (Bull. Atomic Scientists)

Canadian Journal of Botany (Canadian J. Botany)

Canadian Journal of Microbiology (Canadian J. Microbiol.)

Current Contents

DOKLADY—Biochemistry section

DOKLADY—Biological Sciences section

DOKLADY—Botanical Sciences section

Ecology

Evolution

Experimental Cell Research (Exptl. Cell Research)

Federation Proceedings (Federation Proc.)

General Science Quarterly (Gen. Sci. Quart.)

Genetics

Geological Society of America—Bulletin (Geol. Soc. Am. Bull.)

Geophysical Abstracts (Geophys. Abstr.)

Heredity

Herpetologica

Human Genetics

Hydrobiologica

International Abstracts of Biological Sciences (Intern. Abstr. Biol. Sci.)

International Bureau for Plant Taxonomy (Intern. Bur. Plant. Taxonomy)

Journal of Animal Behavior (J. Animal Behavior)

Journal of Animal Ecology (J. Animal Ecology)

Journal of Bacteriology (J. Bacteriol.)

Journal of Biological Chemistry (J. Biol. Chem.)

Journal of Cellular and Comparative Physiology (J. Cellular & Comp. Physiol.)

Journal of Clinical Investigation (J. Clin. Invest.)

Journal of Ecology (J. Ecol.)

Journal of Experimental Biology (J. Exptl. Biol.)

Journal of Experimental Medicine (J. Exptl. Med.)

Journal of Experimental Zoology (J. Exptl. Zool.)

Journal of General Microbiology (J. Gen. Microbiol.)

Journal of Geology (J. Geol.)

Journal of Immunology (J. Immunol.)

Journal of Lipid Research (J. Lipid Research)

Journal of Mammology (J. Mammol.)
Journal of Molecular Biology (J. Molecular Biol.)
Journal of Paleontology (J. Paleontol.)
Journal of Physiology (J. Physiol.)
Journal of Protozoology (J. Protozool.)
Journal of Wildlife Management (J. Wildl. Mgmt.)
Linnean Society of London Journal (Linnean Soc. London J.)
Mutation Research
National Academy of Sciences—Proceedings (Proc. Nat. Acad. Sci.)
National Wildlife (Nat. Wildl.)
Naturalist
Nature
New York Academy of Sciences, Annals of (Ann. NY Acad. Sci.)
Palaeobotanist
Philosophy of Science
Physiological Reviews (Physiol. Rev.)
Physiological Zoology (Physiol. Zool.)
Plant Physiology (Plant Physiol.)
Plant World
Proceedings of the National Academy of Science (Proc. Nat. Acad. Sci.)
Radiation Research (Radiation Res.)
Review of Applied Mycology (Rev. Appl. Mycology)
Science
Science Education (Sci. Ed.)
Scientific American (Sci. Am.)
Scientific American Monthly (Sci. Am. Monthly)
Scientific Monthly (Sci. Monthly)
Soil Conservation (Soil Conserv.)
Stain Technology
Zeitschrift für Zellforschung und mickroskopische Anatomie

Business

Books

Accountant's Index. New York: American Institute of Accountants, 1921-date.
Alexander, Raphael, ed. Business Pamphlets and Information Sources. New York: Exceptional, 1967.
Brown, Stanley M., ed. Business Executive's Handbook. Rev. Lillian Doris. 4th ed. New York: Prentice-Hall, 1953.
Business Books in Print 1975. New York: Bowker, 1975.
Business Periodicals Index. New York: H. W. Wilson, 1958-date.

Clark, Donald T., and Bert A. Gottfried. University Dictionary of Business and Finance. New York: Apollo, 1974.
Coman, Edwin T., Jr. Sources of Business Information. Rev. ed. Berkeley: Univ. of California Press, 1964.
Georgi, Charlotte. Literature of Executive Management: Selected Books and Reference Sources for the International Businessman. New York: Special Libraries Association, 1963.
Harvard University Graduate School of Business Administration. A Classification of Business Literature. Rev. ed. Hamden, Conn.: Shoe String Press, 1960.
Heyer, Carl, ed. The Encyclopedia of Management. 2nd ed. New York: Reinhold, 1973.
Lazarus, Harold. American Business Dictionary. New York: Philosophical Library, 1957.
Lovett, Robert W., ed. American Economics and Business History: Information Sources. Detroit: Gale, 1971.
Munn, Glenn G. Encyclopedia of Banking and Finance. Ed. Ferdinand L. Garcia. 7th ed. Boston: Bankers, 1973.
Nemmers, Erwin E., ed. Dictionary of Economics and Business. 3rd ed. Totowa, N.J.: Littlefield, 1974.
Williams, Robert I., and Lillian Doris, eds. Encyclopedia of Accounting Systems. 5 vols. Englewood Cliffs, N.J.: Prentice-Hall, 1956-57.
Wixon, Rufus, et al., ed. Accountants' Handbook. 5th ed. New York: Ronald Press, 1970.

Journals

Accountants' Digest
Accounting Research
Accounting Review
Advertising Age
American Economic Review
Appraisal Journal
Barron's National Business and Financial Weekly
Best's Review (Life/Health Insurance Edition)
Best's Review (Property/Liability Insurance Edition)
Better Living
Business Horizons
Business Week
Changing Times
Consumers' Research Bulletin
CPA Journal

Dun's Review and Modern Industry
Economic Indicators
Employment Security Review
Factory Management and Maintenance
Federal Reserve Bulletin
Federal Tax Articles
Federal Tax Guide
Financial Executive
Forbes
Fortune
Harvard Business Review
Human Engineering
Journal of Accountancy
Journal of Accounting Research
Journal of Finance
Journal of Insurance Information
Journal of Marketing
Journal of Retailing
Kiplinger Washington Letter
Labor Market and Employment Security
Lloyd's Bank Review
Magazine of Wall Street and Business Analyst
Management Accounting
Management News
Management Review
Monthly Review
Moody's Banks and Finance
Moody's Handbook of Widely Held Common Stocks
Moody's Industrials
Moody's Magazine
National Tax Journal
Nation's Business
Office Executive
Operations Research
Over-the-Counter Securities Review
Personnel Administration
Personnel and Guidance Journal
Personnel Psychology
Sales Management
Social Security Bulletin
Standard and Poor's Corporation Records
Supervisory Management
Survey of Current Business
Systems
Tax Executive
Value Line
Wall Street Journal

Education

Books

Camp, William L. *Guide to Periodicals in Education.* Metuchen, N.J.: Scarecrow, 1968.

Current Index to Journals in Education. New York: Macmillan, 1969-date.
Dewey, John. *Dictionary of Education.* Ed. Ralph B. Winn. 1859; rpt. Westport, Conn.: Greenwood, 1972.
Digest of Educational Statistics. Washington, D.C.: GPO, 1962-date.
Ebel, R. L. *Encyclopedia of Educational Research.* 4th ed. New York: Macmillan, 1969.
Education Abstracts. Fulton, Mo.: Education Clearing House, 1936-date.
Education Index. New York: H. W. Wilson, 1929-date.
Educational Media Index. New York: McGraw-Hill, 1964. Supplements.
Educational Resources Information Center. *Current Index to Journals in Education.* New York: Macmillan, 1969-date.
------------. *Early Childhood Education: An ERIC Bibliography.* New York: Macmillan, 1973.
------------. *Educational Documents Abstracts.* New York: Macmillan, 1968-date.
------------. *Educational Documents Index.* New York: Macmillan, 1966-date.
------------. *Educational Finance: An ERIC Bibliography.* New York: Macmillan, 1972.
Educational Technology Reviews. 12 vols. Englewood Cliffs, N.J.: Educational Technology Pub., 1973.
Encyclopedia of Education. New York: Macmillan, 1971.
Good, Carter V., ed. *Dictionary of Education.* 3rd ed. New York: McGraw-Hill, 1973.
Monroe, Paul, ed. *A Cyclopedia of Education.* 5 vols. 1911; rpt. Detroit: Gale, 1968.
Monroe, Walter S., and Louis Shores. *Bibliographies and Summaries in Education to July 1935.* New York: H. W. Wilson, 1936.
Powell, John P. *Philosophy of Education: A Select Bibliography.* 2nd ed. New York: Humanities Press, 1971.
Richmond, W. Kenneth. *The Literature of Education: A Critical Bibliography, 1945-1970.* New York: Methuen, 1972.
UNESCO. *International Yearbook of Education.* Paris: UNESCO, 1948-date.
------------. *World Survey of Education.* 4 vols. Paris: UNESCO, 1955-66.
U.S. Office of Education. *Biennial Survey of Education in the United States.* Washington, D.C.: GPO, 1921-62.
  Continued by *Digest of Educational Statistics,* 1962-date.

Who's Who in American Education. New York: Who's Who in American Education, 1928-date.

World Year Book of Education. London: Evans, 1932-date. Sometimes titled Yearbook of Education.

Journals

American Educational Research Journal

American School Board Journal

Bulletin of the National Association of Secondary School Principals

California Journal of Educational Research

Childhood Education

Educational Leadership

Elementary School Journal

Elementary School Teacher

Harvard Educational Review

Journal of Education

Journal of Educational Research

Journal of Experimental Education

Journal of Higher Education

Journal of Negro Education

Journal of Secondary Education

Journal of Teacher Education

Junior College Journal

National Elementary Principal

NEA Research Division Reports

Phi Delta Kappan

Review of Educational Research

School Executive

School Life

School Management

Teachers College Record

Theory into Practice

Today's Education

English Language and Literature

GENERAL

Books

Altick, Richard D., and Andrew Wright. Selective Bibliography for the Study of English and American Literature. 4th ed. New York: Macmillan, 1971.

Baldensperger, Fernand, and Werner P. Friederich. Bibliography of Comparative Literature. 3rd ed. 1950; rpt. New York: Russell and Russell, 1960.

Bibliographical Dictionary of Modern Literature. New York: H. W. Wilson, 1942. Supplement, 1955.

Bond, Donald F. A Reference Guide to English Studies. 2nd ed. Chicago: Univ. of Chicago Press, 1971.

Holman, C. Hugh. Handbook to Literature. 3rd ed. Indianapolis: Odyssey Press, 1972.

Kennedy, Arthur G., and Donald B. Sands. A Concise Bibliography for Students of English. Rev. William E. Colburn. Stanford: Stanford Univ. Press, 1972.

Magill, Frank N., ed. Masterplots. 6 vols. New York: Salem Press, 1960. Annual Review.

Modern Language Association of America. MLA International Bibliography of Books and Articles on the Modern Languages and Literature. New York: MLA, 1921-date.

Moulton, Charles Wells. Library of Literary Criticism of English and American Authors. 8 vols. 1901-05; rpt. New York: Peter Smith, 1935-40.

AMERICAN LITERATURE

Books

Blanck, Jacob, comp. Bibliography of American Literature. 6 vols. New Haven: Yale Univ. Press, 1955-73. (In progress)

Cambridge History of American Literature. 4 vols. New York: Putnam, 1917-21.

Clark, Harry Hayden. American Literature: Poe Through Garland. New York: Meredith, 1971.

Davis, Richard Beale. American Literature Through Bryant. New York: Meredith, 1969.

Evans, Charles. American Bibliography. 13 vols. Metuchen, N.J.: Scarecrow, 1967.

Gohdes, Clarence. Bibliographical Guide to the Study of Literature of the U.S. 3rd ed. Durham, N.C.: Duke Univ. Press, 1970.

Hart, James D. The Oxford Companion to American Literature. 4th ed. New York: Oxford Univ. Press, 1965.

Havlice, Patricia Pate. Index to American Author Bibliographies. Metuchen, N.J.: Scarecrow, 1971.

Jones, Howard Mumford, and Richard M. Ludwig. Guide to American Literature and Its Backgrounds Since 1890. 4th ed. Cambridge, Mass.: Harvard Univ. Press, 1972.

Kunitz, Stanley J., and Howard Haycraft, eds. American Authors, 1600-1900. New York: H. W. Wilson, 1938.

Leary, Lewis. *Articles on American Literature, 1900-1950*. Durham, N.C.: Duke Univ. Press, 1954.

------------. *Articles on American Literature, 1950-1967*. Durham, N.C.: Duke Univ. Press, 1970.

Nilon, Charles H. *Bibliography of Bibliographies in American Literature*. New York: Bowker, 1970.

Nyren, Dorothy, ed. *Modern American Literature*. 3rd ed. New York: Ungar, 1964.

Richards, Robert F., ed. *Concise Dictionary of American Literature*. New York: Philosophical Library, 1955.

Spiller, Robert E., et al. *Literary History of the United States*. 4th ed. 3 vols. New York: Macmillan, 1974.

Tate, Allen. *Sixty American Poets*. Folcroft, Pa.: Folcroft Library Editions, 1945.

BLACK LITERATURE

Books

Black African Literature in English Since 1952: Works and Criticism. New York: Johnson Reprint Corp., 1967.

Black List: The Concise Reference Guide to Publications, Films, and Broadcasting Media of Black America, Africa, and the Caribbean. Rev. ed. New York: Panther House, 1974.

Davis, Arthur. *From the Dark Tower: Afro-American Writers from 1900 to 1960*. Washington, D.C.: Howard Univ. Press, 1974.

Deodene, Frank, and William P. French. *Black American Fiction Since 1952: A Preliminary Checklist*. Chatham, N.Y.: Chatham Bookseller, 1970.

Hallie Q. Brown Memorial Library. *Index to Periodical Articles by and About Negroes*. Boston: G. K. Hall, 1971.

Hatch, James V. *Black Image on the American Stage: A Bibliography of Plays and Musicals 1770-1970*. New York: Drama Book Specialists, 1970.

Hughes, Langston, and Arna Bontemps, eds. *Poetry of the Negro, 1746-1970*. New York: Doubleday, 1970.

Irwin, Leonard B. *Black Studies*. Brooklawn, N.J.: McKinley Pub., 1973.

Mitchell, Loften. *Voices of the Black Theatre*. New York: T. J. White, 1974.

Office of Adult Services. *No Crystal Stair: A Bibliography of Black Literature*. New York: New York Public Library, 1971.

Spalding, Henry D. *Encyclopedia of Black Folklore and Humor*. Middle Village, N.Y.: Jonathan David, 1972.

Turner, Darwin T. *Afro-American Writers*. New York: Meredith, 1970.

Welsch, Erwin K. *Negro in the United States: A Research Guide*. Bloomington: Indiana Univ. Press, 1965.

Whitlow, Roger. *Black American Literature: A Critical History of the Major Periods, Movements, Themes, Works, and Authors*. Chicago: Nelson-Hall, 1973.

Work, Monroe Nathan. *A Bibliography of the Negro in Africa and America*. New York: Argosy-Antiquarian, 1965.

Journals

Bibliographic Survey: The Negro in Print
Black Scholar
Black World
Crisis
Ebony
Journal of African Studies
Journal of Black Studies
Journal of Negro History
Negro Heritage
Negro History Bulletin

BRITISH LITERATURE

Books

Arnold, James F., and J. W. Robinson. *English Theatrical Literature 1559-1900: A Bibliography Incorporating Lowe's Bibliographical Account*. New York: British Book Center, 1971.

Baker, Ernest A. *History of the English Novel*. 11 vols. New York: Barnes & Noble, 1924-67.

Baugh, Albert C. *A Literary History of England*. 2nd ed. New York: Appleton, 1967.

Cambridge Bibliography of English Literature. 5 vols. New York: Cambridge Univ. Press, 1940.

Cambridge History of English Literature. 15 vols. New York: Putnam, 1907-33.

Courthope, William J. *A History of English Poetry*. 6 vols. New York: Macmillan, 1895-1910.

Dick, Aliki. *A Student's Guide to British Literature*. Littleton, Colo.: Libraries Unlimited, 1972.

Downs, Robert B. *British Literary Resources: A Bibliographical Guide*. Chicago: American Library Assn., 1973.

Harvey, Paul, comp. and ed. *The Oxford Companion to English Literature.* Rev. by Dorothy Eagle. 4th ed. New York: Oxford Univ. Press, 1967.

Howard-Hill, T. H. *Bibliography of British Literary Bibliographies.* Oxford: Clarendon Press, 1969.

Kunitz, Stanley J., and Howard Haycraft. *British Authors Before 1800: A Biographical Dictionary.* New York: H. W. Wilson, 1952.

------------. *British Authors of the Nineteenth Century.* New York: H. W. Wilson, 1936.

Mellown, Elgin W. *A Descriptive Catalogue of the Bibliographies of Twentieth Century British Writers.* Troy, N.Y.: Whitston, 1972.

Northup, Clark S. *A Register of Bibliographies of the English Language and Literature.* New York: Hafner, 1962.

Ray, Gordon N. *Bibliographical Resources for the Study of Nineteenth Century English Fiction.* Folcroft, Pa.: Folcroft Library Editions, 1964.

Temple, Ruth, and Martin Tucker, eds. *Twentieth Century British Literature.* New York: Ungar, 1966.

Watson, George. *Cambridge Bibliography of English Literature.* 2nd ed. New York: Cambridge Univ. Press, 1965.

Wilson, Percy, and Bonamy Dobree. *The Oxford History of English Literature.* New York: Oxford Univ. Press, 1945-date. (In progress)

Years Work in English Studies. New York: Humanities, annually.

DRAMA

Books

Adelman, Irving, and Rita Dworkin. *Modern Drama: A Checklist of Critical Literature on Twentieth Century Plays.* Metuchen, N.J.: Scarecrow, 1967.

Anderson, Michael, et al. *Crowell's Handbook of Contemporary Drama.* New York: Crowell, 1971.

Baker, Blanch M. *Dramatic Bibliography.* New York: H. W. Wilson, 1933.

------------. *Theatre and Allied Arts: A Guide to Books Dealing With the History, Criticism, and Technic of the Drama and Theatre, and Related Arts and Crafts.* New York: H. W. Wilson, 1952.

Breed, Paul F., and Florence M. Sniderman. *Dramatic Criticism Index.* Detroit: Gale, 1972.

Brockett, Oscar Gross. *A Bibliographical Guide to Research and Dramatic Art.* Glenview, Ill.: Scott, Foresman, 1963.

Chicorel, Marietta, ed. *Chicorel Theater Index to Plays in Periodicals.* New York: Chicorel Library, 1974.

Coleman, Arthur, and Gary R. Tyler. *Drama Criticism.* 2 vols. Denver: Swallow, 1966-71.

Cumulated Dramatic Index. 2 vols. Westwood, Mass.: Faxon, 1950.

Matlaw, Myron. *Modern World Drama: An Encyclopedia.* New York: Dutton, 1972.

Palmer, Helen H., and Anne Jane Dyson. *American Drama Criticism.* Hamden, Conn.: Shoe String, 1967. Supplement, 1970.

------------. *European Drama Criticism.* Hamden, Conn.: Shoe String, 1968. Supplements, 1970 and 1974.

Play Index. New York: H. W. Wilson, 1949-date.

Stratman, Carl Joseph, ed. *Bibliography of American Theatre.* Chicago: Loyola Univ. Press, 1965.

LANGUAGE

Books

Bailey, Richard W., and Dolores M. Burton. *English Stylistics: A Bibliography.* Cambridge, Mass.: The M.I.T. Press, 1968.

Bond, Donald F. *Reference Guide to English Studies.* 2nd ed. Chicago: Univ. of Chicago Press, 1971.

Brenni, Vito J. *American English: A Bibliography.* Philadelphia: Univ. of Pennsylvania Press, 1964.

Craigie, William, and James R. Hulbert. *A Dictionary of American English on Historical Principles.* 4 vols. Chicago: Univ. of Chicago Press, 1936-44.

Kennedy, Arthur G., and Donald B. Sands. *A Concise Bibliography for Students of English.* 5th ed. Stanford: Stanford Univ. Press, 1972.

Modern Humanities Research Association. *Annual Bibliography of English Language and Literature.* New York: Cambridge Univ. Press: 1921-date.

Murray, J. A. *Oxford English Dictionary.* 13 vols. Oxford: Clarendon Press, 1933.

MYTH AND FOLKLORE

Books

Diehl, Katherine S. *Religion Mythologies, Folklores: An Annotated Bibliography.* 2nd ed. Metuchen, N.J.: Scarecrow, 1962.

Eastman, Mary Huse. *Index to Fairy Tales, Myths, and Legends.* 2nd ed. Westwood, Mass.: Faxon, 1926. Supplements 1937, 1952.

Haywood, Charles. *A Bibliography of North American Folklore and Folksong.* 2nd ed. 2 vols. New York: Dover, 1961.

Ireland, Norma O. *Index to Fairy Tales, 1949-1972; Including Folklore, Legends, and Myths in Collections.* Westwood, Mass.: Faxon, 1973.

Larousse Encyclopedia of Mythology. New York: Prometheus Press, 1959.

MacCulloch, John A., et al., eds. *Mythology of All Races.* 13 vols. Boston: Archaeological Institute of America, 1916-32.

Thompson, Stith. *Motif Index of Folk Literature: A Classification of Narrative Elements in Folktales, Ballads, Myths, Fables, Mediaeval Romances. . . .* Rev. and enl. ed. 6 vols. Bloomington: Indiana Univ. Press, 1955-58.

NOVEL

Books

Adelman, Irving, and Rita Dworkin. *The Contemporary Novel: A Checklist of Critical Literature on the British and American Novel Since 1945.* Metuchen, N.J.: Scarecrow, 1972.

Bell, Inglis F., and Donald Baird. *The English Novel, 1578-1956: A Checklist of Twentieth-Century Criticisms.* Denver: Swallow, 1959.

Bufkin, Ernest C. *Twentieth-Century Novel in English: A Checklist.* Athens: Univ. of Georgia Press, 1967.

Drescher, Horst W., and Bernd Kahrmann. *The Contemporary English Novel: An Annotated Bibliography of Secondary Sources.* New York: International Publications Service, 1973.

Gerstenberger, Donna, and George Hendrick. *The American Novel 1789-1959: A Checklist of Twentieth-Century Criticism.* Denver: Swallow, 1961.

Holman, C. Hugh, ed. *American Novel Through Henry James.* Northbrook, Ill.: AHM, 1966.

Kearney, E. I., and L. S. Fitzgerald. *The Continental Novel: A Checklist of Criticism in English, 1900-1966.* Metuchen, N.J.: Scarecrow, 1968.

Nevius, Blake. *American Novel: Sinclair Lewis to the Present.* Northbrook, Ill.: AHM, 1970.

Palmer, Helen, and Jane Dyson. *English Novel Explication: Criticisms to 1972.* Hamden, Conn.: Shoe String, 1973.

Watt, Ian. *British Novel: Scott Through Hardy.* Northbrook, Ill.: AHM, 1973.

Wiley, Paul L. *British Novel: Conrad to the Present.* Northbrook, Ill.: AHM, 1973.

Woodress, James. *American Fiction 1900-50: A Guide to Information Sources.* Detroit: Gale, 1974.

Wright, Lyle H. *American Fiction: A Contribution Towards a Bibliography.* 3 vols. San Marino, Calif.: Huntington Library, 1957-69.

POETRY

Books

Arms, George, and Joseph M. Kuntz. *Poetry Explication: A Checklist of Interpretations Since 1925 of British and American Poems Past and Present.* Denver: Swallow, 1962.

Bruncken, Herbert. *Subject Index to Poetry.* Chicago: American Library Assn., 1940.

English Poetry: Select Bibliographical Guides. Ed. A. E. Dyson. New York: Oxford Univ. Press, 1971.

Sell, Violet, et al. *Subject Index to Poetry for Children and Young People.* Chicago: American Library Association, 1957.

Smith, William J., ed. *Granger's Index to Poetry.* 6th ed. New York: Columbia Univ. Press, 1962.

SHORT STORY

Books

Cook, Dorothy E., and Isabel S. Monro. *Short Story Index.* New York: H. W. Wilson, 1953. Supplements.

Thurston, Jarvis, O. B. Emerson, Carl Hartman, and Elizabeth V. Wright. *Short Fiction Criticism: A Checklist of Interpretations Since 1925 of Stories and Novelettes (American, British, Continental) 1800-1958.* Denver: Swallow, 1960.

Walker, Warren S. *Twentieth-Century Short Story Explication: Interpretations, 1900-1966.* Hamden, Conn.: Shoe String, 1968. Supplement for years 1967-69.

WORLD LITERATURE

Books

Adelman, Irving, and Rita Dworkin. *The Contemporary Novel: A Checklist of Critical Literature on the British and American Novel Since 1945.* Metuchen, N.J.: Scarecrow, 1972.

Buchanan-Brown, John, ed. *Cassell's Encyclopedia of World Literature.* New rev. ed. New York: Morrow, 1973.

Harvey, Paul, and J. E. Heseltine. *The Oxford Companion to Classical Literature.* Oxford: Clarendon Press, 1937.

------------. *The Oxford Companion to French Literature.* Oxford: Clarendon Press, 1959.

Hornstein, Lillian H., ed. *Reader's Companion to World Literature.* Rev. ed. New York: New American Library, 1973.

Morgan, Bayard Q. *A Critical Bibliography of German Literature in English Translation, 1481-1927.* 2nd ed. Metuchen, N.J.: Scarecrow, 1965.

Smith, Horatio, ed. *Columbia Dictionary of Modern European Literature.* New York: Columbia Univ. Press, 1947.

Stipley, Joseph T., ed. *Dictionary of World Literature.* New rev. ed. New York: Philosophical Library, 1953.

Journals

Abstracts of English Studies
American Journal of Philology
American Literature
American Notes & Queries
American Quarterly
American Scholar
American Speech
College Composition and Communication
College English
Comparative Literature
ELH (ELH is the title)
English Language Notes
English Studies
Explicator
Journal of English and Germanic Philology
Modern Drama
Modern Fiction Studies
Modern Language Abstracts
Modern Language Forum
Modern Language Journal
Modern Language Notes
Modern Language Quarterly
Modern Language Review
Modern Philology
New England Quarterly
Nineteenth Century Fiction

Philological Quarterly
PMLA (PMLA is the title)
Renaissance News
Review of English Studies
Romance Philology
Shakespeare Quarterly
Studies in Philology
Victorian Studies

Foreign Languages

GENERAL

Books

Birkmaier, Emma M., and Dale L. Lange. *Selective Bibliography on the Teaching of Foreign Languages, 1920-1966.* New York: Modern Language Assn., 1967.

MLA International Bibliography. New York: Modern Language Assn., 1921-date.

Modern Humanities Research Association. *Year's Work in Modern Language Studies.* New York: Oxford Univ. Press, 1931-date.

Nostrand, Howard L., et al. *Research on Language Teaching: An Annotated International Bibliography, 1945-64.* Rev. ed. Seattle: Univ. of Washington Press, 1965.

Journals

Books Abroad
Modern Language Quarterly
Modern Philology
Philological Quarterly
PMLA
Romance Notes
Romance Philology
Studies in Philology
Symposium
Modern Language Review

FRENCH

Books

Barre, André. *Le Symbolisme: Bibliographie de la poésie symboliste.* 1911; rpt. New York: Burt Franklin, 1968.

Bloch, Oscar, and W. Wartburg. *Dictionnaire étymologique de la langue française.* New York: French & European Publ., 1968.

Bourin, André, and J. Rousselot. *Dictionnaire de la littérature française contemporaine.* Paris: Larousse, n.d.

Cabeen, David Clark. *A Critical Bibliography of French Literature.* 4 vols. Syracuse: Syracuse Univ. Press, 1947.

Cassell's New French Dictionary. New York: Funk & Wagnalls, 1967.

Cioranescu, Alexandre. *Bibliographie de la littérature française du dix-huitième siècle.* Paris: National Center of Scientific Research, 1969.

Dauzat, A., et al. *Nouveau Dictionnaire étymologique.* Paris: Larousse, 1971.

Dictionnaire biographique des artistes contemporains. 3 vols. and supplements. New York: Somerset, 1930-34.

Dictionnaire biographique français contemporain. Paris: Grasset, 1960.

Dictionnaire du français contemporain. Paris: Larousse, 1967.

Dubois, Marguerite, and Marie Dubois. *Dictionnaire de locutions français-anglais: Dictionary of Idioms French-English.* Paris: Larousse, 1973.

Dulong, Gaston. *Bibliographie linguistique du Canada français.* Portland: International Scholarly Book Service, 1966.

Encyclopédie française. 22 vols. Elmsford, N.Y.: Maxwell Scientific International, n.d.

Golden, H. H., and S. O. Simches. *Modern French Literature and Language.* Millwood, N.Y.: Kraus Reprint, 1953.

Grand Larousse encyclopédique. 10 vols. Paris: Librairie Larousse: 1960-64.

Harvey, Paul, and Janet E. Heseltine. *Oxford Companion to French Literature.* Oxford: Clarendon Press, 1959.

Johnson, H. H. *A Short Introduction to the Study of French Literature.* Folcroft, Pa.: Folcroft, 1973.

Kettridge, Julius O. *Dictionary of Technical Terms* (Fr.-Eng., Eng.-Fr.). New York: French & European Publ., n.d.

Klapp, Otto. *Bibliographie der Französischen Literatur, 1956-62.* Frankfurt: Klostermann, 1967-69.

La Grande Encyclopédie. Paris: Larousse, n.d.

Lanson, Gustave. *Manuel bibliographique de la littérature française moderne.* Paris: Hachette, 1920. Supplement, 1935, 1945.

Larousse classique. Paris: Larousse, 1967.

Littré, Emile. *Dictionnaire de la langue française.* Paris: Hachette, 1959.

Malcles, M. *Les Sources du travail bibliographique.* 3 vols. New York: French & European Publ., n.d.

Mankin, Paul, and Alex Szogyi. *Anthologie d'humour français.* Glenview, Ill.: Scott, Foresman, 1971.

Mansion, J. E. *Heath's Standard French and English Dictionary.* 3rd ed. Boston: Heath, 1966.

Marks, Joseph, et al., eds. *New French-English Dictionary of Slang and Colloquialisms.* New York: Dutton, 1971.

Rancœur, René. *Bibliographie de la littérature française du moyen age à nos jours.* Paris: Librarie Armand Colin, 1966-date.

Robert, Paul. *Dictionnaire alphabétique et analogique de la langue française.* 7 vols. New York: French & European Publ., n.d.

Sutherland, D. M., and C. B. Osburn. *Research and Reference Guide to French Studies.* Metuchen, N.J.: Scarecrow, 1968.

Thieme, Hugo R. *Bibliographie de la littérature française de 1800 à 1930.* 2 vols. Geneva: Slatkine, 1933.

Journals

L'Express
French News
French Notes and Queries
French Review
French Studies
Hommes et Mondes
Information Littéraire
Mercure de France
Le Monde (newspaper)
Le Moyen Age
Neophilologus
Nouvelle Revue Française
Les Nouvelles Littéraires (newspaper)
Réalités
Revue des Deux Mondes
Revue d'Esthétique
Revue d'Histoire Littéraire
Revue de Littérature Comparée
Revue de Paris
Revue des Sciences Humaines
Romania
Studi Francesi
Les Temps Modernes
Yale French Studies

GERMAN

Books

Albrecht, Gunter, and Gunther Dahlke, eds. *International Bibliography of the History of German Literature: Index.* New York: International Publications Service, 1969-72.

Allgemeine Deutsche Biographie. 56 vols. Leipzig: Duncker, 1875-1910.

Binger, Norman. *Bibliography of German Plays on Microcards.* Hamden, Conn.: Shoe String, 1970.

Brenner, Emil. *Deutsche Literaturgeschichte.* 15th ed. Wels, Austria: Leitner, 1960.

Brockhaus, F. A., ed. *Sprachbrockhaus.* Rev. ed. Chicago: Adler, 1972.

Brockhaus Illustrated German-English, English-German Dictionary. New York: McGraw-Hill, n.d.

Brockhaus Konversations-Lexikon. *Der Grosse Brockhaus.* 16th ed. 12 vols. Wiesbaden: Brockhaus, 1952-58.

Bruhns, Leo. *Deutsche Künstler in Selbstdarstellungen.* Königstein im Taunus: K. R. Langewiesche, 1957.

Bruns, Friedrich, ed. *Die Lese der Deutschen Lyrik von Klopstock bis Rilke.* New York: Appleton, 1938.

Cassell's New German Dictionary. New York: Funk & Wagnalls, 1965.

Dornseiff, Franz. *Deutscher Wortschatz nach Sachgruppen.* New York: DeGruyter, 1970.

Duden, R., ed. *Der Grosse Duden.* 10 vols. Chicago: Adler, 1971.

Erdelyi, Gabor, and Agnes F. Peterson. *German Periodical Publications.* Stanford: Hoover Institution Press, 1967.

Fleissner, O. S., and E. M. Fleissner. *Deutsches Literaturlesebuch.* 4th ed. New York: Appleton, 1968.

Grimm, Jacob, and Wilhelm Grimm. *Deutsches Woerterbuch: Erstausgabe.* 16 vols. Chicago: Adler, 1954-60.

Groeg, Otto J., ed. *Who's Who in German: A Biographical Dictionary.* 5th ed. New York: International Publications Service, 1974.

Hersch, Gisela, comp. *A Bibliography of German Studies, 1945-1971.* Bloomington: Indiana Univ. Press, 1972.

Internationale Bibliographie zur Geschichte der Deutschen Literatur. 4 vols. Totowa, N.J.: Littlefield, 1974.

Kohlschmidt, Werner, and Werner Mohr, eds. *Reallexikon der Deutschen Literaturgeschichte.* 3 vols. 2nd ed. New York: DeGruyter, 1958-72.

Kopp, W. LaMarr. *German Literature in the United States, 1945-60.* Chapel Hill: Univ. of North Carolina Press, 1968.

Krell, Leo, and Leonhard Fiedler. *Deutsche Literaturgeschichte.* 8th ed. Bamberg: Buchner, 1960.

Magill, C. P. *German Literature.* New York: Oxford Univ. Press, 1974.

Martini, Fritz. *Deutsche Literaturgeschichte von den Anfängen bis zur Gegenwart.* 10th ed. Stuttgart: Kröner, 1960.

Morgan, Bayard Q. *Critical Bibliography of German Literature in English Translation, 1481-1927.* 1938; rpt. Metuchen, N.J.: Scarecrow, 1965. (Supplement for years 1928-55. See below, Smith, Murray F., for a second supplement for years 1956-60.)

Muret, E., and D. Sanders, eds. *German and English Encyclopedia Dictionary.* 2 vols. New York: Ungar, n.d.

Richter, Karl. *Deutsche Heldensagen, Neuerzählt.* München: Droemersche Verlagsanstalt, 1957.

Rose, Ernst. *A History of German Literature.* New York: New York Univ. Press, 1960.

Smith, Murray F. *Selected Bibliography of German Literature in English Translation, 1956-60.* Metuchen, N.J.: Scarecrow, 1972.

Springer, Otto, ed. *The New Muret-Sanders Encyclopedic Dictionary of the English and German Languages.* 2 vols. New York: Hippocrene, 1974.

Verzeichnis Lieferbarer Bücher, 1974. (German Books in Print). 4th ed. New York: Bowker, 1974.

Vexler, Robert I. *Germany: A Chronology and Fact Book.* Dobbs Ferry, N.Y.: Oceana, 1973.

Wer Ist Wer? 2 vols. 17th ed. New York: International Publications Service, 1973.

Wildhagen, Karl, and Will Heraucourt. *New Wildhagen German Dictionary.* Chicago: Follett, 1965.

Journals

German Documentation Literature
German International
German Life and Letters
German News
German Quarterly
German Tribune
Germanic Review
Germanistik
Germany
Kulturbrief
Kunst und Literatur
Kürbiskern
Literat
Ran
Scala International
Spiegel
Stein
Welt und Wort
Wiesbadener Leben

LATIN

Books

Brockelmann, Carl. *Lexicon Syriacum.* 2nd ed. New York: International Publications Service, 1966.

Chevallier, R. *Dictionnaire de la littérature latine.* Paris: Larousse, 1974.

Cole, A. T., and D. O. Ross, eds. *Studies in Latin Language and Literature.* New York: Cambridge Univ. Press, 1972.

Estienne, Robert. *Thesaurus Linguae Latinae.* 4 vols. 1740; rpt. Chicago: Adler, 1974.

Faider, Paul. *Repertoire des index et lexiques d'auteurs latins.* 1926; rpt. New York: Burt Franklin, 1971.

Glare, P. G., ed. *Oxford Latin Dictionary.* New York: Oxford Univ. Press, 1968-date. (In progress)

Graesse, Johann G. *Orbis Latinus: Lexikon lateinischer geographischer Namen des Mittelalters und der Neuzeit.* 3 vols. New York: International Publications Service, 1970.

Hoffmann, Samuel F. *Bibliographisches Lexikon der Gesammten Litteratur der Griechen.* 2nd ed. 1830; rpt. New York: Burt Franklin, n.d.

International Guide to Classical Studies. Darien, Conn.: American Bibliographic Service, 1961-date.

Kittredge, George L. *Some Landmarks in the History of Latin Grammars.* 1903; rpt. New York: Burt Franklin, 1974.

Lewis, Charlton T., and Charles Short. *Latin Dictionary: Founded on Andrews' Edition of Freund's Latin Dictionary.* 1879; rpt. New York: Oxford Univ. Press, 1974.

MacDonald, Gerald. *Antonio de Nebrija: Vocabulario de romance en latin.* Philadelphia: Temple Univ. Press, 1974.

Mackail, John W. *Latin Literature.* Folcroft, Pa.: Folcroft, 1973.

Mantinband, James H. *Dictionary of Latin Literature.* Totawa, N.J.: Littlefield, 1956.

Norton, Mary E. *Selective Bibliography on the Teaching of Latin and Greek, 1925-69.* New York: Modern Language Assn., 1974.

Sandys, John E. *Companion to Latin Studies.* 3rd ed. 1935; rpt. New York: Hafner, 1963.

Journals

American Classical Review
American Journal of Philology
AREPO
Arethusa
Arion
Athenaeum
Classical Bulletin
Classical Journal
Classical Outlook
Classical Philology
Classical Quarterly
Classical Review
Classical World
Greek, Roman and Byzantine Studies
Hellenism
Modern Greek Studies Association Bulletin
Nestor
Philological Quarterly
Phoenix
Quarterly Check-List of Classical Studies
Ramus

RUSSIAN

Books

Alford, M. H., and V. L. Alford. *Russian-English Scientific and Technical Dictionary.* 2 vols. Elmsford, N.Y.: Pergamon, 1970.

Blum, A. *Concise Russian-English Scientific Dictionary for Students and Research Workers.* Elmsford, N.Y.: Pergamon, 1965.

Crowther, Peter A. *Bibliography of Works in English on Early Russian History to 1800.* New York: Barnes & Noble, 1969.

Gilbert, Martin. *Russian History Atlas.* New York: Macmillan, 1972.

Harkins, William E. *Dictionary of Russian Literature.* 1956; rpt. Westport, Conn.: Greenwood, 1971.

Horecky, Paul L. *Basic Russian Publications: A Selected and Annotated Bibliography on Russian and the Soviet Union.* Chicago: Univ. of Chicago Press, 1962.

Institute for the Study of the U.S.S.R., et al. *Who Was Who in the U.S.S.R.* Metuchen, N.J.: Scarecrow, 1972.

Line, Maurice B., et al. *Bibliography of Russian Literature in English Translation to 1945.* 1963; rpt. Totawa, N.J.: Littlefield, 1972.

Muller, V. K., ed. *English-Russian Dictionary.* 14th ed. New York: Dutton, 1973.

Neiswender, Rosemary, ed. *Guide to Russian Reference and Language Aids.* SLA Bibliography Series No. 4. New York: Special Libraries Association, 1962.

Parker, W. H. *Historical Geography of Russia.* Chicago: Aldine, 1969.

Smirnitsky, A. I., ed. *Russian-English Dictionary*. Rev. ed. New York: Dutton, 1973.

Zenkovsky, Serge A., and David L. Armbruster, eds. *Guide to the Bibliographies of Russian Literature*. Nashville: Vanderbilt Univ. Press, 1970.

Journals

Literatura V Shkole
Moskva
Russian
Russian Language Journal
Russian Review
Slavic Review

SPANISH

Books

Aquino-Bermudez, et al. *Mi diccionario ilustrado*. New York: Lothrop, Lee and Shepard, 1972.

Bryant, Shasta M. *The Spanish Ballad in English*. Lexington: Univ. Press of Kentucky, 1974.

Celorio, Marta, and Annette C. Barlow. *Handbook of Spanish Idioms*. New ed. New York: Regents Publishing Co., 1974.

Chatham, James R., and Enrique Ruiz-Fornells. *Dissertations in Hispanic Languages and Literatures: 1876-1966*. Lexington: Univ. Press of Kentucky, 1970.

Fitzmaurice-Kelly, J. *Chapters on Spanish Literature*. Folcroft, Pa.: Folcroft Library Editions, 1973.

Flores, A. *Spanish Literature in English Translation: A Bibliographical Syllabus*. Staten Island: Gordon Press, n.d.

Hernández, José G. *Chicano Dictionary*. Los Gatos, Calif.: Polaris Press, 1974.

Jones, Willis K. *Latin American Writers in English Translation: A Classified Bibliography*. 1944; rpt. Detroit: Blaine-Ethridge, 1972.

McCready, Warren T. *Bibliografía temática de estudios sobre el teatro español antiguo*. Toronto: Univ. of Toronto Press, 1966.

MacCurdy, Raymond R., ed. *Spanish Drama of the Golden Age: Twelve Plays*. New York: Prentice-Hall, 1971.

Medina, Jeremy T. *Introduction to Spanish Literature: An Analytical Approach*. New York: Harper & Row, 1973.

Newmark, Maxim. *Dictionary of Spanish Literature*. Totowa, N.J.: Littlefield, 1956.

Peers, Edgar A., ed. *Cassell's Spanish Dictionary*. New York: Funk & Wagnalls, 1966.

Russell, P. E. *Spain: A Companion to Spanish Studies*. New York: Pitman, 1973.

Zimmerman, Irene. *Guide to Current Latin American Periodicals: Humanities and Social Sciences*. Gainesville, Fla.: Kallman, 1961.

Journals

Actualidad Española
Bulletin of Hispanic Studies
Cosmopolis
Cuaderno Cultural
Cultura Hispánica
Eco
Ediciones el Caracol Marino
Época
Exilio
Gaceta Ilustrada
Hispania
Hispanic Review
Hispanofila
Journal of Spanish Studies
Latin American Literary Review
Latin American Theatre Review
Lecturas
Lookout
Mexico Quarterly Review
Pan American Review
Revista Chicano-Requeña
Revista De Estudios Hispánicos
Semana
Spain Today
Spanish Today

Health and Physical Education

Books

American Alliance for Health, Physical Education and Recreation. *Abstracts of Research Papers*. Washington, D.C.: AAHPER, 1970-date.

------------. *Annotated Bibliography on Perceptual-Motor Development*. Washington, D.C.: AAHPER, 1972.

------------. *Completed Research in Health, Physical Education, and Recreation*. Washington, D.C.: AAHPER, 1967-date.

------------. *Dance Directory*. Washington, D.C.: AAHPER, 1971.

------------. *Kinesiology*. Washington, D.C.: AAHPER, 1974.

------------. *Research in Dance*. Washington, D.C.: AAHPER, 1973.

------------. *Research in Outdoor Recreation*. Washington, D.C.: AAHPER, 1973.

------------. *Research Methods in Health, Physical Education, Recreation.* Washington, D.C.: AAHPER, 1973.

------------. *Topical List of Theses and Dissertations in Health Education.* Washington, D.C.: AAHPER, 1970.

Barrow, Harold M., and Rosemary McGee. *A Practical Approach to Measurement in Physical Education.* 2nd ed. Philadelphia: Lea & Febiger, 1971.

Belknap, Sara. *Guide to Dance Periodicals.* Metuchen, N.J.: Scarecrow, 1950-date.

Besford, Pat. *Encyclopedia of Swimming.* New York: St. Martin's Press, 1971.

Beyrer, Mark K., et al. *Directory of Selected References and Resources for Health Instruction.* Rev. ed. Minneapolis: Burgess, 1969.

Bucher, Charles A. *Foundations of Physical Education.* 6th ed. St. Louis: Mosby, 1972.

Chujoy, Anatole, and P. W. Manchester, comps. and eds. *The Dance Encyclopedia.* Rev. and enl. ed. New York: Simon & Schuster, 1967.

Cummings, Parke. *The Dictionary of Sports.* New York: Barnes & Noble, 1949.

Gadan, Francis, et al., eds. *Dictionary of Modern Ballet.* New York: Corner, 1959.

Greenwood, Frances A. *Bibliography of Swimming.* New York: H. W. Wilson, 1940.

Higginson, Alexander Henry. *British and American Sporting Authors: Their Writings and Biographies.* Berryville, Va.: Blue Ridge Press, 1949.

Lovell, Eleanor C., and Ruth M. Hall. *Index to Handicrafts, Modelmaking, and Workshop Projects.* Westwood, Mass.: Faxon, 1936. Supplements, 1943, 1950, 1965, 1969.

Magriel, Paul David. *A Bibliography of Dancing.* New York: H. W. Wilson, 1936. Supplements.

Menke, Frank G. *The Encyclopedia of Sports.* 5th ed. New York: Barnes & Noble, 1974.

Minneapolis Public Library, Music Dept. *Index to Folk Dances and Singing Games.* Chicago: American Library Association, 1936. Supplement, 1949.

National Recreation Association. *Guide to Books on Recreation.* New York: Bowker, 1956.

Spalding's Official Athletic Almanac. New York: American Sports Publishing Co., 1893-1941.

Sportsman's Encyclopedia. New York: Grosset & Dunlap, 1971.

Van Dalen, Deobold B., et al. *A World History of Physical Education.* Englewood Cliffs, N.J.: Prentice-Hall, 1956.

------------. *World History of Physical Education: Cultural, Philosophical, and Comparative.* 2nd ed. Englewood Cliffs, N.J.: Prentice-Hall, 1971.

Weber, Jerome C., and David R. Lamb. *Statistics and Research in Physical Education.* St. Louis: Mosby, 1970.

Williams, Kathleen N., comp. *Health and Development: An Annotated Indexed Bibliography.* N.p.: Department of International Health, 1972.

Journals

American Journal of Public Health and the Nation's Health
American Recreation Journal
American Recreation Society Newsletter
Aquatic Artist
Athletic Journal
Ballroom Dance Magazine
Collegiate Baseball
Dance Magazine
Dance Observer
Dance Perspectives
Dance Scope
Field and Stream
Health Bulletin
Health, Education, and Welfare Indicators
Health, Education, and Welfare Trends
Hygeia
Hygiene and Physical Education
International Journal of Physical Education
Journal of Health and Physical Education
Journal of Health, Physical Education and Recreation
Journal of Hygiene
Journal of School Health
Modern Gymnast
Physical Education Newsletter
Physical Educator
Playground
Public Health Reports
Outdoor Life
Outing
Recreation
Research Quarterly of AAHPER
Scholastic Coach
School Health Review
Sports Illustrated
Today's Health
Track and Field News

Update
World Health
World Tennis

Home Economics

Books

Axford, Lavonne. *English Language Cookbooks by Title.* Detroit: Gale, 1974.

Bitting, Katherine Golden. *Gastromic Bibliography.* San Francisco: priv. pr., 1939; rpt. Detroit: Gale, 1971.

Compton, Norma, and Olive Hall. *Foundations of Home Economic Research: A Human Ecology Approach.* Minneapolis: Burgess, 1972.

Dodd, Marguerite. *America's Homemaking Book.* Rev. ed. New York: Scribner's, 1968.

Forsman, John, ed. *Recipe Index—1970: The Eater's Guide to Periodical Literature.* Detroit: Gale, 1972.

Gourley, James E. *Regional American Cookery, 1884-1934: A List of Works on the Subject.* New York: New York Public Library, 1936.

Hauser, Gaylord, and Ragnar Berg. *Dictionary of Foods.* Simi Valley, Calif.: Lust, 1971.

Iowa State College of Agriculture and Mechanic Arts. *Basic Books and Periodicals in Home Economics.* Ames: Iowa State College Library, 1942. Supplement, 1949.

Johnson, Arnold, and Martin Peterson. *Encyclopedia of Food Technology.* Milwaukee: Aviation, 1974.

Lincoln, Waldo. *American Cookery Books, 1742-1860.* Rev. and enl. by Eleanor Lowenstein. Worcester, Mass: American Antiquarian Society, 1954.

Lowenstein, Eleanor. *Bibliography of American Cookery Books, 1742-1860.* New York: Corner, 1972.

Montagné, Prosper. *Larousse Gastronomique: The Encyclopedia of Food, Wine, and Cookery.* Ed. Charlotte Turgeon and Nina Froud. New York: Crown, 1961.

Robertson, Annie I. *Guide to the Literature of Home and Family Life.* 1924; rpt. Detroit: Gale, 1971.

Simon, André. *Bibliotheca Bacchica Wine and Cooking Bibliography.* 2 vols. West Orange, N.J.: Saifer, 1974.

------------. *Bibliotheca Gastronomica: A Catalogue of Books and Documents on Gastronomy.* London: Wine and Food Society, 1953.

------------, and Robin Howe. *Dictionary of Gastronomy.* New York: McGraw-Hill, 1970.

Stevenson, Bob, and Vera Stevenson. *Illustrated Almanac for Homemakers.* New York: Grossett & Dunlap, 1974.

Treves, Ralph. *The Homeowner's Complete Guide.* New York: Dutton, 1974.

Ward, Artemas. *Encyclopedia of Food.* 1923; rpt. Ann Arbor: Finch Press, 1974.

U.S. Dept. of Agriculture. *Home Economics Research Report.* Washington, D.C.: GPO, 1957-date.

Vicaire, Georges. *Bibliographie Gastronomique.* New York: Burt Franklin, 1890.

Journals

AHEA Newsletter
Better Homes and Gardens
Canadian Home Economics Journal
Changing Times
Consumer Reports
Cookbook Digest
Cuisine et vins de France
Domestic Science
Family Economics Review
Food and Cookery Review
Good Housekeeping
Home Economics Research Abstracts
Home Economics Research Journal
Homemaker
Journal of Food Science
Journal of Home Economics
Journal of Marriage and the Family
Journal of Nutrition
McCall's
Mademoiselle
Vogue
What's New in Home Economics
Woman's Day

Music

• Books

Apel, Willi. *Harvard Dictionary of Music.* 2nd rev. ed. Cambridge, Mass.: Harvard Univ. Press, 1969.

Bahle, Bruce, ed. *The International Cyclopedia of Music and Musicians.* 10th ed. New York: Dodd, Mead, 1974.

Baker, Theodore. *Baker's Biographical Dictionary of Musicians.* 5th ed. New York: Schirmer, 1958. Supplement, 1971.

------------. *Dictionary of Musical Terms.* New York: Schirmer, 1923.

Basart, Ann P. *Seventy-Five Years of New Music: An Information Guide.* Detroit: Gale, 1974.

Besterman, Theodore. *Music and Drama.* Totowa, N.J.: Littlefield, 1971.

Bingley, William. *Musical Biography.* 2 vols. 1834; rpt. New York: Da Capo, 1971.

Blom, Eric. *General Index to Modern Musical Literature in the English Language Including Periodicals for the Years 1915-1926.* 1927; rpt. New York: Da Capo, 1970.

Brown, Len, and Gary Friedrich. *Encyclopedia of Country and Western Music.* New York: Tower, 1971.

Champlin, John. *Cyclopedia of Music and Musicians.* 3 vols. New York: Gordon, 1974.

Charles, Sydney R. *Handbook of Music and Music Literature.* New York: Free Press, 1972.

Clough, Francis F., and G. J. Cuming. *The World's Encyclopaedia of Recorded Music.* 3 vols. London: Gramaphone Corp., 1952. Supplements, 1953, 1957.

Davies, J. H. *Musicalia: Sources of Information in Music.* 2nd ed. Elmsford, N.Y.: Pergamon, 1969.

Duckles, Vincent. *Music Reference and Research Materials.* 2nd ed. New York: Free Press, 1967.

Evans, May G. *Music and Edgar Allan Poe: A Bibliographical Study.* Westport, Conn.: Greenwood, 1968.

Farish, Margaret K. *String Music in Print.* 2nd ed. New York: Bowker, 1973.

Feather, Leonard. *Encyclopedia of Jazz in the Sixties.* New York: Horizon, 1974.

Fuller-Maitland, John A. *A Consort of Music.* Plainview, N.Y.: Books for Libraries, 1973.

Grant, W. Parks. *Handbook of Music Terms.* Metuchen, N.J.: Scarecrow, 1967.

Grove, George. *Dictionary of Music and Musicians.* Ed. Eric Blom. 5th ed. 10 vols. New York: St. Martin's Press, 1954-61.

Hampton, Barbara. *American Music: An Information Guide.* Detroit: Gale, 1974.

Heyer, Anna Harriet. *Historical Sets, Collected Editions, and Monuments of Music: A Guide to the Contents.* 2nd ed. Chicago: American Library Association, 1969.

Jacobs, Arthur, ed. *The Music Yearbook.* New York: St. Martin's Press, annually.

Kenneson, Claud. *Bibliography of Cello Ensemble Music.* Detroit: Information Coordinators, 1973.

Keohn, Ernst C. "The Bibliography of Music." *Musical Quarterly,* 5 (1919), 231-54.

King, Alexander Hyatt. "Recent Work in Music Bibliography." *The Library,* 26 (Sept.-Dec. 1945).

Loewenberg, Alfred. *Annals of Opera, 1597-1940.* 2nd ed. 2 vols. Geneva: Societas Bibliographica, 1955.

Markewich, Reese. *Definitive Bibliography of Harmonically Sophisticated Tonal Music.* New York: Markewich, 1970.

Mixter, K. E. *General Bibliography for Music Research.* Detroit: Information Coordinators, 1962.

Music Article Guide. Philadelphia: Music Article Guide, 1966-date.

The Music Index. Detroit: Information Coordinators, 1949-date.

Musician's Guide. 3 vols. New York: Music Information Service, 1954-57.

Oxford History of Music. 8 vols. 2nd ed. London: Oxford Univ. Press, 1929-38.

Pratt, Waldo Selden. *The New Encyclopedia of Music and Musicians.* Rev. ed. New York: Macmillan, 1929.

Roxon, Lilian. *Encyclopedia of Rock.* New York: Grosset & Dunlap, 1969.

Sainsbury, John F. *Dictionary of Musicians from the Earliest Time.* 2 vols. 2nd ed. New York: Da Capo, 1969.

Scholes, Percy A. *Concise Oxford Dictionary of Music.* 2nd ed. New York: Oxford Univ. Press, 1964.

Shapiro, Nat. *Popular Music: An Annotated Index of American Popular Songs.* 5 vols. New York: Adrian Press, 1964- . (In progress)

Stambler, Irwin. *Encyclopedia of Popular Music.* New York: St. Martin's Press, 1965.

Strunk, Oliver, ed. *Source Readings in Music History.* 5 vols. New York: Norton, 1950.

Thompson, Kenneth. *St. Martin's Dictionary of Twentieth-Century Composers 1910-1971.* New York: St. Martin's, 1973.

Thompson, Oscar, ed. *International Cyclopedia of Music and Musicians.* 9th rev. ed. 1964. New York: Dodd, Mead, 1964.

Vinton, John, ed. *The Dictionary of Contemporary Music.* New York: Dutton, 1974.

Weichlein, William J. *A Checklist of American Music Periodicals, 1850-1900.* Detroit: Information Coordinators, 1970.

Westrup, J. A., and F. L. Harrison, eds. *New College Encyclopedia of Music.* New York: Norton, 1960.

Who's Who in Music: Musicians' International Directory. Riverside, N.J.: Hafner, 1972.

Journals

ACTA Musicologia
American Music Teacher
Brass and Percussion
British Catalogue of Music
Choral Journal
Clavier
Current Musicology
Educational Music Magazine
Journal of the American Musicological Society
Journal of Band Research
Journal of Music Theory
Journal of Music Therapy
Journal of Renaissance and Baroque Music
Journal of Research in Music Education
Modern Music
Music and Letters
Music Index
Music Journal
Music Journal Biographical Cards
Music Review
Musica Disciplina
Musical America
Musical Quarterly
Musical Record
Musical Times
Musician
Notes
Opera Journal
Piano Quarterly
Sonorum Speculum

Philosophy

Books

Baldwin, James Mark. *Dictionary of Philosophy and Psychology.* 3 vols; rpt. Gloucester, Mass.: Peter Smith, 1960.

Bibliography of Philosophy, 1933-36. 4 vols. New York: Journal of Philosophy, 1934-37.

Copleston, Frederick. *A History of Philosophy.* 8 vols. Garden City, N.Y.: Doubleday, 1962.

Davidson, R. F. *Philosophies Men Live By.* 2nd ed. New York: Holt, Rinehart, & Winston, 1974.

DeGeorge, Richard T. *Guide to Philosophical Bibliography and Research.* Century Philosophy Series. New York: Appleton, 1971.

Edwards, Paul, ed. *Encyclopedia of Philosophy.* 4 vols. New York: Free Press, 1973.

Higgins, Charles L. *Bibliography of Philosophy.* Ann Arbor: Campus, 1965.

Passmore, John. *A Hundred Years of Philosophy.* Baltimore: Penguin, 1968.

Rand, Benjamin, comp. *Bibliography of Philosophy, Psychology and Cognate Subjects.* 2 vols. New York: Macmillan, 1905.

Runes, Dagobert D., ed. *The Dictionary of Philosophy.* Totowa, N.J.: Littlefield, 1960.

U.S. Library of Congress. General Reference and Bibliography Division. *Philosophical Periodicals: An Annotated World List.* Ed. David Baumgardt. Washington, D.C.: U.S. Library of Congress, 1952.

Urmson, J. O., ed. *The Concise Encyclopedia of Western Philosophy and Philosophers.* New York: Hawthorn, 1960.

Weingartner, Rudolph H. *Philosophy in the West: Readings in Ancient and Medieval Philosophy.* New York: Harcourt, Brace, 1965.

Journals

American Philosophical Society, Proceedings
Bibliography of Philosophy
Diogenes
Ethics
Humanist
International Journal of Ethics
Journal of Existentialism
Journal of the History of Ideas
Journal of Philosophy

*Journal of Philosophy, Psychology, and
   Scientific Method*
Journal of Symbolic Logic
Journal of Thought
Mind
Pacific Philosophy Forum
Personalist
Philosopher's Index
Philosophia Mathematica
Philosophical Quarterly
Philosophical Review
Philosophical Studies
Philosophy and Phenomenological Research
Philosophy of Science
Review of Metaphysics
Self-Realization Magazine
Southwestern Journal of Philosophy
Soviet Studies in Philosophy
Studies in Soviet Thought

Psychology

Books

Annual Review of Psychology. Palo Alto, Calif.: Annual Reviews, 1950-date.

Bachrach, Arthur J. *Psychological Research: An Introduction.* 3rd ed. New York: Random House, 1974.

Beigel, Hugo G. *Dictionary of Psychology and Related Fields.* New York: Ungar, 1974.

Bell, James E. *Guide to Library Research in Psychology.* Dubuque: William C. Brown, 1971.

Columbia University. *Cumulated Subject Index to Psychological Abstracts, 1927-1960.* 2 vols. Boston: G. K. Hall, 1966. Supplements.

English, Horace B., and Ava C. English. *A Comprehensive Dictionary of Psychological and Psychoanalytical Terms.* New York: McKay, 1958.

Eysenck, H. J., et al. *Encyclopedia of Psychology.* New York: Seabury, 1972.

Goldenson, Robert M. *Encyclopedia of Human Behavior.* 2 vols. Garden City, N.Y.: Doubleday, 1974.

Gowen, John Curtis, comp. *Annotated Bibliography on Creativity and Giftedness.* Northridge, Calif.: San Fernando Valley State College Foundation, 1965.

Grinstein, Alexander. *The Index of Psychoanalytic Writings.* 5 vols. New York: International Universities Press, 1956-60. Supplements, 1964- . (In progress through vol. 14)

Harvard University. *The Harvard List of Books in Psychology.* 4th ed. Cambridge, Mass.: Harvard Univ. Press, 1971.

Kiell, Norman. *Psychiatry and Psychology in the Visual Arts and Aesthetics: A Bibliography.* Madison: Univ. of Wisconsin Press, 1965.

Lathrop, Richard. *Introduction to Psychological Research: Logic, Design, Analysis.* New York: Harper & Row, 1969.

Louttit, Chauncey M. *Bibliography of Bibliographies on Psychology, 1900-1927.* 1928; rpt. New York: Burt Franklin, 1970.

------------. *Handbook of Psychological Literature.* New York: Gordon, 1974.

Mental Health Book Review Index. New York: American Foundation for Mental Hygiene, 1956-date.

Murchison, C. A., ed. *A Handbook of Social Psychology.* 1935; rpt. New York: Russell & Russell, 1967.

Narramore, Clyde M. *Encyclopedia of Psychological Problems.* Grand Rapids: Zondervan, 1966.

Psychological Abstracts. Lancaster, Pa.: American Psychological Assn., 1927-date.

Psychological Index, 1894-1935. 42 vols. Princeton, N.J.: Psychological Review Co., 1895-1936.
   Superseded by *Psychological Abstracts.*

White, Owen R. *Glossary of Behavioral Terminology.* Champaign, Ill.: Research Press, 1971.

Wilkening, Howard E. *The Psychology Almanac: A Handbook for Students.* Monterey, Calif.: Brooks-Cole, 1970.

Journals

American Journal of Psychology
American Journal of Psychotherapy
American Psychologist
Annual Review of Psychology
Behavioral Science
*Child Development Abstracts and
   Bibliography*
Contemporary Psychology
Journal of Abnormal & Social Psychology
Journal of Applied Behavioral Science
Journal of Applied Psychology
Journal of Clinical Psychology
Journal of Educational Psychology
Journal of Experimental Psychology
Journal of General Psychology
Journal of Individual Psychology
Journal of Psychology
Journal of Social Psychology

Menninger Quarterly
Psychological Bulletin
Psychological Monographs
Psychological Record
Psychological Review

Religion

Books

Attwater, Donald, ed. *A Catholic Dictionary.* 3rd ed. New York: Macmillan, 1961.

Barrow, John Graves. *A Bibliography of Bibliographies in Religion.* Ann Arbor: Edwards, 1955.

Butler, Alban. *Lives of the Saints.* Ed. Bernard Kelley. 5 vols. Westminister, Md.: Christian Classics, 1962.

Buttrick, George A., et al. *The Interpreter's Bible.* 12 vols. New York: Abingdon, 1951-57.

------------, ed. *The Interpreter's Dictionary of the Bible.* 4 vols. New York: Abingdon, 1962.

Case, Shirley J., ed. *A Bibliographical Guide to the History of Christianity.* Chicago: Univ. of Chicago Press, 1931.

The Catholic Encyclopedia. 18 vols. New York: Gilmary Society, 1950-59.

The Catholic Periodical and Literature Index. New York: Catholic Library Association, 1972.

Coulson, John, ed. *The Saints: A Concise Biographical Dictionary.* New York: Hawthorn, 1958.

Cross, F. L., ed. *The Oxford Dictionary of the Christian Church.* New York: Oxford Univ. Press, 1957.

Crow, Paul A., Jr. *The Ecumenical Movement in Bibliographical Outline.* New York: Dept. of Faith and Order, National Council of the Churches of Christ in the U.S.A., 1965.

Ellison, John W., ed. *Nelson's Complete Concordance of the Revised Standard Version of the Bible.* New York: Nelson, 1957.

Ferm, Vergilius T. A., ed. *An Encyclopedia of Religion.* New York: Philosophical Library, 1945.

Frazer, James George. *The New Golden Bough.* Abridged ed. Ed. Theodore H. Gastner. New York: S. G. Phillips, 1959.

Gibb, H. A., and J. H. Kramers, eds. *Shorter Encyclopedia of Islam.* Ithaca, N.Y.: Cornell Univ. Press, 1953.

Gilkey, Langdon. *Naming the Whirlwind: The Renewal of God-Language.* New York: Bobbs, 1969.

Hastings, James, ed. *Dictionary of the Bible.* Rev. ed. New York: Scribner's, 1963.

------------, ed. *Encyclopedia of Religion and Ethics.* 2nd ed. 12 vols. New York: Scribner's, 1908-27.

Hick, John, ed. *Philosophy of Religion.* 2nd ed. Englewood Cliffs, N.J.: Prentice-Hall, 1973.

Hutchinson, John A. *Paths of Faith.* New York: McGraw-Hill, 1969.

Ince, Richard B. *A Dictionary of Religion and Religions.* Ann Arbor: Finch Press, 1935.

International Association for the Study of History of Religions. *International Bibliography of the History of Religions.* Leiden, Netherlands: E. J. Brill, 1952.

Jacquet, Constat H., Jr., ed. *Yearbook of American Churches.* New York: Abingdon, 1972.

Joy, Charles R., ed. *Harper's Topical Concordance.* Rev. ed. New York: Harper & Row, 1962.

Kaster, Joseph. *Putnam's Concise Mythological Dictionary: A Dictionary of the Deities of All Lands.* New York: Putnam, 1964.

Landman, Isaac. *Universal Jewish Encyclopedia and Reader's Guide.* 11 vols. New York: Ktav, 1944.

Loetscher, Lefferts A., ed. *Twentieth-Century Encyclopedia of Religious Knowledge.* Grand Rapids: Baker Book House, 1955.

Lyon, Quinter M. *Meditations from World Religions.* New York: Abingdon, 1960.

May, Herbert G., and G. H. S. Hunt, eds. *Oxford Bible Atlas.* New York: Oxford Univ. Press, 1974.

Mayer, Frederick E., ed. *The Religious Bodies of America.* 2nd ed. St. Louis: Concordia, 1956.

Mazar, Benjamin, and Michael Avi-Yonah, eds. *Illustrated World of the Bible Library.* 5 vols. Hartford: Davey, Daniel, & Co., 1961.

Mead, Frank Spencer. *Handbook of Denominations in the United States.* 5th ed. New York: Abingdon, 1970.

Meissner, William W. *Annotated Bibliography in Religion and Psychology.* New York: Academy of Religion and Mental Health, 1961.

Miller, Madeleine S., and J. Lane Miller. *Harper's Bible Dictionary*. New York: Harper & Row, 1952.

Morris, Raymond P. *A Theological Book List*. Cambridge, Mass.: Greeno Hadden, 1971.

Parrinder, Geoffrey. *A Dictionary of Non-Christian Religions*. Philadelphia: Westminster, 1973.

------------. *Faiths of Mankind: A Guide to the World's Living Religions*. New York: Crowell, 1965.

Peltz, John, ed. *Index to Religious Periodical Literature*. South Pasadena, Calif.: William Carey Library, 1974.

Roth, Cecil, ed. *The Standard Jewish Encyclopedia*. Rev. ed. Garden City, N.Y.: Doubleday, 1962.

Schaff, Philip, and Joann Herzog. *The New Schaff-Herzog Encyclopedia of Religious Knowledge*. 12 vols. 1908-12; rpt. Grand Rapids: Baker Book House, 1940-50.

Strong, James. *The Exhaustive Concordance of the Bible*. 1894; rpt. New York: Abingdon, 1958.

Thompson, Newton W., and Raymond Stock. *Complete Concordance to the Bible* (Douay Version). St. Louis: Herder, 1945.

Tylor, Edward. *Religion in Primitive Culture*. Gloucester, Mass.: Peter Smith, 1972.

Union Theological Seminary. *Essential Books for a Pastor's Study*. Richmond, Va.: Union Theological Seminary, 1960.

Wach, Joachim. *Types of Religious Experience*. Chicago: Univ. of Chicago Press, 1951.

Watts, Harold H. *Modern Reader's Guide to Religions*. New York: Barnes & Noble, 1964.

Wright, George E., and Floyd V. Filson. *The Westminster Historical Atlas to the Bible*. Rev. ed. Philadelphia: Westminster, 1956.

Zaehner, Robert C., ed. *The Concise Encyclopedia of Living Faiths*. Boston: Beacon Press, 1959.

Journals

America
American Judaism
The Biblical Archaeologist
Catholic Digest
Christian Century
Christian Herald
Christian Scholar
Christianity and Crisis
Church History
Commentary

Commonweal
Cross Currents
Dialog
Ecumenical Review
Ecumenist
Encounter
The Expository Times
Hibbert Journal
History of Religions
International Journal of Religious Education
International Review of Missions
Interpretation: A Journal of Bible and Theology
Journal for the Scientific Study of Religion
Journal of Religion
Motive
Religion in Life
Religious and Theological Abstracts
Religious Education
Risk

Social Sciences

GENERAL

Books

Belson, W. A., and B. A. Thompson. *Bibliography on Methods of Social and Business Research*. New York: Halstead Press, 1973.

Boehm, Eric H. *Blueprint for Bibliography: A System for the Social Sciences and Humanities*. Santa Barbara: ABC-CLIO, 1965.

Clarke, Jack A., ed. *Research Materials in the Social Sciences*. 2nd ed. Madison: Univ. of Wisconsin Press, 1967.

Ducharme, Raymond A., et al. *Bibliography for Teachers of Social Studies*. New York: Teachers College Press of Columbia Univ., 1968.

Ferman, Gerald S., and Jack Levin. *The Student Handbook of Social Science Research*. Cambridge, Mass.: Schenkman, 1973.

Freides, Thelma K. *Literature and Bibliography of the Social Sciences: A Guide to Search and Retrieval*. New York: Wiley, 1974.

Gopal, M. H. *Introduction to Research Procedure in Social Sciences*. 2nd ed. New York: Asia, 1970.

Gould, Julius, and W. J. Kolb. *UNESCO Dictionary of the Social Sciences*. New York: Free Press, 1964.

Hoselitz, Bert F., ed. *A Reader's Guide to the Social Sciences.* Rev. ed. New York: Free Press, 1972.

Legters, Lyman H. *Research in the Social Sciences and Humanities.* Santa Barbara: ABC-CLIO, 1967.

Lewis, Peter R. *Literature of the Social Sciences.* London: Library Association, 1960.

London Bibliography of the Social Sciences. London: London School of Economics, 1931-date.

New York State Library. *Checklist of Books and Pamphlets in the Social Sciences.* Albany: New York State Library, 1956-date.

Rothschild, Max, ed. *Cumulative Index of Jewish Social Studies.* 25 vols. New York: Conference on Jewish Social Studies, 1967.

------------. *Jewish Social Studies Cumulative Index.* New York: Ktav, 1968.

Seligman, Edwin R., ed. *Encyclopedia of the Social Sciences.* 8 vols. New York: Macmillan, 1937.

Sills, D. E., ed. *International Encyclopedia of the Social Sciences.* 17 vols. New York: Macmillan, 1968.

Simon, Julian. *Basic Research Methods in Social Science: The Art of Empirical Investigation.* New York: Random House, 1968.

Social Sciences and Humanities Index. 25 vols. New York: H. W. Wilson, 1907-73.

Social Sciences Index. New York: H. W. Wilson, 1973-date.

Tompkins, Dorothy C. *Methodology of Social Science Research: A Bibliography.* Berkeley: Univ. of California Press, 1936.

United Nations Statistical Yearbook. New York: Publishing Service, United Nations, 1948-date.

U.S. Library of Congress. *Monthly Checklist of State Publications.* Washington, D.C.: GPO, 1912-date.

U.S. Superintendent of Documents. *Monthly Catalog of United States Government Publications.* Washington, D.C.: GPO, 1895-date.

Wall, C. Edward, ed. *Book Review Index to Social Science Periodicals.* 2 vols. Ann Arbor: Pierian Press, 1970-71.

White, Carl M., et al. *Sources of Information in the Social Sciences.* 2nd ed. Chicago: American Library Association, 1973.

ECONOMICS

Books

Batson, Harold E. *Select Bibliography of Modern Economic Theory 1870-1929.* Clifton, N.J.: Kelley, 1930.

Belson, W. A., and Thompson, B. A. *Bibliography on Methods of Social and Business Research.* New York: Halstead Press, 1973.

Berenson, Conrad, and Raymond Colton. *Research and Report Writing for Business and Economics.* New York: Random House, 1971.

Cohen, J. *Special Bibliography in Monetary Economics and Finance.* New York: Gordon, 1973.

Commodity Year Book. New York: Commodity Research Bureau, 1939-date.

Cumulative Bibliography of Economic Books: 1954-1962. New York: Gordon, 1965.

Cumulative Bibliography of Economic Books: 1963-1967. New York: Gordon, 1972.

Dasgupta, A. K., ed. *Methodology in Economic Research.* New York: Asia, 1974.

Dorfman, Robert, and Nancy S. Dorfman. *Economics of the Environment: Selected Readings.* New York: Norton, 1972.

Economic Almanac. New York: National Industrial Conference Board, 1949-date.

Ferber, Robert, and P. J. Verdoorn. *Research Methods in Economics and Business.* New York: Macmillan, 1962.

Geiger, H. Kent. *National Development 1776-1966: A Selective and Annotated Guide to the Most Important Articles in English.* Metuchen, N.J.: Scarecrow, 1969.

Greenwood, Douglas. *The McGraw-Hill Dictionary of Modern Economics: A Handbook of Terms and Organizations.* 2nd ed. New York: McGraw-Hill, 1973.

Houston, Samuel R., et al., eds. *Methods and Techniques in Business Research.* New York: MSS Information, 1973.

Huchinson, William K. *American Economic History: An Information Guide.* Detroit: Gale, 1974.

Hughes, Catherine, and Elaine Youngers. *Economic Education: An Information Guide.* Detroit: Gale, 1974.

International Bibliography of Economics. Chicago: Aldine, 1955-date.

Kooy, Marcelle, ed. *Studies in Economics and Economic History*. Durham: Duke Univ. Press, 1972.

Melnyk, Peter. *Economics: Bibliographic Guide to Reference Books and Informational Resources*. Littleton, Conn.: Libraries Unlimited, 1971.

Murdick, Robert G. *Business Research: Concept and Practice*. New York: Intext, 1969.

Palgrave, H. Inglis. *Palgrave's Dictionary of Political Economy*. Ed. Henry Higgs. 3 vols. London: Macmillan, 1925-26.

Rummel, Francis J., and Weley C. Ballaine. *Research Methodology in Business*. New York: Harper & Row, 1963.

Sloan, Harold S., and Arnold J. Zurcher, eds. *A Dictionary of Economics*. 5th ed. New York: Barnes & Noble, 1970.

Spitz, Allan A. *Developmental Change: An Annotated Bibliography*. Lexington: Univ. Press of Kentucky, 1969.

United Nations Bureau of General Economic Research and Policies. *World Economic Survey*. New York: United Nations Dept. of Economic and Social Affairs, 1945-47-date.

Zaremba, Joseph. *Econometrics and Economic Statistics: An Information Guide*. Detroit: Gale, 1974.

Journals

ACES Bulletin
American Economic Review
American Economist
Barron's
Business Economics
Economic and Business Digest
Economic and Business Review
Economic Bulletin
Economic Indicators
Economic Journal
Economic News
Economic Notes
Economic Studies
Federal Reserve Bulletin
Journal of Economic Abstracts
Journal of Economic Education
Journal of Economic Literature
Journal of Political Economy
Quarterly Check-List of Economics and Political Science
Quarterly Journal of Economics
Review of Economics and Statistics
Southern Economic Journal
Wall Street Journal
Western Economic Journal

GEOGRAPHY

Books

American Geographical Society. *Current Geographical Publications: Additions to the Research Catalogue of the American Geographical Society*. New York: American Geographical Society of New York, 1938-date.

------------. *Research Catalogue of the American Geographical Society*. 15 vols. Boston: G. K. Hall, 1962.

Brewer, J. Gordon. *The Literature of Geography: A Guide to Its Organization and Use*. Hamden, Conn.: Shoe String, 1973.

Durrenberger, Robert W. *Geographical Research and Writing*. New York: Crowell, 1971.

Goode's World Atlas. 13th ed. Chicago: Rand McNally, 1971.

Harris, Chauncy D., and Jerome D. Tellmann. *International List of Geographical Serials*. 2nd ed. Chicago: Univ. of Chicago, Dept. of Geography, 1971.

International Bibliography of Geography. New York: International Publications Service, 1974.

Lock, Muriel. *Geography: A Reference Handbook*. Rev. 2nd ed. Hamden, Conn.: Shoe String, 1972.

Martinson, Tom L. *Introduction to Library Research in Geography*. Metuchen, N.J.: Scarecrow, 1972.

Minto, C. S. *How to Find Out in Geography*. Elmsford, N.Y.: Pergamon, 1967.

Monkhouse, Francis J. *Dictionary of Geography*. 2nd ed. Chicago: Aldine, 1970.

Statesman's Yearbook. New York: St. Martin's Press, 1961-date.

Time's Atlas of the World. Boston: Houghton Mifflin, 1959.

United Nations. *Statistical Yearbook*. New York: United Nations, 1960-date.

United Nations Statistical Office. *Demographic Yearbook*. New York: International Publications Service, 1961-date.

U.S. Bureau of Census. *Census of Business*. Washington, D.C.: GPO, 1966.

------------. *Current Population Reports*. Washington, D.C.: GPO, 1970-date.

------------. *1970 Census of Population*. Washington, D.C.: GPO, 1972.

------------. *Statistical Abstract of the United States*. Washington, D.C.: GPO, 1878-date.

U.S. Department of Commerce. *Census of Agriculture*. Washington, D.C.: GPO, 1972.

Journals

Annales de Geographie
Annals of the Association of American Geographers
Die Erde
Economic Geography
Geographical Review
Journal of Geography
Journal of Regional Science
Landscape
The Professional Geographer

HISTORY

Books

Adams, James T. *Dictionary of American History*. 2nd ed. 6 vols. New York: Scribner's, 1942-63.

American Historical Association. *Guide to Historical Literature*. Ed. George F. Howe, et al. New York: Macmillan, 1961.

Beers, Henry Putney. *Bibliographies in American History: Guide to Materials for Research*. New York: H. W. Wilson, 1942; rpt. New York: Octagon, 1973.

Bengtson, Hermann. *Introduction to Ancient History*. Trans. R. I. Frank and Frank D. Gilliard. Berkeley: Univ. of California Press, 1970.

Besterman, Theodore. *History and Geography*. 4 vols. Besterman World Bibliographies Series. Totowa, N.J.: Littlefield, 1972.

Bradford, T. C. *Bibliographer's Manual of American History*. 5 vols. New York: Gordon, n.d.

Brooks, Philip C. *Research in Archives: The Use of Unpublished Primary Sources*. Chicago: Univ. of Chicago Press, 1969.

Bury, J. B., et al. *The Cambridge Ancient History*. 12 vols. New York: Cambridge Univ. Press, 1923-39.

Clark, G. Kitson, and G. R. Elton. *Guide to Research Facilities in History in the Universities of Great Britain and Ireland*. 2nd ed. New York: Cambridge Univ. Press, 1965.

Cooper, William R. *Archaic Dictionary*. 1876; rpt. Detroit: Gale, 1969.

Coulter, Edith M., and Melanie Gerstenfeld. *Historical Bibliographies: A Systematic and Annotated Guide*. Berkeley: Univ. of California Press, 1935; rpt. New York: Russell & Russell, 1965.

Dell, W. R., ed. *Britannica Book of the Year*. Chicago: Encyclopaedia Britannica. Annually.

Facts on File. New York: Facts on File, 1946-date.

Facts on File Master Indexes. New York: Facts on File, 1951-date.

Gwatkin, Henry M., et al. *The Cambridge Medieval History*. 8 vols. New York: Cambridge Univ. Press, 1911-36.

International Bibliography of Historical Sciences. New York: H. W. Wilson, 1930-date.

Langer, William Leonard, comp. and ed. *An Encyclopedia of World History: Ancient, Medieval, and Modern*. 4th ed. Boston: Houghton Mifflin, 1968.

Laqueur, W., and G. L. Mosse. *New History: Trends in Historical Research and Writing Since World War Two*. Gloucester, Mass.: Peter Smith, n.d.

McDermott, John F., ed. *Research Opportunities in American Cultural History*. Lexington: Univ. Press of Kentucky, 1961.

Morris, Richard B., and Graham W. Irwin, eds. *Harper Encyclopedia of the Modern World: A Concise Reference History from 1760 to the Present*. New York: Harper & Row, 1970.

New York Public Library. *Dictionary Catalog of the History of the Americas Collection*. 28 vols. Boston: G. K. Hall, 1961.

Poulton, Helen J., and Marguerite S. Howland. *The Historian's Handbook*. Norman: Univ. of Oklahoma Press, 1972.

Radice, Betty. *Who's Who in the Ancient World*. Baltimore: Penguin, 1973.

Roach, John, ed. *Bibliography of Modern History*. New York: Cambridge Univ. Press, 1968.

Sabin, J., et al. *Bibliotheca Americana: A Dictionary of Books Relating to America from Its Discovery to the Present Time*. 29 vols. 1936; rpt. 15 vols. New York: Hafner, 1962.

Sanderlin, David. *A Guide to Historical Research*. Woodbury, N.Y.: Barron's Educational Series, 1973.

Schlesinger, Arthur M., and Dixon R. Fox, eds. *A History of American Life*. 12 vols. New York: Macmillan, 1927-44.

Ward, A. W., et al. *The Cambridge Modern History*. 13 vols. New York: Cambridge Univ. Press, 1902-13.

Winsor, Justin, ed. *Narrative and Critical History of America*. 8 vols. Boston: Houghton Mifflin, 1884-89.

Woodcock, Percival G., ed. *Concise Dictionary of Ancient History*. New York: Philosophical Library, 1955.

Journals

American Historical Review
Economic History Review
English Historical Review
Hispanic American Historical Review
History
History Today
Journal of American History
Journal of Economic History
Journal of the History of Ideas
Journal of Modern History
Journal of Southern History
New Statesman
North American Review
Pacific Historical Review
Past and Present
Renaissance News
Social Studies
Speculum

POLITICAL SCIENCE

Books

Baier, C. W., et al., eds. *Documents on American Foreign Relations.* Mystic, Conn.: Verry, Lawrence, 1966.

Beer, Samuel H., and Adam B. Ulam. *Patterns of Government: The Major Political Systems of Europe.* 3rd ed. New York: Random House, 1972.

Bergholt, Joan, and Alfred De Grazia, eds. *The Universal Reference System.* New York: Plenum, 1968. Annual supplements.

Brock, Clifton. *The Literature of Political Science: A Guide for Students, Librarians, and Teachers.* New York: Bowker, 1969.

Garceau, Oliver, ed. *Political Research and Political Theory.* Cambridge, Mass.: Harvard Univ. Press, 1968.

Garson, G. David. *Handbook of Political Science Methods.* Boston: Holbrook, 1970.

Golembiewski, Robert T., et al. *Methodological Primer for Political Scientists.* Chicago: Rand McNally, 1969.

Griffith, Ernest S., ed. *Research in Political Science.* Port Washington, N.Y.: Kennikat, 1969.

Harmon, Robert B. *Methodology and Research in Political Science: An Annotated Bibliography.* Bibliographical Information, 1972.

-----------. *Political Science: A Bibliographical Guide to the Literature.* Metuchen, N.J.: Scarecrow, 1965. Supplements, 1968, 1972, 1974.

-----------. *Political Science Bibliographies.* Metuchen, N.J.: Scarecrow, 1973.

Holler, Frederick L. *The Information Sources of Political Science.* Santa Barbara: ABC-CLIO, 1971.

Holt, Robert T., and John E. Turner, eds. *The Methodology of Comparative Political Research.* New York: Free Press, 1970.

International Bibliography of Political Science. Chicago: Aldine, 1954.

McLaughlin, Andrew C., and Albert B. Hart, eds. *Cyclopedia of American Government.* 3 vols. 1914; rpt. Gloucester, Mass.: Peter Smith, 1949.

Palgrave, H. Inglis. *Palgrave's Dictionary of Political Economy.* Ed. Henry Higgs. 3 vols. London: Macmillan, 1925-26.

Plano, Jack C. *Dictionary of Political Analysis.* New York: Holt, Rinehart, & Winston, 1972.

Pogany, Andras H., and L. Hortenzia. *Political Science and International Relations.* Metuchen, N.J.: Scarecrow, 1967.

Roberts, G. K. *Dictionary of Political Analysis.* New York: St. Martin's Press, 1971.

Sperber, Hans, and Travis Trittschuh. *American Political Terms: An Historical Dictionary.* Detroit: Wayne St. Univ. Press, 1962.

Statesman's Yearbook. New York: St. Martin's Press, annually.

Stebbins, Richard P. *Political Handbook and Atlas of the World.* New York: Simon & Schuster, 1970.

United Nations Yearbook. New York: Columbia Univ. Press, annually.

U.S. Congress. *Biographical Directory of the American Congress, 1724-1961.* Washington, D.C.: GPO, 1961.

The Yearbook of World Affairs. New York: Praeger, annually.

Journals

Administrative Science Quarterly
American Bar Association Journal
American Political Science Review
Annals of the American Academy of
Political and Social Science
Atlantic Community Quarterly
Canadian Journal of Political Science
Center Magazine
China Quarterly
Columbia Law Review
Commentary
Comparative Political Studies
Comparative Politics
Comparative Studies in Society and History
Congressional Digest
Congressional Quarterly Almanac

Congressional Quarterly Weekly Report
Congressional Record
Cornell Law Review
Current History
Daedalus
Dissent
Foreign Affairs
Government and Opposition
International Affairs (Great Britain)
International Review of Administrative
 Sciences
International Social Science Journal
International Studies Quarterly
Journal of Applied Behavioral Science
Journal of Inter-American Studies
Journal of Inter-American Studies and
 World Affairs
Journal of Law and Economics
Journal of Political Economy
Journal of Politics
Journal of Public Law
Journal of Social Issues
Midwest Journal of Political Science
Orbis
Parliamentary Affairs
Political Science Quarterly
Political Science Review
Political Studies
Politics
Politics and Society
Polity
Public Administration Review
Public Interest
Public Opinion Quarterly
Review of Politics
Science & Society
State Government
State Government Administration
Studies in Soviet Thought
Urban Affairs Quarterly
Washington Monthly
Western Political Quarterly
World Affairs
World Politics
Yale Review

SOCIOLOGY

Books

Andriot, John L. Guide to U.S. Government
 Statistics. Arlington, Va.: Documents In-
 dex, 1961.
Current Sociological Research. New York:
 American Sociological Association, 1953.

Fairchild, Henry Pratt, ed. Dictionary of
 Sociology and Related Sciences. Totowa,
 N.J.: Littlefield, 1970.
Faris, R. E. L., ed. Handbook of Modern
 Sociology. Chicago: Rand McNally, 1964.
Goslin, David E., ed. Handbook of Sociali-
 zation Theory and Research. Chicago:
 Rand McNally, 1969.
International Bibliography of Sociology.
 Chicago: Aldine, 1952.
Lazarsfeld, Paul F., et al. The Uses of Soci-
 ology. New York: Basic Books, 1967.
March, James G., ed. Handbook of Organi-
 zations. Chicago: Rand McNally, 1965.
Morris, Robert, ed. Encyclopedia of Social
 Work. New York: National Association of
 Social Workers, 1965-date.
Social Science Index. New York: H. W.
 Wilson, 1974-date.
Sociological Abstracts. New York: Sociologi-
 cal Abstracts, 1952.
Statistical Abstract of the United States.
 Washington, D.C.: GPO, annually.
Theodorson, George, and Achilles G. Theo-
 dorson. A Modern Dictionary of Soci-
 ology. New York: Crowell, 1969.

Journals

American Journal of Sociology
American Sociological Review
British Journal of Sociology
Contemporary Sociology
Human Organization
International Social Science Journal
Journal of Educational Sociology
Journal of Health and Social Behavior
Journal of Marriage and the Family
Social Education
Social Science
Social Science Abstracts
Social Science Review
Sociological Quarterly
Sociology and Social Research
Sociometry

WOMEN'S STUDIES

Books

Cisler, Lucinda. Women: A Bibliography. 6th
 ed. New York: The Compiler, 1974.
Davis, Audrey B. Bibliography on Women:
 With Special Emphasis on Their Roles in
 Science and Society. New York: Science
 History Pub., 1974.

Ireland, Norma. *Index to Women of the World from Ancient to Modern Times: Biographies and Portraits.* Westwood, Mass.: Faxon, 1970.

Krichmar, Albert. *Women's Rights Movement in the U.S., 1948-1970: A Bibliography and Sourcebook.* Metuchen, N.J.: Scarecrow, 1972.

Lerner, Gerda. *Black Women in White America.* New York: Pantheon, 1972.

O'Connor, Patricia Ann, et al. *Women: A Serial Bibliography.* Springfield, Ohio: Wittenberg Univ., 1973.

U.S. Women's Bureau. *Guide to Sources of Data on Women and Women Workers for the United States and for Regions, States, and Local Areas.* Washington, D.C.: GPO, 1972.

Wheeler, Helen Rippier. *Womanhood Media: Current Resources About Women.* Metuchen, N.J.: Scarecrow, 1972.

Who's Who of American Women. Chicago: Marquis-Who's Who, Inc., 1965-date.

The World's Who's Who of Women. Totowa, N.J.: Littlefield, 1973.

Journals

Collegiate Woman's Career Magazine
Ms.
Womanpower
Woman Activist
Woman's Journal
Women Studies Abstracts
Women's Studies
Women's World

Speech and Drama

Books

Auer, J. Jeffery. *Introduction to Research in Speech.* New York: Harper & Row, 1959.

Berlo, David K. *The Process of Communication.* New York: Holt, Rinehart, & Winston, 1960.

Besterman, Theodore. *Music and Drama.* Besterman World Bibliographies Series. Totowa: N.J.: Littlefield, 1971.

Broderick, Gertrude G., and Patricia Beall Hamill. *Radio and Television: A Selected Bibliography.* Washington, D.C.: U.S. Dept. of Health, Education, and Welfare, 1960.

Cheney, Sheldon. *The Theatre: Three Thousand Years of Drama, Acting and Stagecraft.* New York: McKay, 1972.

Chicorel, Marietta. *Chicorel Theater Index to Plays in Anthologies, Periodicals, Discs, and Tapes.* 8 vols. New York: Chicorel Library, 1970-73.

Connor, John M., and Billie M. Connor. *Ottemiller's Index to Plays in Collections.* 5th ed. Metuchen, N.J.: Scarecrow, 1971.

Cooper, Lane, trans. *The Rhetoric of Aristotle.* New York: Appleton, 1932.

Cumulated Dramatic Index, 1909-1949: A Cumulation of the F. W. Faxon Company's Dramatic Index. 2 vols. Boston: G. K. Hall, 1965.

Duker, Sam. *Time-Compressed Speech.* 3 vols. Metuchen, N.J.: Scarecrow, 1973.

Firkins, Ina T. E., comp. *Index of Plays, 1800-1926.* 2 vols. New York: H. W. Wilson, 1927. Supplement, 1935.

Gassner, John, and Edward Quinn, eds. *Reader's Encyclopedia of World Drama.* New York: Crowell, 1969.

Granville, Wilfred. *Theater Dictionary: British and American Terms in the Drama, Opera, and Ballet.* Westport, Conn.: Greenwood, 1974.

Greg, W. W. *A Bibliography of the English Printed Drama to the Restoration.* London: The Bibliographical Society, 1962.

Haberman, Frederick W., and James W. Cleary, comps. *Rhetoric and Public Address: A Bibliography: 1947-1961.* Madison: Univ. of Wisconsin Press, 1964. Continued annually in *Speech Monographs.*

Harbage, Alfred. *Annals of English Drama, 1575-1700.* Rev. S. Schoenbaum. London: Methuen, 1964.

Hiler, Hilaire, and Meyer Hiler, comps. *Bibliography of Costume.* Ed. Helen Grant Cushing and Adah V. Morris. New York: H. W. Wilson, 1939.

Hunter, Frederick J., ed. *Drama Bibliography.* Boston: G. K. Hall, 1971.

Index to Full-Length Plays. 3 vols. Westwood, Mass.: Faxon, 1956-65.

Keller, Dean H. *Index to Plays in Periodicals.* Metuchen, N.J.: Scarecrow, 1971. Supplement, 1973.

Logasa, Hanna, and Winifred Ver Nooy, comps. *An Index to One-Act Plays, 1900-1924.* Westwood, Mass.: Faxon, 1924. Supplements, 1932-date.

McGraw-Hill Encyclopedia of World Drama. 4 vols. New York: McGraw-Hill, 1972.

Mulgrave, Dorothy, et al. *Bibliography of Speech and Allied Areas, 1950-1960*. Philadelphia: Chilton, 1962.

New York Public Library. *Catalog of the Theatre and Drama Collections*. Boston: G. K. Hall, 1967.

The New York Times Theatre Reviews 1920-1970. 8 vols. New York: Arno, 1972.

Ottemiller, John H. *Index to Plays in Collections*. 4th ed. Metuchen, N.J.: Scarecrow, 1964.

Smith, Bruce L., and Chitra M. Smith. *International Communication and Political Opinion: A Guide to the Literature*. Princeton, N.J.: Princeton Univ. Press, 1956.

Stratman, Carl J. *Bibliography of the American Theatre*. Chicago: Loyola Univ. Press, 1965.

------------. *Bibliography of English Printed Tragedy*. Carbondale: Southern Illinois Univ. Press, 1966.

------------. *Bibliography of Medieval Drama*. Berkeley: Univ. of California Press, 1954.

------------. *Britain's Theatrical Periodicals, 1720-1967: A Bibliography*. 2nd ed. New York: New York Public Library, 1972.

Summers, Montague. *A Bibliography of the Restoration Drama*. London: Fortune Press, 1934.

Thompson, Wayne N. *Quantitative Research in Public Address and Communication*. New York: Random House, 1967.

Thonssen, Lester, and Elizabeth Fatherson. *Bibliography of Speech Education*. New York: H. W. Wilson, 1939. Supplement, 1950.

Journals

Audio-Visual Communication Review
Business Screen
Education Theatre Journal
Film News
Film Quarterly
Modern Drama
New York Guide and Theatre Magazine
New York Theatre Critic's Reviews
Quarterly Journal of Speech
Radio and Television News
Speech Monographs
The Speech Teacher
Studies in Public Communication
Television Magazine
Television Quarterly
Theatre
Theatre Arts
Theatre Arts Monthly
Tulane Drama Review

INDEX